You won't want to miss this exceptional book! Dr Sartori is uniquely qualified. She conducted one of the most important prospective near-death experience studies ever reported. As a nurse she works daily with dying patients. This book is scholarly in content, yet easy and delightful to read. This highly recommended book contains a treasure trove of wisdom that is powerful, inspiring, and could change your life.

**Jeffrey Long, MD, author of the *New York Times* bestselling *Evidence of the Afterlife: The Science of Near-Death Experiences***

With more than twenty years experience of nursing dying people in an intensive therapy unit, plus a PhD in Near-death Experiences, Dr Sartori is very well qualified to discuss issues of death and dying. She believes that NDEs provide us with a greater understanding of the dying process and that care of terminally ill patients could be enhanced if NDEs would more widely studied. A greater acceptance of the inevitability of death would help the situation of terminally ill people. At present they are increasingly exposed to invasive and burdensome treatments even when prospects for recovery are recognised as minimal. This book is an immensely valuable contribution to current debates about patient care.

**Professor Paul Badham, Professor Emeritus of Theology and Religious Studies at the University of Wales, Trinity St David**

Nurse Penny Sartori was driven by an experience with a traumatized dying patient to study near-death experiences, not to pursue what might happen in an afterlife but rather to improve what happens in this life. Her goal was to learn all she could about the dying process in order to help her patients find meaning in their illness and restore a sense of well-being in their lives. *The Wisdom of Near-Death Experiences*, the fruit of her labors, is an invaluable resource for health care workers, for dying patients and their families, and for all of us who will face death eventually.

**Professor Bruce Greyson, MD, Carlson Professor of Psychiatry & Neurobehavioral Sciences, Charlottesville, Virginia**

Dr Sartori has masterfully crafted a comprehensive summary of research on near-death and related experiences that is both accessible to the interested public and informative for many healthcare professionals. This work has the power to remind people of their purpose in living and to provoke a revolution in the more humane treatment of the dying.

**Janice Holden, EdD, LPC-S, LMFT, NCC, Chair, Department of Counseling and Higher Education and Professor, Counseling Program, College of Education, University of North Texas**

# Also by Penny Sartori

*The Near-Death Experiences of Hospitalized Intensive-Care Patients: A Five-Year Clinical Study*

# The Wisdom
# of Near-Death
# Experiences

## HOW UNDERSTANDING NDEs
## CAN HELP US LIVE MORE FULLY

Dr Penny Sartori

WATKINS PUBLISHING

LONDON

This edition first published in the UK and USA 2014 by
Watkins Publishing Limited
PO Box 883
Oxford, OX1 9PL
UK

A member of Osprey Group

For enquiries in the USA and Canada:
Osprey Publishing
PO Box 3985
New York, NY 10185-3985
Tel: (001) 212 753 4402
Email: info@ospreypublishing.com

Some extracts summarized from *Near-Death Experiences of Hospitalized Intensive Care Patients: A Five-Year Clinical Study* (2008) by Penny Sartori are reproduced with kind permission from The Edwin Mellen Press.

5 7 9 10 8 6 4

Typeset by JCS Publishing Services Ltd, www.jcs-publishing.co.uk

Printed and bound in the US

A CIP record for this book is available from the British Library

ISBN: 978-1-78028-565-8

Watkins Publishing is supporting the Woodland Trust, the UK's leading woodland
conservation charity, by funding tree-planting initiatives and woodland maintenance.

www.watkinspublishing.co.uk

# Acknowledgements

There are so many people I would like to thank and express my gratitude to because without their help this book would not have been written. First of all, thank you to my husband Enrico for his support (both emotional and financial) since I first became interested in this subject. If he hadn't worked the long hours he did then I would not have been able to reduce my hours working in ITU and dedicate so much time to this all-consuming work. Thanks also to the rest of my family, in-laws and friends for their help, support and understanding of my preoccupation with my studies!

To Professor Paul Badham and Dr Peter Fenwick, who both supervised my PhD between 1997 and 2005 and who continue to support me to this day with their invaluable advice and help. To the Lifebridge Foundation in New York, which funded my university fees when I embarked on this research.

To my colleagues in ITU at both Morriston and Singleton hospitals, there are far too many of you to name individually. I was very blessed to work with an amazing team of people and I will always have very fond memories of working in both hospitals. It was an absolute privilege and one that I will never forget. I will always be very proud to say that I worked on those intensive-care units. Whereas I miss the work, the patients and my colleagues, I don't miss working nights, working every weekend or getting up at 5.45am for a morning shift!

Thank you so much to Dr Pim van Lommel. Although I'd been in email contact with Pim, we didn't meet until 2006 when we both spoke at the IANDS conference in Houston, Texas and then again in 2012 when we both spoke at the Bioethics Forum, Madison, Wisconsin. The work of Dr van Lommel and his colleagues was a breakthrough for the field of NDE research when their study was published in The Lancet in 2001. It is a true honour that he has been kind enough to write the foreword for this book.

The greatest thanks of all go to all of the patients I have nursed throughout my career, especially the one whose death motivated me to learn more about death, and to the near-death experiencers (NDErs) who have contacted me over the years. A big thank you to all of you who have so graciously given up your time for me to interview you and then allowed me to describe your experience in this book. You have all been my greatest teachers.

# Note

Most of the examples that I have used in this book are from people who have written to me or emailed me over the years. Although everyone gave their permission for me to use their stories, many of the people preferred to be anonymous and this has been respected.

Where I have drawn on examples that I encountered during my nursing career, these are all actual events that occurred but some details and names have been changed to ensure the patients cannot be identified.

# Contents

*Dedicated to Nanna Beryl 1927–2009,*
*my husband Enrico,*
*my brother Julian and his civil partner Christopher*
*and the spring and summer that we all shared in 2009.*
*It was a true gift.*

# Foreword

In this well-written and open-hearted book Penny Sartori describes how near-death experiences (NDEs) can have a great impact for our healthcare system as well as for our death-denying and materialistic society. By doing research into NDE and being able to listen with an open mind to critically ill and dying patients in the intensive-care unit she totally changed her ideas about life and death, a change that specifically started after her encounter with a dying patient.

Unfortunately for their patients, the majority of healthcare workers still apparently do not have enough knowledge about NDEs and recent NDE research. I know from many personal accounts that an NDE, or an experience of enhanced consciousness during a life-threatening medical crisis, still gives rise to many unbelieving and critical questions, because within our Western culture this experience is completely at odds with conventional wisdom. As long as one has not experienced an NDE themself it seems impossible to really understand the impact and the life-changing after-effects of this overwhelming experience. So, of course, an NDE is still an incomprehensible and unknown phenomenon for most physicians, psychologists, and for patients and their family. How could it scientifically be explained that people can have clear memories of a period of obvious unconsciousness? Or how is it possible that permanent life changes occur after a cardiac arrest of several minutes' duration? An NDE seems to be an unforgettable confrontation with unlimited dimensions in our consciousness. The existing worldview has radically changed: 'It felt as if I had become another person but with the same identity.' So it seems obvious that in our Western world a near-death experience cannot only be defined as a medical but also as a psychological or spiritual crisis.

In the past a lot has been written about special or 'altered' states of consciousness. But surprisingly, many people and many healthcare practitioners nowadays still have never heard of or read about NDEs, nor about the life-changing effects of this experience. One has to realize that according to our current medical concepts it is not possible to experience consciousness during a cardiac arrest, when circulation and breathing have ceased, during a deep coma with a severely disturbed EEG, or during a life-threatening crisis in the end stage of cancer. However, during the period of unconsciousness associated with cardiac arrest or coma, patients may report the paradoxical occurrence of enhanced consciousness experienced in a realm without our conventional constraints of time and space, with cognitive functions, with emotions, with self-identity, with memories from early childhood and sometimes with perception from a position out and above the lifeless body. Since the publication of the book *Life after Life* by Raymond Moody these extraordinary conscious experiences are called near-death experiences. Such an NDE can be defined as the reported memory of a range of impressions during a special state of enhanced consciousness, including a number of 'universal' elements such as an out-of-body experience, pleasant feelings, seeing a tunnel, a light, deceased relatives, a life review or the conscious return into the body. NDEs are reported during many different types of circumstances: cardiac arrest (clinical death), shock after loss of blood (childbirth), coma following traumatic brain injury or stroke, near-drowning (children) or asphyxia, but also in serious diseases that are not immediately life-threatening, during depression ('existential crisis'), isolation, meditation ('enlightening experience' or 'experience of oneness'), during imminent traffic accidents ('fear-death' experience), during the terminal stage of illness ('end-of-life experience'), or sometimes without any obvious reason at all. The NDE is transformational, always causing profound changes of life-insight, enhanced intuitive sensibility and the loss of fear of death. Near-death experiences occur with increasing frequency because of improved survival rates resulting from modern techniques of resuscitation, and from better treatment of life-threatening diseases.

The content of an NDE and the effects on patients seem similar worldwide. However, the subjective nature and absence of a frame of reference for this experience leads to individual cultural and religious factors determining the vocabulary used to describe and interpret this ineffable experience. According to a recent random poll in Germany and the USA about 4 per cent of the total population in the Western world should have experienced an NDE. So, surprisingly, 2.5 million people in the UK, more than 20 million people in Europe, and 9 million people in the USA are likely to have had an NDE.

Because of her curiosity about the cause, content and after effects of NDEs, and because of her confrontation with the widespread ignorance about NDE in her own hospital, Penny Sartori started her own prospective study on NDE. She knew that many healthcare workers dispute the validity of an NDE. When cases of NDEs had been reported anecdotally there was no way of ascertaining if these accounts were factual, particularly when out-of-body experiences (OBE) were reported. There was no way of knowing if the person really did come close to death, if their hearts had stopped, if they really were unconscious, what drugs had been given or if their blood levels were deranged. However, once Penny had started to conduct her prospective hospital research, which was providing all these medical details, it became far more difficult to dismiss NDEs and simply reduce them to materialist factors such as anoxia and drugs.

Her study of NDEs in critically ill patients consisted of three samples of patients. The first sample consisted of all patients who survived their admission to ITU during the first year of data collection. Out of 243 patients only two reported an NDE (0.8 per cent), and two reported an OBE (0.8 per cent) but no other NDE component. The second sample consisted only of survivors of cardiac arrest during the five years of data collection. There were far fewer patients in this sample but the frequency of NDEs increased markedly. Out of 39 patients seven reported an NDE (17.9 per cent). The percentage of NDEs found in her study was about the same as had been found in three recent prospective studies in survivors of cardiac arrest. The third sample of her study consisted of all of those patients who reported a NDE during the five years' data collection. Some of these NDEs were associated with cardiac arrest, and some occurred during a period of unconsciousness associated with a medical emergency. In total there were 15 patients who reported a NDE during these five years. There were eight reports of out-of-body type experiences.

Since the publication of several prospective studies on NDEs in survivors of cardiac arrest, with strikingly similar results and conclusions, the phenomenon of the NDE can no longer be scientifically ignored. It is an authentic experience which cannot be simply dismissed as imagination, fear of death, hallucination, psychosis, the use of drugs, or oxygen deficiency. Likewise, Penny Sartori concludes also that, according to mainstream science, it is quite impossible to find a scientific explanation for the NDE as long as we 'believe' that consciousness is only a side effect of a functioning brain. The fact that people report lucid experiences in their consciousness when brain activity has ceased is, in her view, difficult to reconcile with current medical opinion. The current materialistic view of the relationship between the brain and consciousness held by most physicians, philosophers and psychologists is too restricted for a proper understanding of this phenomenon. There are good reasons to assume that our consciousness does not always coincide with the functioning of our brain: enhanced consciousness can sometimes be experienced separately from the body. Several NDE researchers from Europe and the USA have come to the inevitable conclusion that most likely the brain must have a facilitating and not a producing function to experience waking consciousness, and one should consider the function of the brain as a transceiver, a transmitter-receiver or interface. By making a scientific case for consciousness as a non-local and thus ubiquitous phenomenon, we should of course question a purely materialist paradigm in science.

Despite the surprising findings and conclusions of recent NDE-research there is still a widespread ignorance by healthcare workers as there is simply not enough education about NDE. If healthcare workers are not fully aware of the complexities of NDEs then responding appropriately becomes a very difficult task. Healthcare workers are usually the first people who come into contact with a person after their NDE and in some instances they are also involved in their long-term recovery. Most people don't know that adjusting to life after the NDE can be very difficult as no one else can understand exactly what has been experienced. People are afraid to discuss their experience because they are concerned that they will be ridiculed or disbelieved. An unfavourable attitude can result in the person never discussing the experience again. NDErs are not attention seekers and have a great reluctance to publicly speak about their experience. Penny explains that many examples used in this book are from people who have requested anonymity.

This fascinating book is the result of twenty years of Penny trying to make sense of death and in the process learning important lessons about life. It has opened Penny's eyes to things she had never previously acknowledged simply because they had never been brought to her attention. She quotes many impressive stories of patients who reported their NDE to her, and she shares with us her new insight: live your life well and don't leave things left undone until the time of your death. It is important that we take notice and hear what these people have to say without any comment or prejudice. Our ideas about life and death will change forever.

By reading this important book with an open mind we are able to reap the benefits of the NDE without having to nearly die. I can highly recommend this book, not only for healthcare workers and for patients with an NDE, but also for terminally ill patients and their families.

Pim van Lommel, cardiologist,
author of *Consciousness beyond Life*

# Introduction

*Everyone knows they're going to die but nobody believes it. If we did,
we would do things differently . . . Learn how to die and you learn
how to live.*

Morrie Schwartz[1]

I was about to change my patient's position in the bed when I heard
the unmistakable ring of the cardiac arrest buzzer. I stopped what I
was doing, asked my colleague to keep an eye on my patient and ran to
the bed area where the patient who had suffered a cardiac arrest was.
I could feel the adrenaline surge inside me. I was the first to assist and
quickly commenced chest compressions as my colleague attended to the
patient's airway. Within seconds several other colleagues arrived – one
deflated the air mattress on the bed, one got the defibrillator, one opened
the emergency drugs, one counted the cycles of cardiopulmonary
resuscitation (CPR) and others stood waiting to take over CPR or run
for other drugs if required.

'Come on, Bob, come back to us,' I said out loud as I continued the
chest compressions. By now my arms felt as though they were going to
drop off but I was determined to keep this man alive. After a further 15
minutes the cardiac monitor registered an erratic heart rhythm which
became more regular and he regained his cardiac output. I was thrilled
to bits – I'd helped to save this man's life, it was a great feeling!

Over the next few days I made a point of going to see 'Bob' even
though I hadn't been allocated to look after him. He remained connected
to the ventilator and infusions of drugs were used to maintain his blood
pressure. He was not communicative and he did not smile or wave at
me as he had done previously. His condition gradually deteriorated and
ten days later he died when there was no further treatment that could
be offered. I was upset as we'd tried our best to help him recover from
his illness. I had only been working in the Intensive Therapy Unit (ITU)

for about a month at that point and felt proud that I was helping to save all these lives: it felt heroic in some way. I was young and enthusiastic. I'd never thought about how the patients might feel; to me it was about saving their lives and making them better. I never really considered what might be going through the minds of patients who didn't recover.

Then, about 18 months later, in 1995, my life changed. I was working a night shift and looking after a man who was clearly dying. He had been a patient in ITU for 14 weeks so I'd got to know him well. That night I said hello to him and, after I had taken hand over from the nurse on the previous shift, checked the equipment at his bedside and prepared to give him a bed bath – the usual ritual in the ITU where I worked. As I touched the handset of the electric bed to adjust its height the patient almost jumped out of bed in agony. His whole body tensed, his arms flew up in the air and his face twisted into a contorted mass. Our eyes connected and it was as if everything around us just stopped – I was no longer aware of the noise around me, the ventilator doing the breathing for him, the flashing intravenous pumps administering the drugs, the turning of the pumps on the dialysis machine, my colleagues talking in the background – my surroundings disappeared and I suddenly seemed to understand everything that the patient was feeling. He couldn't speak, as he was connected to a ventilator via a tracheostomy, but he mouthed pleadingly to me, 'Leave me alone, let me die in peace . . . just let me die.' I will never forget the look in his eyes; it will stay with me forever. They were filled with tears, pain and frustration. The whole experience had a huge impact on me and I just stood there unable to move for about five minutes in a state of shock. I called the doctor, who increased the pain-killing infusion, but the patient remained in obvious distress. I was in a dilemma about what to do – if I didn't bed-bath him I would be reprimanded by the nurse in charge for not doing so, but if I did I would cause him further discomfort.

I pulled the screens around the bedside and reassured him as best I could. He began to settle a little, then, with his permission, I washed the parts of his body that I could reach and just sat with him, holding his hand. After a few hours he eventually became more peaceful and closed his eyes and fell into a light sleep. For the rest of the shift I couldn't stop thinking about how he must feel. He was at the end of his life and, for the past 14 weeks, he had not had a voice, he had been hooked up to numerous different machines, the function of almost every organ in his body had been taken over by mechanical pumps, he had not had any proper sleep and every aspect of his life was under the control of the nurses. I cried as I drove home that morning and couldn't sleep as he was constantly on my mind. I phoned work mid-morning, to be told that he had died two hours after my shift had ended. I was so profoundly affected by the whole experience that I came very close to giving up nursing.

Every time I went into work after that I noticed more patients who were going through similar experiences at the end of their life. I seemed to develop a heightened sense of empathy with the patients and their relatives. I just wanted to hug them all and make things better for them but was powerless to do so. It also made me wonder – is death that bad that we must do everything in our power to prevent patients from dying? What is death anyway? What happens when we die? Why are we so afraid of it? Why don't we ever talk about it?

For the next few months I became very depressed; I felt like I was on autopilot every time I went into work. I made enquiries about nursing courses that would help me to have a greater understanding of how to care for patients dying in critical-care areas, but there was nothing of relevance to ITU (and still isn't!). So I began reading about death, I read every book on death that I could find. Wherever I went I had a book in my hand. Then I came across the concept of near-death experiences (NDEs) and thought: 'Wow! These people are telling us that death is nothing to be afraid of!' My scientific training as a nurse told me that these must be simply hallucinations or wishful thinking but I became more and more curious about them. I began asking patients I looked after if they had had any such experiences but none of them reported anything like that.

In the meantime one of the nursing sisters began to get concerned that I was so withdrawn and there were no signs of my usual sense of humour. She arranged a staff development review so that we could discuss my thoughts. Over the next two hours I let the frustrations and the emotions of the past few months pour out. All the very shocked sister could say was, 'Well, you've got some very valid points there, so how are we going to deal with them?' The discussion ended with me setting some goals for the long term. I said that the only thing that would keep me in ITU was if I could research NDEs. She laughed and said it was highly unlikely as I would have to go to the Ethics Committee, get the permission of the consultants, etc., and she doubted that any of them would agree to this – it seemed so unlikely that we didn't even write it down as one of my goals. However, I was certain that was what I wanted to do and *nothing* was going to dissuade me.

Two years later I had managed to obtain the permission of the Ethics Committee, my manager and the consultants and embarked on the UK's first long-term prospective study on NDEs under the supervision of the UK's leading authorities on NDEs, Professor Paul Badham and Dr Peter Fenwick.

The study began in 1997 and for eight years my life was totally consumed by my research, driven by that initial encounter with the dying patient. I really wanted to understand death so that I could help future patients and ensure that no one else had to go through what that patient had. For the more technical and scientifically orientated reader I have already published an academic book which has the full details of my research methods, results, statistics, discussion and conclusion.[2]

As my lectures have been so well attended, especially the public ones, it is apparent that there is a real interest in this subject and both the general public and healthcare workers have a thirst for knowledge in this area. In response to newspaper articles about my research I've been contacted by many people from all over the world. I was totally unprepared for all the attention my work received, and shied away from the publicity as much as possible as I found it to be quite unnerving. I was thrown in at the deep end and appeared on TV and spoke on radio shows in the UK and as far away as Colombia, Brazil and New Zealand. Wherever I go, people want to know more about my research.

Unfortunately, there have been a lot of misconceptions regarding the research I have undertaken, very often being associated with the concept of life after death. I want to make it clear that I am not trying to prove or disprove an afterlife – what I have been trying to do is gain a greater understanding of the dying process so that care for dying patients can be enhanced. Obviously, what I have written about the encounter with the dying patient at the beginning of this introduction cannot begin to express the depth of emotion that I felt that night. I have spared you the full details of what he had to endure. The connection I made with that man in 1995 is what continues to motivate me to persevere with my research to this day. I have no agenda other than to improve care for dying patients – this is an issue that affects each one of us as death is the only certainty in *everyone's* life and I know that *I* don't want to go through what that man went through.

Although the research that I undertook in the hospital predominantly investigated NDEs that occurred during cardiac arrest, NDEs can occur in other contexts, which will also be described. Over the years I have gathered hundreds of examples of NDEs from members of the general public who have contacted me. I have included a number of examples but deciding which ones to add was very difficult as I have so many interesting cases on file and each one is of value. The testimonies appear in their original form and have not been altered except for spelling corrections and removal of names – most of the people preferring to remain anonymous. This book, I hope, is an easy read which draws on my 21 years' experience as a nurse, my doctoral research into NDEs and the personal insights I have gained during the course of my career. It seeks to bring these experiences to a wider audience and give examples of NDEs and, I hope, convey why these experiences are more than mere alleged hallucinations and are something that we can all learn from. I hope you will be able to engage with these experiences and gain a greater awareness of all the complexities that they encompass. More importantly, I hope you will think twice if ever you find yourself in the company of someone who has been brave enough to discuss their NDE and that you will respond with respect, whatever your personal perspective.

It has been a real privilege to have been in a position where I have been able to learn so much from the patients I have cared for throughout my career, as well as the patients who formed the basis for my study and from the people who have shared their NDE with me. There is something very humbling about being in the presence of someone who has had an NDE and I consider it a true honour that all of these people have shared such an intensely emotional and personal experience with me.

For any sceptical reader, I would suggest not just taking the NDE at face value but to try to get a deeper understanding and engage with the full range of experiences of this very complex phenomenon before making any judgements. Especially I would recommend sitting down and just *listening* to several people describe their NDE – it is one thing to read about NDEs and it is quite another thing to be in the presence of an NDEr while they recount their experience.

The crucial point I want to make with this book is that NDEs undoubtedly occur and have very real, life-changing effects on those who have them. Further to that, the wisdom gained during the NDE can be life enhancing and have hugely positive effects on those who have not experienced an NDE – all we have to do is take notice and *hear* what these people have to say. By trying to pathologize the NDE we are missing out on very important insights.

Paradoxically, the biggest thing I have learned since undertaking my research is not about death but about life. With our current technology and consumerist, materialist way of life, we have forgotten the most important thing – how to live. My new perspective on death and consequently life has not only helped me to continue working in ITU for the past 17 years but has also greatly helped when caring for dying members of my own family. I do not profess to know all of the answers – all I am doing is presenting experiences described to me and I hope I am able to convey some of what I have learned from the patients and from my work as a nurse and my doctoral research. I encourage everyone who reads this book to have an open mind and I hope you too will be inspired to embark on your own journey and discover more about this great mystery that we call death.

# 1

# The Near-Death Experience

*Fear of death has caused more suffering than all physical diseases combined. NDEs are a cure for suffering because they suggest that consciousness transcends the dying brain and body. NDErs learn this during their experience, and return with the permanent absence of the fear of death and certainty of immortality.*

Larry Dossey[1]

By the time you have read this book you will have a greater understanding of:

- What an NDE is
- How NDEs can affect people who have them
- The contexts in which the NDE can occur
- Cultural variations of NDEs
- Current scientific theories proposed as an explanation for the NDE
- The findings of my prospective hospital study
- A brief history of cultural attitudes to death, leading up to the present day
- The implications NDEs can have for our healthcare system
- How the positive message of NDEs can enhance the way we live our lives.

When I began my nurse training in 1989, I'd never heard of an NDE and it was never something I was taught. During my first year I recall looking after a patient on the medical ward; I had worked ten consecutive shifts so got to know her really well. On the tenth shift, while I was helping her to wash, she sheepishly told me that she had 'gone to heaven' when her heart had stopped in the coronary-care unit. I remember listening to her experience of looking down on her own body in the bed and going to a beautiful meadow where her dead mother was waiting for her. I thought to myself, 'She must have been hallucinating or had too much diamorphine.' I never gave it a second thought and I didn't question her further; I simply listened. It was a few years later, after I had qualified as a staff nurse, that I was to realize the significance of what she had said.

I would like everyone to read this book with an open mind and to discard any pre-conceived ideas about how to explain or explain away the NDE. This book is trying to convey a thorough and wider understanding of the NDE and all of the complexities that go with it, such as psychological, spiritual, sociological and physical after effects. Further to that, this book considers the implications that a wider understanding of this phenomenon can have for our society and the way we live our lives. At the end of the book is a discussion highlighting the sociological research which shows that engaging with and embracing the NDE as a valid experience can give great meaning to our lives and promote love, respect and compassion for others, ourselves and our planet.

## What is an NDE?

Many readers may be quite familiar with the term 'near-death experience'. Some may have never heard of it before, whereas there may be many readers who recognize this type of experience as actually having happened to them at some point in the past and have never understood it or told anyone what they experienced.

NDEs are not a new phenomenon; they have been reported through-out history. They feature in the Bible (2 Corinthians 12: 1–9), Plato's *Republic*, in Roman times[2] and are commonly described in medieval literature.[3] Similar experiences have been recorded within different world cultures, such as the Tibetan Book of the Dead,[4] along with experiences of Tibetan delogs.[5] Works of art by Hieronymus Bosch (c1450–1516) and William Blake (1757–1827) depict images that parallel an NDE.

In the early 1970s NDEs were reported and investigated by Dr Johan Hampe and Dr Elisabeth Kübler-Ross. However, it wasn't until Dr Raymond Moody classified and named them as 'near-death experiences' in 1975 that they became popularized when his book *Life After Life* became an international best-seller. Moody defined the NDE as an experience undergone while unconscious, occurring close to death, in which the person reports a set of components, described below.

## Previous Research

Since the recognition of the NDE in the 1970s extensive research has been conducted and much has been written on the NDE. Pioneers in the field were Dr Raymond Moody, Professor Kenneth Ring, Professor Bruce Greyson, Dr Michael Sabom, Dr Melvin Morse, Nancy Evans-Bush, and P. M. H. Atwater in the USA and Professor Paul Badham and Dr Linda Badham, Dr Susan Blackmore and Dr Peter Fenwick and Elizabeth Fenwick, Dr Margot Grey and David Lorimer in the UK to name but a few. In the 1980s the International Association of Near-Death Studies (IANDS) was formed in the USA. Currently, in the UK, the Horizon Research Foundation performs a similar function and seeks a greater understanding of consciousness.

Further research was undertaken in hospitals by Dr Michael Sabom,[6] Dr Melvin Morse,[7] Professor Janice Holden,[8] Dr Madelaine Lawrence[9] and Dr Maurice Rawlings.[10] The past decade has seen the development of prospective hospital research undertaken by Dr Pim van Lommel in the Netherlands,[11] Janet Schwaninger[12] and Professor Bruce Greyson[13] in the USA. In 1997 Dr Sam Parnia[14] and I both embarked on similar research projects at the same time independently of each other in the UK.

## Recent NDEs

Two recent high-profile cases have seen a surge of media interest in NDEs and created much debate. Anita Moorjani[15] had an NDE when she was admitted to intensive care. At the time, she was suffering from advanced lymphoma and was expected to die. Her family had been prepared for the worst and her brother had flown to be at her bedside. As she got close to death, Anita went into a coma and experienced an NDE. Remarkably, she recovered from that acute phase of her illness and she now believes that her lymphoma has completely gone. Her experience has totally changed the way in which she lives her life and she now regularly speaks about her experience to audiences all over the world.

Probably one of the most surprising of recent reports of an NDE has come from Dr Eben Alexander III.[16] Not only is his NDE one of the deepest NDEs I have come across but the fact that he is a neurosurgeon and not afraid to talk publicly about his experience is highly unusual and very commendable. Dr Alexander contracted a rare form of meningitis and was a patient in intensive care, where he was in a drug-induced coma for seven days.

A particularly fascinating aspect of his NDE transpired after it had occurred. During the NDE Eben was accompanied by a beautiful guardian angel with butterfly wings; this beautiful face was very vivid but he didn't recognize it as anyone he knew. Dr Alexander was adopted and hadn't met his birth family until the year before his NDE. His birth sisters explained that his younger sister Betsy had died. Four months after being discharged from intensive care they sent him a photograph of Betsy (whom he had never seen before) and he realized he was looking at the face that was on the butterfly wings during his NDE.

His NDE was very extensive and, as he is a neurosurgeon, he tried to rationalize his experience in terms of neurophysiology. However, despite his medical training and extensive knowledge of the brain, he was unable to understand his NDE in terms of the current scientific beliefs about consciousness. Consequently, he is now convinced that the current belief that consciousness is created by the brain is incorrect.

Having worked with many doctors over the years, I spoke to a few who confided that they had actually experienced an NDE. Most often the doctors would try to explain their NDE away or attribute it to one physiological factor or another and they would certainly never tell anyone else about their experience due to peer pressure and fear of ridicule. The fact that Dr Alexander has chosen to speak about his NDE publicly highlights just how powerful his NDE was in changing his mind about everything he had been taught about consciousness in medical school.

In March 2013 I spoke at a conference in Marseille, France, organized by Sonia Barkallah of S17 Productions. There I met NDEr Rajaa Benamour, from Casablanca, Morocco. It was really fascinating talking with Rajaa but as my French is not very good I had to rely on a translator. She first explained that she was wearing dark sunglasses indoors because she had developed sensitivity to light as a result of her NDE and the lighting was really affecting her eyes.

The conference had instant translation facilities via headphones so I could understand what she said during her talk. Following an injection of anaesthetic, Rajaa underwent an intense NDE where she gained highly detailed knowledge, had a life review that took her back to her own birth and also a more extensive review of the birth of the whole universe. She also described experiencing everything at a quantum level and having acquired an in-depth understanding of quantum physics that she didn't previously have. She has since been motivated to study quantum physics at university level.

During the conference a video recording of an interview with Rajaa's university professor was broadcast. He stated how puzzled he was about Rajaa's level of knowledge of quantum physics. The knowledge and understanding that she has cannot be acquired by attending an accelerated course or reading lots of books about quantum physics. What I found particularly intriguing was that he said that not even he understood some of what Rajaa was writing about but her work had since been confirmed by recent papers that had been published in physics journals.

Rajaa is currently writing a book about her NDE but, as she mentioned at the conference, her NDE was so extensive that it will be three volumes long. I'm really looking forward to learning more about her experience and I hope her books are translated into English.

## Components of the NDE

*Hearing the News of Being Close to Death*
Some people report hearing bystanders saying that they are dead or the doctor/nurse saying such things as 'She's arrested', 'We're losing him' or that the person is not going to survive.

*Noise*
As the person 'leaves' the body they may report hearing a buzzing, whistling, whirring or humming sound, or a click.

*The Out-of-Body Experience (OBE)*
The out-of-body component can occur alone, with no other components of the NDE. People report suddenly being drawn upwards out of their body and finding themselves at a point close to the ceiling, above the

emergency situation, looking down on themselves. At first they may not recognize themselves, but then notice other people such as doctors or nurses attending to their body. Often there is a sense of weightlessness and they feel that the 'real them' is the one looking down on the body, which is something they no longer identify with or associate as a part of themselves. Remarkably, some blind people have reported NDEs which also contain the OBE component.[17]

The following example of an OBE was sent to me in response to a newspaper article I wrote:

*I was most interested in your article and believe that this field needs more research. Twenty years ago I was galloping a racehorse, on my own on top of a mountain when he lost his footing, the bridle snapped and we went headlong into the ground, with a ton of racehorse doing 30 miles an hour rolling over me. I woke up some two hours later with rain gently falling, looking down on myself. My crash helmet was smashed and someone told me that I would be all right but that I needed to get up as it wasn't time for me to go as I was still needed by my daughter. I had a feeling that I was 'halfway to heaven', watching from above with a voice talking to me.*

*I watched from this hovering position as my body raised itself and started to walk off the mountain and down a steep stony forestry track (some two miles). When I reached the forestry car park a man came to my body and helped me into his car and drove towards the main road. I was now hovering above the car as it approached my friend, who stopped the car; they transferred my body into her car and she drove me to the hospital, her husband ran up the mountain to recover the horse. I was examined by a doctor in the hospital but I was actually above the bed watching. They x-rayed my head and told my friend to take me home, this she refused to do. I was hovering above her, telling her to get another doctor. Another doctor arrived and I was wheeled into a small theatre and they undertook a thoracotomy on my collapsed lungs. As I drew my first breath I went back into my body and felt pain for the first time, some three and a half hours after the accident.*

*The next day my consultant also diagnosed a crushed left leg as well as my fractured ribs, severe concussion, etc. She was enthralled with my story as it should have been impossible for me to even stand up, never mind walk – she likened my injuries to someone who had had a tractor roll over them. It was a life-changing experience, I have always felt a better person for it – there is without doubt a greater power. Some ten years later I was in a GP's surgery waiting for my father's repeat prescription when a man, someone that I had never met before, sat down beside me. He turned to me and said that he had had an out-of-body experience recently when he had a massive heart attack and now recognized someone like me who had also experienced it. It was quite something as he also felt that he had an aura around him, like me – and that it had made him a much better person. Good luck with your research, if I can help in anyway, please let me know.*

## The Tunnel/Darkness and Light

Not all people report a tunnel; in fact in some cultures it appears that the tunnel is absent and people report transitions from darkness into light.[18] For those who report a very dark tunnel, sometimes the inside will have a specific texture such as velvet, corrugated, muddy or concrete. The person may be propelled very quickly through or just gently float through. At the end of the darkness is a bright light that usually gets brighter. Despite the brightness it does not hurt the eyes and sometimes has almost a magnetic quality that seems to pull the person towards it.

## The Life Review

During the life review living images of the person's life are literally played out and relived from a third-person perspective. It is described by some people as panoramic and everything occurs at once. The life review can include all of the important events in their life as well as the insignificant. The images have been described as holographic with a simultaneous matrix of impressions.[19] It can be in chronological order or just random images that don't have any particular relevance. In some cases during the life review the person may be accompanied by a non-judgemental presence that appears to provide a source of strength and comfort as the images unfold. The person is confronted with the consequences of their actions – good or bad – and can feel the effects that their actions have had on others. They may experience a strong feeling of self-judgement as they review their life from this third-person perspective. For example, they may report feeling deeply upset by an inconsiderate remark they made to someone as they relive it in the life review. Equally they may feel elated after experiencing from the other person's perspective how their actions had helped someone.

## Heightened Senses
During and sometimes after the NDE the person may experience more acute senses such as hearing and sight. There is a heightened sense of awareness and heightened sense of consciousness. Often the experience has been described to me as 'realer than real'.

## Meeting Deceased Loved Ones
The person may be met by deceased relatives or friends. In fact this was the most commonly reported component in the study that I undertook. Interestingly, sometimes they met people who they did not know to be dead at the time of their experience. Very often the deceased person will tell the person experiencing the NDE that it's not their time and that they have to return.

## Presence or 'Being of Light'
A 'being of light' sometimes appears during the experience. It can be a religious figure associated with the person's culture or it can just appear as a presence. Great love and bright light usually emanate from this being/presence.

## Telepathic Communication
Any communication between the person and the deceased loved ones/being of light is through telepathy as opposed to verbal communication.

## Entering into Another Realm/Beautiful Gardens and Landscapes
Once they reach the light, the person may find themselves in a beautiful garden with lovely landscapes full of lush green grass and vividly coloured flowers. There may be a stream or river in the background.

## Feelings of Peace, Joy and Tranquillity and the Absence of Pain
The most prevalent components of the NDE are feelings of immense joy, peace, euphoria, calm and tranquillity. Any pain that the individual was previously experiencing disappears during the NDE.

*Barrier or Point of No Return*
A barrier such as a gate, a river or a doorway often symbolizes the end of the experience. The person knows that if they cross this barrier they will not return to life.

*Feelings of Unity/Interconnectivity*
During the experience some people feel a great sense of unity and interconnectivity between all people.

*Coming Back/Sent Back*
Some people feel as if they float gently backwards into their body, some feel as if they suddenly jolt back into their body, some feel as though they re-entered their body through their head, while others just 'wake up' in their body, wondering what just happened. Most people are sent back by the deceased loved ones or 'being of light' that they meet. They are often told that it is not their time or that they still have work to do. Often the individual is left with a sense that there is a mission in their life they need to accomplish, though they do not know what that mission is.

*Glimpse of a Future Event*
Some people report a glimpse of an event that is in the future. It may be related to their personal future or the future of the planet.

*Time Distortion*
Time seems to have no meaning during an NDE. In many cases the experience may seem as if it had lasted for hours yet the time of unconsciousness was literally seconds or minutes. Sometimes it feels as if time is greatly speeded up; sometimes it goes slower. Most of the time, the person cannot put a timescale on the duration of the experience. It is quite remarkable how people can report such lengthy and detailed descriptions of what they experienced during such a brief period of unconsciousness.

*Ineffability*
When people try to make sense of the experience or try to verbalize it they find that words fail them. They have experienced something with which they have nothing to compare, and to try to find words to describe it is impossible. Due to the ineffability of the experience, even when the person writes it down, words do not do it justice. So for me to

report what others have described is tainted and somewhat diluted from its original form. When NDEs are reproduced for TV shows or movies it is unfortunate that the full essence of such a profound experience can never be adequately captured for the audience.

## Greater Ecological Awareness
Many NDErs recognize the importance of ecological issues and the impact that humans are having on the planet.

## Recalling an NDE
Another aspect for people to be aware of is that the recall of the NDE can evoke a lot of emotion and it may take several attempts to talk about the experience because the person can become so moved when thinking of their experience (they weren't really upset; most of the time it was tears of joy). I have spoken to men and women who have been unable to tell me about their NDE because they cannot stop crying. It was easier for them to write down their experience because they were too overcome by their emotions to talk. These are not tears of sadness, but an overwhelming emotion triggered by memory of the immense love that they felt during the experience.

Some people are quite disappointed or even angry at being successfully resuscitated.[20] They were so happy where they were that they did not wish to return to life. In cases of childhood NDEs and some adult NDEs there remains a longing or yearning to return to the place they visited during their NDE.

The following is an example sent to me by email from a 43-year-old lady called Jules Lyons:

*I have started to talk more openly about my NDE, which I kept pretty much to myself for the past 22 years. It only lasted a few minutes (earthly time, according to medics that's how long I was 'gone'), yet it felt like SO much longer. It was simply the most amazing, beautiful thing I have ever, ever experienced . . . just talking about it still makes my whole body tingle and sort of glow inside. It's as clear and vivid as if it happened only an hour ago.*

*I was in a very bad way, in the Accident & Emergency unit, it was summer 1987. I was slipping in and out of consciousness. Anyway, I remember the doctor's voice, saying, 'there's nothing else we can do'* to someone, at the same moment I realized I had somehow floated upwards, out of my own body, and was floating upwards towards the ceiling of the hospital room. I could actually feel my back physically pressing against the ceiling of the hospital room. I was watching the doctor and two nurses moving around my own body, lying on the bed below. They were talking, I could clearly hear what they were saying ... it wasn't very positive! I felt that I was floating there, against the ceiling, for about a minute. I felt strangely calm, deeply calm and incredibly peaceful, just observing, quietly.

I was 'pulled up' through the ceiling and seemed to whizz off somewhere else, at incredible speed. Next thing I knew, I was floating/flying down a very long tunnel, miles and miles long, very dark and empty, and I could feel the speed I was flying at was fast, as it was like wind flowing over me and through my hair, etc. I felt incredibly calm and peaceful still, no fear at all. I felt a sense of release, if anything: of immense freedom and lightness of being. I could see miles into the distance and at the end of this long dark tunnel was a massively bright white light. Intensely bright white; almost blinding. The tunnel felt cold, dark and windy, yet I felt an OVERWHELMING, all-pervasive sense of deep, deep peace, joy and calm. Like being enveloped in a warm bubble bath or a blanket of sheer calm, bliss and peace. It was like nothing I can ever adequately describe, nor anything I have ever experienced on earth (prior or since the NDE).

When I got to the end of the tunnel, and to the brilliant white light, I found myself now floating along on what seemed to be thin air. Just clear, light, empty space; bright and clear, like crystal-clear air. I suddenly felt a rush of immense joy welling up inside me, felt SO uplifted and SO peaceful and incredibly happy. And, I very clearly remember, for the first time ever, I experienced what it felt like to feel truly FREE, as if every atom of my being was free and glowing with joy.

As I was floating along (more like 'being floated along' by some external force), there appeared a quite high stone wall, running for miles and miles on my right hand side, and even though it was high (maybe ten feet high?), I could actually float myself upwards a little bit and see over the top of it.

What I saw, over this stone wall, was simply the MOST BEAUTIFUL, MOST PEACEFUL and most AMAZING place I could ever imagine. Wide, panoramic gardens/landscape with rivers, ponds, fountains, flowers, trees, hills, meadows, valleys, etc. It was breathtakingly beautiful. Yet, the most incredible thing about this place was the colour. The colours of everything were so incredibly bright and vivid, almost iridescent and glowing, as if they were alive in some strange way. It was like no landscape at all on earth ... more like a super-technicolour, really vivid and amazingly beautiful colours, almost like crystal-clear, vibrant, radiating colours.

There were a few distinct features which stood out immediately to me: a few pathways which looked like iridescent glass or something, astonishingly beautiful colours; these paths led off into an invisible distance, as there seemed to be no end to the landscape. I could see fountains, rivers, the most beautiful trees and flowers.

There was also one very interesting and unusual building, the only building I could see in the whole place. It was quite small, quite simple, and I can only accurately describe it as like a cross between a garden gazebo/summer house and a domed temple, almost like a mosque dome, of what appeared to be gold and light. The most intense golden light was shining out through this building, almost in rays, out onto the surrounding landscape. I somehow knew that one by one everyone had to go inside this building at some point.

There were comfortable seats and benches dotted around, all over the gardens and into the distance, with quite a lot of people. Yes, what seemed to be perfectly ordinary people, all sat around, peacefully chatting, all in a quiet, gentle way, like a sense of soft whispering, some were in small groups under trees, some sat on the grass, some walking down the pathways. I couldn't hear any actual words or distinguish any voices, it was as if they were communicating with each other without speech, and I had an awareness that they were having conversations. They seemed to be wearing some kind of robes, or garments, not earthly clothes, but they were very definitely human! There was a DEEP sense of peace and calm amongst everyone. I felt very clearly like they were 'waiting'. As if this was some kind of 'waiting' or 'reception' area. Everyone in this landscape was waiting.

It felt like a gentle summer day, warm, comfortable, not too hot, and I was happily floating along this wall, looking over the top into this landscape, when quite suddenly a gate appeared just up ahead.

An ordinary-looking, old-fashioned tall wooden garden gate: the type they used to have in old stone walls or gardens. As I was floating nearer this gate, I could see a figure stood (floating on this crystal clear air just like me!) next to it.

It seemed to take me a while to get up close (the floating sensation/ my movements were not being dictated by me, but by some other energy/power carrying me along, at a gentle pace). Anyway, I finally reached this gate, and there in front of me, large as life and as real as I am sat here now, was my maternal grandmother, bless her soul, who passed away when I was five years old (over 38 years ago). My family never really talked about her (nor about any of our grandparents!), so I didn't really have many memories of her when I was a child and growing up.

There she was, real as anything, no ghostly apparition, but real and solid, I could have reached out and touched her, she was calmly stood there, totally alive, well, real and looking lovely and radiant (she 'died' of lung cancer).

She smiled such a warm and loving smile, and I felt her hug me, even though she didn't touch me at all, I could physically feel her arms wrapping around me and such a huge wave of love. She gave me the most warm and loving cuddle ever. It was wonderful, and so real, even though it appeared she didn't actually move or touch me at all. I felt the most incredible love and peace and happiness and calm, both inside me and in this place, in all these people, like nothing I've ever felt here on earth. Such deep calm and peace and love.

I clearly remember all of this like it just happened this morning. I felt SO happy. My gran spoke to me, her voice clear and alive, even though her mouth didn't move from the smile she was wearing, I sensed she was talking directly to my brain/mind, like there were no spoken words, yet I could clearly understand what she was saying. She gave me a very clear message (three very clear sentences which will live with me forever) including: 'We are not ready for you yet' and that 'You have to go back' and finally that 'There is something you have to do. Your purpose.' She then smiled at me so warmly, it seemed to infuse me with peace and love and joy.

Then, in what felt like a split second, I was being 'floated' backwards, at far greater speed this time, all the way back along the wall, as I watched my gran disappearing in the distance, I was *'floated' all the way back towards and through the tunnel, all the time backwards, still facing where I had just been, and then I felt myself actually going back into my body, which coincided with such a resounding 'THUD' that my whole body did a massive jolt/ spasm (like those dreams where you're falling off a cliff and you jolt as you wake up, only 100x greater in strength). And this is when I apparently suddenly 'awoke', and regained 'vital signs', on the hospital trolley/bed.*

*Well, that was over 22 years ago; I made a full recovery and had good health for many years afterwards. It was a miracle to me. And it was the start of a lot of things happening for me in my life, including my awakening/interest in spiritual matters (I was 21, had no prior knowledge or exposure to anything spiritual or related to near-death experiences or the afterlife).*

*After that, for a few years, I'd sometimes have a really strong sense that my gran was around me, like I could sense her in the room occasionally, and once or twice I could have sworn I actually heard her speak, but I convinced myself I must have been imagining it! I never spoke about these things to anybody for years and years, apart from one close friend. I never did anything to 'contact' my gran, or to develop any 'skills' in that area (to be honest, the idea of that sort of thing scared me a bit!), but I did start to read a lot of books about all sorts of spiritual subjects, including reading the Bible for the first time.*

As the experience demonstrates, time seems to have no relevance during an NDE. The whole complex scenario reported occurred in a matter of seconds while Jules was unconscious and had no vital signs. How can something so structured and lucid be described in such detail when the brain is so severely dysfunctional? It should not be possible. Jules's NDE was described in great depth; not all NDEs are as deep as that. Some may just have one or two of the components while others may have the majority of them. Each NDE is unique. The components don't appear in any particular order but the out-of-body experience and the tunnel and light are usually at the beginning. In fact it has been reported that some experiencers have embellished their NDE to include a tunnel so that it corresponded with the classic NDE.[21]

\* \* \*

An individual's reactions to an NDE are varied; they can continue indefinitely or dissipate with time. The following example is from a lady who was changed temporarily by her NDE:

*I suffered a car accident many years ago and ended up with fractures of my pelvis, femur and clavicle. I also suffered some brain injury though not very serious. I was not in ITU and awoke on the ward. It was explained to me what had happened and I went back to 'sleep'.*

*I, too, travelled along a dark tunnel and towards a very bright light. I reached the light to find beautiful pastures and vivid blue skies. What struck me most was the sensation of utter contentment and bliss. I am unable to put into words the exact feeling that I experienced. I saw no dead relatives or friends, just a little wooden fence and I knew that if I crossed that fence, there was no return.*

*I was brought up in a Christian culture but I am agnostic. After my 'experience', I did have religious fervour and began to wear a crucifix. I knew without doubt that there was an afterlife and that physical matters were really insignificant. I'm afraid the feeling only lasted a few months and the hustle and bustle of working and general living soon returned me to my cynical self! In saying that, even taking into consideration other factors that may have prompted the experience, e.g. morphine, blood loss, I still have the memory of the peace that I felt and the fact that I had never experienced it before or have done since. Maybe it is the body's natural endorphins preparing for death and making it a pleasant sensation rather than a frightening one. It doesn't explain 'out-of-body' experiences, though! It is a fascinating subject and maybe one day there will be an answer.*

## Distressing NDEs

Not all NDEs are pleasant; some can be quite distressing and people who experience these are inclined to suppress the memory.[22] They can evoke such terror that the person will not speak about it, as even to recall the memory is too traumatic.[23] Unfortunately, not much attention has been paid to these types of NDEs but they do occur and, so far, there is no explanation as to why some people report pleasant NDEs whereas a minority of cases are distressing. There is no evidence to suggest that the pleasant NDEs happen to 'good' people and the distressing NDEs happen to 'bad' people.

The medieval otherworld journeys reported by Zaleski[24] and distressing spiritual experiences[25] (which occur in circumstances which are not life threatening) are comparable with distressing NDEs. One of the first people to report such a distressing experience was cardiologist Maurice Rawlings,[26] who resuscitated a patient who screamed that he was in hell as he regained consciousness. On a follow-up visit two days later the patient had no recollection of being in hell and Rawlings suggested that this was due to suppression.

In 2006 I was contacted by a 40-year-old man in response to one of my newspaper articles. His NDE is very interesting as it is not characteristic of the usual positive NDE and has left him with some very irksome after effects, which will be discussed in Chapter 2. The NDE occurred during an accident while he was playing rugby at the age of 15, which resulted in a broken neck. He described his experience as not being pleasant or unpleasant:

*The last thing I remember is hearing three loud cracks – snap, snap, snap. It was my neck breaking. The very next thing I was rapidly accelerating headfirst, back arched, arms outstretched down a huge endless void, pitch-black save for a pin prick of brilliant white light that sped away from my grey featureless feet. It almost felt as though I had been dropped head first down a well or tunnel. What was happening, how had I got from the rugby pitch to here? How can I make it stop? Everything happened at tremendous speed.*

*I'd heard that your life flashes before your eyes when you die. Well, that didn't happen to me. What I experienced was thoughts and images from the whole of my life whooshing rapidly past me as if they were being sucked out of my brain. It's as if all of my memories were being downloaded and removed from my brain. The images were so fast ... whoosh ... then another thought ... whoosh ... then another image. I tried to focus on a couple as they left my mind and could see what they were but only for a fraction of a microsecond ... me fishing? ... a familiar face? ... but I had to get my focus back on what was happening to me ... I was 'falling' after all ... I could see all of the images disappearing from my memory banks. I realized this as I was falling, I was scrabbling for words, they were all being broken down until I got to the very last smallest word, 'Nooooooooo'. It was as if that was the last word left before my brain was completely empty. I know that if I hadn't said 'No' then I would have died. I just managed to get that word out and it all just stopped.*

*It was warm and comfortable there. It was pitch black, the darkest black you can imagine, but there was a bright white light in the top right-hand corner of my vision and I was sure there was some distant warmth coming from it. It was bright white; it was comforting and gave me just enough light to see by. I looked down and could see my fingers and they were grey but when I looked at my feet I couldn't see my toes, it was as if I was wearing grey socks. I was scared to move because it felt as though I was balancing on a ledge and if I made any sudden movements I'd roll off and start to fall again. I was hovering in space, I was feeling underneath me and there was nothing there. I was worried but wasn't panicking. I moved my head to the left then to the right and there was just blackness; it was the darkest room. It was a holding place or waiting room. I was left there while a decision was being made by someone else. It's as if there is more than one God – if there was only one person to make the decision then it would have been quick. There must have been more than one person because the decision would have been made sooner. Then it was like lying on the bottom of a swimming pool looking up and slowly coming to the surface. I could make out movement, then silhouettes of light and dark moving like smoke, then outlines, then I recognized it was faces, then mouths, then sounds, then sentences I recognized – I was alive again.*

Distressing accounts were investigated by British researcher Dr Margot Grey, who categorized the distressing experiences as:[27]

- Fear and a feeling of panic
- Out-of-body experience
- Entering a black void
- Sensing an evil force
- Entering a hell-like environment.

Basing their study on 50 accounts of distressing NDEs, Greyson and Bush[28] later classified them as:
- The prototypical NDE but interpreted in an unpleasant way

- Void experience (common during childbirth) where the person believes that they are in a dark eternal 'nothingness'
- Hellish, where the person believes that they are in hell or encounter demons who are trying to take them to hell.

Dr Barbara Rommer[29] added in a fourth category, where the person experiences a distressing life review in which they are judged by a higher power. However, Dr Rommer believed that despite the NDE being distressing, it still had positive, life-changing effects such as the NDEr becoming less judgemental and feeling an increased love of life and heightened sense of morality.

I was chatting to a colleague at the university who had heard that I was interested in NDEs and she casually mentioned that she'd had an NDE about 35 years ago when she was 17. Immediately my ears pricked up and I listened intently to what she had to say. She was ventilated in intensive care and, while unconscious, over a period of 10 days, underwent some unpleasant subjective experiences. The most vivid experience was standing on a platform, like the ones used by window cleaners who are cleaning windows on the outside of tall buildings. Immediately in her line of vision were scenes of a sexual nature that she was forced to watch. She didn't wish to elaborate on these scenes as they were so disturbing. Every time she tried to turn her head away, she would find herself facing the same scene until she had watched it all play out. She then progressed to the next level, where she again had to watch similar scenes.

Another part of her NDE appears to be similar to the void experience. It was all very difficult to put into words but she described watching a scroll of paper unfolding before her eyes. Every time she tried to look at something different her attention was taken back to the same place on the scroll of unfolding paper. She described it as 'eternal boredom' just watching the same thing over and over and over and wondering if it was ever going to end. Once she 'accepted' or 'gave in' to the feeling of boredom and became interested, then something changed and the boredom was brought back.

It has been suggested that distressing NDEs are the result of increased levels of carbon dioxide[30] or due to anaesthetics[31] but I did not find this to be the case in the research that I undertook.

As a student nurse I remember looking after a lady who was dying. She was in obvious spiritual distress and was tormented by something.

Each time I or my colleagues went near her she would grab hold of our uniforms and claw at our arms, digging her nails into our skin, begging us to save her from death. Her eyes were wide and bulging and had a terrified look. She said that she had died before and it was a horrible place. None of us knew how best to help this lady but she was obviously terrified by what she had previously experienced. We discussed this with her family, who said that many years ago she had had a cardiac arrest but they didn't know why she was so frightened. It was only on reflection several years later, after I became acquainted with NDEs, that it seems likely that the lady had experienced a distressing NDE during her cardiac arrest many years previously. At the time, my colleagues and I had never heard of such an experience. Hence it is so important that we are aware of these experiences so that future patients may be helped through such psychological trauma. Had we been aware of these types of experiences we would have been able to provide greater psychological support and maybe the patient would have had a more pleasant transition into death.

Clearly these distressing experiences evoke great concern, and often distress, in those who experience them. In an email, a hospital chaplain had this to say about distressing NDEs:

*I had one patient who had a frightening NDE. He had feelings of being utterly alone, with black shadowy figures moving in and out around him (I actually wondered if his anaesthesia was light and he might have been seeing the surgeons, etc. moving around). Whatever may have happened, afterwards he was in spiritual distress. He was concerned that: (a) death wasn't the end, (b) was this waiting for him when he dies, (c) to him, this meant there was a spiritual realm. We had long conversations about his life, God, the universe and everything.*

Below is a brief example of a prototypical NDE interpreted in a distressing way:

*This is something which I experienced when I was 27 years old, more than 26 years ago. At that time I only told my husband what had happened. Whenever I read about NDEs everyone always states how calm they were – my experience was quite the opposite.*

*I was in hospital in a lot of pain; my husband was sitting by the bed. I felt that I was falling in and out of sleep. I looked out of the window and I could see a very bright tunnel leading up to the sky and the clouds parted. Every time my eyes closed I was drawn towards the tunnel. I became very agitated and did not want to go. I remember saying to somebody, 'I don't want to come, my son is only 3, he needs me.' I told my husband that he must not let me go to sleep because I knew if I closed my eyes I would have gone through the tunnel.*

The following experience was sent to me by Tony, aged 44:

*In 1994 I suffered a very severe head injury, when I was knocked off my bicycle by a car. I spent eleven months in hospital: seven weeks at one and nine months at another. As a result of the accident I was in a coma for four weeks, a wheelchair user for eight months and unable to read and write for a long period.*

*Immediately following this accident, a neighbour (who was also a qualified nurse) took the necessary action to ensure that it did not have fatal consequences by ensuring that I did not lose more blood, that I was able to breathe more comfortably and, perhaps most significantly, she telephoned for an ambulance. She has since advised me that I remained conscious, continually muttering, 'help me, help me.' However, she thought that my injuries were so severe that when an ambulance eventually arrived, I would not survive the journey to the hospital.*

*On my arrival at the hospital, my friend was contacted and asked to identify my body. On arrival, he has advised me that I was described as being in a 'touch and go' predicament. However, following a blood transfusion I was sufficiently stable to be taken by ambulance to a different hospital and was placed on a life support machine for three days.*

*At the time of the accident I was a 'lapsed' Roman Catholic. However, I have been 'reborn' since (but have not become 'overtly religious').*

*Some 'red angels', who I later perceived to be 'devil's demons', asked me to join them. After refusing this request some more 'red angels' came down from what I assumed to be heaven and fought the 'devil's demons' . . . I can vaguely recall a 'heavenly angel' piercing a 'devil's demon' in his/her heart with a spear. In retrospect the physical appearance of 'heavenly angels' and 'devil's demons' should not be dissimilar because the devil (Lucifer) had once been a 'heavenly angel'. I understand that a similar depiction of a 'near-death' experience is depicted in the 'Book of Revelation'.*

*In some respects this experience gave me cause for concern because I felt that if the 'devil's demons' had thought it worthwhile approaching me it was possible that I had been (am) such a bad person that I might deserve to 'rot in hell'.*

There have been cases recorded where a distressing NDE has turned into a pleasant NDE once the person has relaxed into the experience.[32] After being knocked down by a car, a seven-year-old boy reported that he had been in darkness and he had found himself in a tunnel, which he floated through and subsequently came across two doors. On entering one door he was confronted with a devil, who he conversed with. He walked out of that room to encounter a very bright light that didn't hurt his eyes. The light told him not to be afraid and put him in a dungeon. Everything went blurry and he woke up in the hospital.[33]

As I was completing the final editing of this book I received an email out of the blue from former Chief of Anesthesiology at Heart Hospital in Bakersfield, California, Dr Rajiv Parti.[34] I was taken aback as he described a fascinating NDE and it is quite unusual for a doctor to share such an experience. As I've already mentioned, most doctors I have spoken to took years to confide their experience in me and then were most insistent that I would never tell any one else about it. The fact that Dr Parti has spoken publicly about his NDE reiterates the transformative power of NDEs.

In 2008 his life was changed when he was diagnosed with prostate cancer. He suffered complications from his initial surgery and underwent three further surgeries later that year. He was left with several debilitating medical conditions and was in chronic excruciating pain, which led to addiction to pain medication and eventually depression.

In December 2010 he had further surgery but developed post-operative sepsis and was admitted to intensive care. In the early hours of Christmas Day Dr Parti was prepared for an emergency surgical procedure and had a very deep NDE.

He has kindly agreed to share some of his very intricate and detailed NDE in this book. It began with an OBE where he could see his sleeping body in the hospital room and then in the operating room. He described his senses as being hyper vivid and he was aware of the conversations that were going on in the operating room, which were later verified by the staff. Although he was in hospital in Los Angeles, he was also aware of the conversation of some family members in India – he felt as though his awareness was everywhere at once.

After this he was taken to a place that he believed to be hell. He could see himself being dragged to a place where there appeared to be a raging lightning storm with lots of dark clouds. He encountered grotesque entities and could smell burning meat. He witnessed the suffering of others and was himself subjected to tortures such as being stabbed with needles and made to lie on a bed of nails and blood oozed from wounds on his body.

Interestingly, Dr Parti gained valuable personal insights during this distressing phase of the NDE. The experience of hell came with a revelation about his life which he described as being one of materialism and a selfish attitude of putting himself before others. He realized his life had been lived without being loving, kind and compassionate. There had been no forgiveness in his life – for himself or others. He had also acted badly to others whom he believed to be of a lower social class than himself. He was deeply remorseful for the way in which he'd lived his life up until that point. As soon as he realized this, the whole experience changed and his father and grandfather appeared at his side and guided him towards a tunnel with a bright light. Dr Parti then went on to experience a very deep NDE where he believed he went to what could be described as heaven. He is currently writing a book about his NDE which will have the full details of what he experienced.

It has been suggested that renouncing attempted control over the experience is what influences how the NDE proceeds.[35] Distressing NDEs can appear to have a positive long-term effect as people re-evaluate the ways in which they live their lives.[36] Those who reported a hell-like experience considered it to be a warning to modify their attitude to others.[37] However, this may just be the case for those who have managed to integrate the experience into their life.

Distressing NDEs have been considered in depth by Nancy Bush (who experienced a distressing NDE) in her book *Dancing Past the*

*Dark*.[38] She highlights the complete lack of attention given to the 'dark night' aspects of spirituality and considers cultural and religious beliefs that may influence these distressing experiences. She offers useful advice on how to understand and deal with these experiences.

The distressing NDEs have also been examined by Professor Christopher Bache. He has suggested that distressing NDEs occur because the experiencer is accessing the deepest levels of the collective unconscious.[39] However, more research in this area is required before such conclusions can be firmly established.

Consideration has been given to distressing NDEs being the result of suicide attempts, but this was not found to be the case as positive NDEs have also been reported during such situations.[40] Indeed, the case of Jules presented earlier occurred during a suicide attempt. Interestingly, Jules's NDE left her with the certainty that suicide is *not* the answer and would *not* have been a solution to her problems.

Although distressing NDEs are far less common than the pleasant type, statistics vary amongst researchers. One researcher[41] found almost equal reports of distressing and pleasant visions in the 36 survivors of heart attacks interviewed. Out of 55 people who underwent a close encounter with death, 11 reported distressing experiences.[42] Out of 41 NDEs, Grey[43] found five terrifying and one to be hell-like (i.e. approximately 15 per cent were distressing). Out of over 700 NDEs, Atwater[44] found 105 to be distressing (again, approximately 15 per cent). In over 300 NDEs, Dr Rommer[45] reported 18 per cent to be distressing. However, methodologies varied between each researcher so there will be more of an idea as to how common distressing NDEs are with the advent of prospective research.

The NDE is not just about the single event: the experience is one that is never forgotten and has a big impact on the rest of the lives of the NDErs, as the next chapter will show.

# 2

# The After Effects of the NDE

*. . . Adjusting to life again was like learning to walk all over again . . .*
*Then I began to appreciate sounds, colours and music and I thought,*
*my God, I've taken all of this for granted . . .*

The words of the actress Elizabeth Taylor[1]

The NDE is a very complex phenomenon and there are many life changes associated with it.[2] Adjusting to life after an NDE can be very difficult as no one else can understand exactly what has been experienced.[3] The NDE is something that in many cases totally transcends all human experiences – the person has nothing else to compare with it. Often people are reluctant to discuss their experience because they are afraid of being ridiculed or disbelieved. In fact, the reaction the person gets from the first person they discuss their experience with can greatly impact on the way in which the NDE is integrated into their life. A dismissive or unsympathetic attitude can result in the person never discussing the experience again and bottling it all inside. NDErs are not attention seekers and have a great reluctance to speak publicly about their experience – many examples used in this book are from people who have requested anonymity.

Relationship problems may arise between the person and their spouse as their values can change so dramatically; it is not uncommon for couples to divorce[4] following an NDE. Failure of others to acknowledge such an experience can also have a huge impact on the person.[5] A few years ago I was contacted by a lady who described to me some components of the NDE which occurred as she lost consciousness during a road traffic accident. She was severely debilitated for some months due to her injuries and more than three years after the accident she could still not get over what had happened. She had been treated by several psychologists but she could not quite work through her psychological problems. By chance she had read an article in a magazine about my research and recognized what was described as being similar to what she had experienced. After a few emails the lady was able to understand what she had experienced and was able to move on. It seems incredible that something as simple as a greater understanding of NDEs could potentially save the NHS millions of pounds while being of great benefit to patients.

IANDS is one of the most important resources and source of support for someone who has had an NDE. In 2006, 25 NDErs attended a retreat in order to share their experiences with others who had undergone an NDE.[6] The outcome of the retreat was the identification of six major challenges that the NDErs were faced with:

- Processing a radical shift in reality
- Accepting the return to life
- Sharing the experience
- Integrating new spiritual values with earthly expectations
- Adjusting to heightened sensitivities and supernatural gifts
- Finding and living one's purpose.

## Unpleasant After Effects

Contrary to most reports on NDEs, many people are left with some negative after effects. Some exhibit increased personal distress[7] and there is a higher divorce rate.[8] Often people yearn to return to the state that they were in during their NDE, especially if the NDE was experienced during childhood.[9] People can feel very isolated and unable to express their feelings and may become depressed.[10] Some may seek help while others prefer to deal with it alone in silence. However, it has been suggested that these psychological problems may actually signify the beginning of psychological growth.[11]

Here are some interesting insights described by a man whose NDE is on pages 16–17:

*I would like to add this important perspective, please. Not all NDE experiencers remain uplifted and joyously positive throughout every day of their lives post event. The article in the newspaper made it sound as if all NDErs were. My NDE made me drop out of my BA Honours Sports Studies degree course because I couldn't deal with the back-biting, the competitiveness, the 'posiness', . . . it all seemed so artificial . . . I later got a job in the NHS and have been very happy in my role . . . but this led to a 'burn-out' moment where I was trying to up-hold the rights of the elderly, trying to ensure that the sick were getting the best quality in all the investigations they received.*

*I have put everyone else's health and happiness before my own, so that now at 40 I realize I have very little for myself, . . . I have gone through great bouts of depression . . . even repeatedly considering 'going back to that peaceful place' . . . as an NDEr you feel like a misplaced person . . . and you no longer have that thing which gives ordinary people strength to go on, that 'fear of death' you no longer have . . . it also made me more serious and considerate, I am able to 'see the wood for the trees' . . . because I see hundreds of sad, sick, unhappy faces with no trace of hope in them, of dreams all gone, . . . this look has haunted me because I felt I was 'responsible' for uplifting everyone . . . but I can't do it for everyone all the time . . . so, no. An NDE is both a good thing and a bad thing. It has two sides like any coin. An NDE gives you strength in some situations but it is a weakness in other situations. Do not be fooled into thinking it is a wondrous thing. It can be a 'thanatos' too.*

In a further conversation five years later he added:

*I can recall my NDE immediately, that dark place, at any time of the day or night, and I don't even have to close my eyes. It doesn't fill me with fear, I am still in awe of it, but why was I given the experience? I will never know. Some days and moments I have a yearning to get back there, it was such a peaceful place. You are the first person to take me seriously since it happened when I was 15 years old. It's always in the back of my mind and I often wonder, 'is this a dream (real present life, the here and now) or am I still in the tunnel?' I am very scientific but sit between religion and science now. I'm not devout but I also recognize the limitations of our science. I know* what I experienced. I have kept it 'pure' . . . uncluttered by either scientific or religious learning. I've changed from being almost an atheist before the NDE to being more open minded now.

I'm a healthcare worker and there have been numerous times when I have participated in cardiac arrests and the first thing I do is ask the patient's name and talk to them and call them by name even if there are no signs of life on the monitors. If the resuscitation is not successful then I wish them a safe journey whilst looking to the corners of the ceiling just 'in case' they are in their out-of-body experience. My colleagues think I'm a bit strange doing this. I asked one elderly lady not very long after we had resuscitated her if she recalled anything and a big grin came over her face. She remembered being at peace in a place that was so bright and warm; she was ever so pleased to be asked and that I actually understood her and what she had just experienced.

The biggest effect the NDE has had on me is that some colleagues see me as being very annoyingly self-righteous and adhering to an impossibly strong moral ethical code of living and working. It's affected my work relationships because I stand up for the rights of down-trodden colleagues or neglected patients, putting my own career safety in the workplace at risk. Because of my NDE I myself want to be a good person. My beliefs are so strong I can no longer work in my usual workplace. The NDE seemed to magnify those aspects of my personality; it's not easy to fit into society. To me everything is black or white, right or wrong, good or evil – there is no grey. I don't fit in because I don't 'toe the line' and just agree with things.

When I was younger I was always a kindly boy. I was also competitive and always wanted to be the best. After the NDE I started to loathe competitiveness and see how it could also be very destructive; I'm more interested in working together in a team or leading a team but have had my progress to leadership blocked by others so these days I would love to be my own boss and even work alone.

I used to be quite shy and withdrawn whereas after the NDE I became more sociable and tactile. In public I'm very people orientated. I am always very attentive to the elderly patients I see in work. I'm hyper-sensitive to people's moods and can tell what emotions they are feeling. If they come in and they are depressed, *by the time they leave they are uplifted and much happier – I've had many complimentary thank-you letters. My empathic feelings have magnified. I appreciate life and the lives of others. However, it's a double-edged sword because I often value and put first the health and welfare of complete strangers before my own.*

*Light sensitivity is a big after effect that I've noticed. I am very aware of the seasonal changes in light and how that affects my mood. I now strongly believe that during the NDE my pineal gland was deprived of oxygen and damaged; it which has resulted in an imbalance of my serotonin and melatonin levels and disrupted my circadian rhythms. In the sunshine I'm ok but the light levels definitely affect my moods. One minute I can feel invincible and all things are possible, the next I just hit a brick wall and I feel depressed and suicidal. I have become a bit obsessed with this thought in recent years. There is some important research that needs doing here.*

*Before the NDE I was good at predicting things. I could guess the coloured pegs people chose in that game called Mastermind. I could often throw ones or sixes when rolling a dice. When I played rugby I always knew where the ball was going to bounce and I'd run there and catch it. I could tell when people were going to have an accident. For example, I was out cycling with my brother and I could see, in my mind, his pedal hit the kerb. I warned him about this and he moved out but a few minutes later he did hit the kerb and ended up in the road. I even knew or sensed something bad was about to happen the moment I ran out onto the pitch for my last rugby game, the game I broke my neck in and had my NDE. I've lost that ability since the NDE, it just doesn't happen any more but I have an almost constant feeling of impending doom or that the 'boogeyman' is around the next corner along my tortuous life-path, or that I am on 'borrowed time'. This has led me to be very time conscious. I hate wasting my life time in pointless tasks or in the company of stupid people.*

*What I've also become very good at since the NDE is seeing things in the 'third person', projecting myself into a corner of the room and watching myself from an almost 'out-of-body perspective'. I do this during meetings sometimes and I can even project into other people's bodies. With my eyes open or closed I can imagine that I am slipping my arms into their arms like slipping on a jacket and step into their skin, growing or shrinking my imagined new self to fit . . . and feel what it feels like to be them, male or female, and see my real self interacting with these other people. I even get flashes where I can see my own face, eyes and mouth whilst talking to people. I've got much better at this over the years. I'm glad you have recorded my experience because of my 'boogeyman' feelings. I hope this doesn't mean that I am about to 'go' now.*

Other changes are generally pleasant for most people after the NDE.

## No Fear of Death

For many who undergo an NDE, their attitude to death changes. I found in my prospective study that those who didn't attach much significance to their NDE still had a degree of uncertainty about death but those who reported a significant NDE with many components were adamant that death is nothing to fear. That's not to say that the person wants to die but they know that when it's their time to die then death will not be anything to be afraid of as they have been there already and know what to expect. In fact, one patient who was discharged to the ward kept coming to visit ITU because he wanted to tell the other patients that death was so lovely and not to be afraid.

The following was in response to a newspaper article:

*I remember with clarity my own experience many years ago at the age of 49. It was summer 1985, I had my first heart attack and one week later I had my second attack and a week after that had a cardiac arrest. I was told I had to be given 18 defibrillations to keep me alive. After I came round I remembered what happened during this time. I was in a dark tunnel with a light at the end which I was walking towards. I passed through the tunnel into the sunlight, where I walked along a path with grass verges and flowerbeds either side. I have never before felt so happy and contented; no pain, just a feeling of wellbeing. I did not, however, meet anyone and woke what seemed like a short while later. I was back in a bed in the recovery room, which was two days later. The whole experience left me with a feeling of no fear of dying. I hope you may find this of interest to you.*

## More Tolerant, Loving and Compassionate

Most people feel that they are more tolerant of others as a result of their NDE. Many experience indescribable unconditional love. They become more loving and more compassionate and their values change dramatically. Many NDErs go on to work in the caring profession and some train as nurses[12] or doctors[13] or volunteer in hospices.

Pam Williams from Swansea had an NDE when she haemorrhaged after childbirth:

*The doctor came in his car. Even though it was physically impossible I saw the doctor get out of his car and run up our path; he threw off his jacket, rolled up his sleeves and examined me, he appeared to be trying to pull something out. He then banged me on the chest and inserted a needle into my heart and injected me with something. He breathed into my mouth. All the time this was happening I felt fine; warm, happy, full of joy, peaceful, gently floating towards brilliant light. Suddenly in the distance I heard my eldest daughter shout, 'Mam'. I remember thinking, 'Oh dear, Jacquie needs me,' and I came back with a jolt. The doctor had already sent my husband to phone for the emergency maternity ambulance (no mobile phones in those days). The ambulance came with a specialist doctor in attendance. I was stabilized and bundled with my newborn daughter into the ambulance and with the sirens blaring was raced to hospital.*

*When I went for my postnatal appointment six weeks later I told the doctor what I had seen. He was amazed that I could describe the event in such detail but didn't have any explanation. This near-death experience left me with a special legacy: I know for certain that death is not to be feared. I am not a religious person but I believe there is a warm peaceful beautiful place after death. I also felt I had somehow been given the choice as to whether I should continue my journey towards the bright light or return; I chose the latter.*

*This experience was put to the back of my mind. I was an uneducated miner's wife with four small children. I did odd jobs cleaning and being a dinner lady when at the age of 34 a number of seemingly accidental events led me back into education. Within the next six years I became a nursery nurse, a RNMS and a staff nurse RGN. Within four years of qualifying I became a sister on the coronary-*

*care unit in Sheffield. Then everything seemed to fall into place: it was not serendipity or chance that had given me skills and knowledge. I humbly felt that this was the right place for me since my own near-death experience enabled me to give help and support to the dying and newly bereaved patients and families. My own non fear of dying helped me explore aspects of death, firstly at degree, and then at masters level, by which time I was a lecturer in nursing and palliative care.*

*I truly believe that had I not experienced near death, I would not have striven to explore death issues and would probably have remained content not to return to education. As a person I changed from the moment of my near-death experience; I felt an overwhelming sense of joy, and a need to help and support others. I believe strongly in the philosophy of everyday doing something or giving something to help others, often random strangers. I also strongly believe that religion is just a word and that each individual person is responsible for how they choose to live their lives.*

## No Longer Materialistic/Status Orientated

Following an NDE, their whole lives are usually re-evaluated and whereas money, status and wealth were once striven for, following the NDE the simple things in life, such as spending time with their loved ones, take priority.

## Enhanced Appreciation of Life

People realize how important their life is and stop worrying about things that would have previously bothered them.

## Spiritual Values Change

It is common for people to change their spiritual beliefs as a result of the NDE. Effects can be varied. Whereas some people tend to become more religious and may even train to become a minister,[14] some feel that their religion no longer adequately supports what was 'revealed' or felt during their NDE. Regardless of religious/spiritual values, the people are generally more considerate of others. Often NDErs are grateful to have another chance to live their life and feel a sense of spiritual purpose.[15]

Marie-Claire's NDE demonstrates quite a few of the after effects:

*I became ill with meningitis and was sent to hospital, where I stayed for a month. I remember being in the most terrible pain, like my head was being crushed and not liking bright lights. I was put on a drip and then felt myself falling and I pinched my hand to see if I was dreaming – **I was not!** Suddenly I was in what felt like a dark tunnel, travelling at enormous speed and at the end was a brilliant golden light which didn't hurt my eyes. When I reached the end I saw my family and patients (I used to be a nurse), all standing with beautiful smiles and open arms, enveloping me in such love. It was amazing! Even our family pets that had died years before were welcoming me. Some were patients who had had amputations before they died, but now they had limbs and were walking. A voice, which came into my head, asked me if I wanted to remain with them or return back to where I'd come from.*

*I remember very clearly I said, 'Oh goodness I'd love to stay but first I must return to tidy my bedroom!' I'm a children's nanny and I'd left books on the floor before I collapsed. Suddenly I felt myself being pulled back very rapidly by what looked like a silver cord, a very fine one, and then I was screaming in pain because I was woken up by doctors and nurses. I told them – why didn't you leave me alone, I was blissfully happy to be free from pain? Their response shocked me! They said, **but you had died**, we saved your life, and I felt terribly guilty having shouted at them, not appreciating what had happened to me. Of course once I was on the road to recovery I was grateful for my life being saved and I've never looked back.*

*Since I died I became a spiritualist and I'm not afraid to die; I know for certain, this life is one of many, and we do meet our loved ones eventually. Also it's made me a better person and I try to do at least five kind things a day for other people. I love helping my friends and family and I give most of my salary to others who need it much more than I do. Whoever spoke to me on the other side, spoke with such love, it made me cry just thinking about it once I recovered. I shall never forget the love and kindness when I came back; it's something I've never experienced since. Hopefully when my time comes I'll meet the same people I saw before and more!*

*Also, the colours were very different to those here on earth, I can't tell you the colours because I've never seen them before, just that they were absolutely stunning. The flowers were really glorious too, mostly white and the green grass looked like green velvet, it's hard to explain! Sometimes – just sometimes – I wish I could travel back because my precious twin sister passed away five years ago. How I miss her; we were so very close and I loved her dearly. I hope this has not been too boring for you but it's absolutely true and, as I've mentioned, I'm not scared of dying. I know it's just **pure** love on the other side wherever it is in God's universe!*

This was sent in response to one of my newspaper articles:

*I too have had an NDE. It happened nearly 30 years ago and the whole thing stands out as clearly in my memory as if it happened yesterday. I believe that it has nothing to do with hallucinations or medication. I had a pulmonary embolism in hospital after major surgery. I could neither move nor shout for the nurse, it was as if someone had stabbed me in the back and all the air had gone from my lungs. I distinctly remember a nurse looking at me then running to my bed with oxygen and mask, putting the mask on my face. Then I saw two doctors rush to my bed, one was sounding my chest with a stethoscope and the other was pressing hard on the veins in my legs (I found out later he was looking for a DVT). I still couldn't breathe and the pain in my upper back was awful.*

*Suddenly I felt completely calm and felt myself gliding to the corner of the room at ceiling height. I rushed through a tunnel in the corner of the room and it was full of bright lights and vivid colours and at the front was my grandmother, smiling as she always did when alive. Behind my grandmother were other members of our family and friends, all smiling and welcoming me. Suddenly I had to go back to my family and two young sons. I hovered and looked down at my hospital bed. I could see myself lying there on a drip and oxygen, my eyes were closed but the two doctors, and now three nurses, were no longer rushing about. Two days later I woke up (my husband informed me of the time span) with tubes everywhere and acute pain in my lungs. I did not have the pain either while floating above my bed or in the tunnel. I began to recover and then about four days later I had another breathing attack.*

*This time I was in intensive care so a nurse came immediately with oxygen. She pulled the curtains around the bed and said she would return immediately with a doctor. During this time (seconds, apparently) a man all in white clothing came into the cubicle and sat on the end of my bed with his back to me. My breathing was bad and he actually sat on my feet (I am a tall lady) and I remember clearly having trouble moving my feet from under him. Then he said to me, 'Fight it, fight it' over and over again. Then he disappeared in front of my eyes. When my breathing returned to normal I asked the nurse who it was who had come into the cubicle before she came back with the doctor. She informed me that no one had been in with me. Today I believe it was my guardian angel.*

*I would like to add that my experience changed my life. I have spent a lot of my life as a carer for family and friends and also in my employment with the blind. Before that NDE I was quite self-centred and an introvert. So I can say the experience did me a lot of good. One of the first people I looked after was my mother, who passed away 18 months after my NDE. Twenty years later I nursed my father through terminal cancer so perhaps I was saved because I had work to do.*

## Sense of 'Mission' or Purpose in Life

When NDErs are sent back to life it is often with the notion that they have a purpose to fulfil but very often they are at a loss as to what this purpose is. This becomes quite an intense issue for some, and a very interesting course has been devised by Carolyn Matthews[16] to help NDErs discover their 'mission'. The course is the result of her MA in transpersonal studies undertaken at Atlantic University, Virginia.

An example of someone trying to understand their life purpose is below:

*I am writing with reference to an experience I had whilst in hospital in summer 1995. I had been taken into hospital with suspected appendicitis. An operation was scheduled for the morning, and they gave me a morphine injection as I was by this time doubled up in a* lot of pain. To cut a long story short, it was over 18 hours before I was taken down to theatre and just felt like letting go. They thought they had me under the anaesthetic, but I became aware my stomach was being painted in something cold like a fluid, which alarmed me but I couldn't do anything?

The next thing was the strange bit. I felt no pain at all during this experience. I felt as though I was in mid-air a couple of feet above a hospital trolley bed looking down at a baby, and I couldn't figure out who it was until it just came to me that it was me, when the figure instantly changed to an adult body which I didn't recognize until I then realized it was me. I then felt as though I was in a dark place and went towards a figure which had long hair and a beard but with a broad forehead. The figure was like looking at a NEGATIVE photo – black on white, similar to the Turin Shroud but a wider forehead, which had a very soft light behind it. The figure seemed to be much larger than me, and I seemed to rise towards it, but I couldn't see anything below his shoulders (similar to a child against an adult). The light behind the figure seemed to be a very soft white light, and even though I couldn't see anybody else I was sure I was being led on the way back, and I just seemed to float along. It was a very calm experience, apart from looking into the other cavern on the way back, after seeing the figure, but I am still not sure what was in there.

I could only see the head and shoulders, and felt at peace, but the figure looked to its right and I drifted off to my left, with a feeling that it wasn't my time and I had things to do. The only thing that alarmed me, if that's the right word, was when I was going back down a large tunnel or something like it, was when I looked off to my left into an opening of another large cavern, where all I could see was a mist across the floor but it seemed to have lots of sharp points sticking up through the mist, which made me alarmed. I felt that I was being led back all the time but didn't see by whom.

The next thing, I felt as though I was back in my body, in the worst pain I have ever known, and was physically struggling with someone who was moving me bodily, but everything was black and I couldn't see anything, only hear voices. I felt something strange attached to my right side and grabbed it, and then I heard my mother's voice telling me to not grab the pipe, and let them put me into bed. It was her voice that I recognized and I let them move me from the trolley *into the ward bed, even though the pain was unbearable. The pipe was a drain from the wound in my stomach to a bag for the fluid, as it seems, when they finally opened me up, the appendix had burst a long time before and it had turned into peritonitis.*

*I kept asking what had happened as I knew I had experienced something, but all the surgeon would say was that it had been pretty serious and they had to wash my insides out with antibiotics as I was so ulcerated with the peritonitis infection. I just wanted to be left alone as I felt so ill. I was given over 20 morphine jabs to ease the pain during that week. During the first three days every time that I closed my eyes I could see a vivid green tunnel off to my left in the wall, and felt that all I had to do was to let go because of the constant pain. I stopped having the tunnel visions as my temperature dropped on the fourth day.*

*When I finally managed to get out of bed after the fourth day, I noticed my chest looked very red and couldn't understand why. It was when I mentioned this later to my mother she explained, that they had probably shocked me with the paddles, if there had been problems during the operation, which she thought that there had been.*

*I was a practising Catholic before this happened and am not frightened to die, as I know this is all just a stepping stone to something better, which is what I tell people. I am now 46 and have had a son since, but I don't think he was the reason I came back. I know the docs just said the experiences might have been the morphine, but I know it was something different. I fly helicopters and have rescued people, but I still don't feel that I have reached the point which I feel that I was sent back for yet. I sometimes wonder if I am doing the right job for me now, which is strange considering how keen I was to fly before this experience. I have mentioned to some rich individuals who I have come across through my flying that they should set up a charity that would respond faster, to help the sick and children in need around the world, and I feel this has something to do with what I know I was sent back for. I am more interested in the spiritual side of life than I was before, and always said at the time of the operation anybody younger or older wouldn't have got through the pain, as I felt like giving up at times myself. I now feel everything in life is fate, and know it's just a stepping stone to something much better. The strange thing that I still think about is that the being I saw; it was like a negative film image with a soft light behind it. There was no speech but the thoughts were passed to me somehow. I know it was real. I don't think my NDE was anything to do with the morphine either, as I had 20 injections through that week and the out-of-body experience only happened at the start of my stay in hospital. I don't know if this experience resembles anybody else's with the negative image I saw, but thought I would share it with you. Good luck with your work.*

## NDE is Vivid in Mind

The NDE appears to remain etched in the person's mind. Even many years after the NDE it is very vivid, as if it had just happened the day before. I have spoken to people in their eighties and nineties who had had NDEs over 50 years previously, but it remains foremost in their mind.

The account below was sent to me anonymously in response to a newspaper article:

*After reading your reports about NDEs in the newspaper, I feel you might like to hear about mine. This happened when I was a young teenager. I am now over 90. Although I tried to think it was a dream it has remained very vivid in my memory. I was rushed into hospital with acute appendicitis. In those days the anaesthetic used was chloroform. A most unpleasant smell which soon knocked me out. I then felt myself being pushed into a long dark tunnel with a tiny speck of light which seemed a long distance away. It was a horrible journey, I could not resist. As I travelled, the light grew bigger until it became so strong it dazzled me. At that point I shot out of the tunnel to be faced by a gleaming golden gate. A man wearing a long white robe stood there. He had a beard and the most gentle yet radiant face I had ever seen. I looked through the gate and saw my grandparents and others who had passed on. They seemed to be behind a cloud. I could only see them from the waist upwards. They had such a look of peace and happiness on their faces and there was an indescribable peace around me. I pleaded with the man to let me in. How I longed to join them but all he said was, 'No, not yet'. As I pleaded, he raised a flat hand towards me, saying, no not yet. I felt myself being sucked into the tunnel in tears. The light grew less until it was just a pin point and I fell out of the tunnel. I heard voices and found myself surrounded with beds and a very bad pain in my tummy. It took a while to shake off my confusion. Since my NDE I have no fear of death. I do not wish to have my name published because a lot of people here would say I am demented. Nevertheless those magical moments will live with me forever. Thank you for your work.*

## Heightened Concern for the Environment/ Ecological Issues

Many people develop an increased concern for the environment and their relationship to it. Instead of focusing on their personal needs they have a renewed respect for nature and see the wider picture of the effect humans are having on the environment.

Heather Leese had an NDE while a patient in intensive care after a severe infection in which she nearly died. She has had numerous after effects, including an enhanced appreciation for the welfare of the planet:

*It can be really tiring for me coming to terms with what's happening right now for me and tuning into this new powerful energy! Some days I really just cannot function and become overwhelmed.*

*My experience with the human relationship and the environment have changed, I would say, after the NDE. I have always tried to be respectful of life and the environment but after the last NDE I had, with going into the coma and experiencing the white light room, I began to feel an overwhelming connection to mother earth's pain. It's like I experienced the sadness she was feeling with how she was being treated; with tiredness on top of this it was a heavy burden to bear.*

*I tried to do as much as I could but soon realized I can't control how other people treat the land. I can only do my best as one being and started living a more clean life by trying to use eco-friendly cleaning products. My body could not take a high exposure to chemicals so I can only use organic shampoo and salt crystal deodorant, etc. and I downgraded my car to an eco-friendly 1.1-litre engine. I recycle and when I can afford it buy only organic food and I will pick up litter on the street if it is possible (my dad laughs at me when I do this!). My thoughts on other things like emissions and stuff I can't really go into or I choose not to because it makes me angry and that doesn't feel beneficial to me right now. I have come to the general conclusion and have been told by spirits that people are already working on environmental issues and that my job is elsewhere at the moment, but I am in the space right now that if mother earth chooses to wipe us out for the pain we have caused her I am at total peace with this because that is her and God's business! My family and I do what we can and a lot of people do the best they can with the knowledge they are given. Hope this makes a little sense.*

Dr Parti, whose NDE was briefly described in Chapter 1, was profoundly changed in many of the above-mentioned ways as a result of his NDE. His health was transformed, he healed remarkably quickly and was discharged within 72 hours of being operated on for sepsis. As time passed he realized his addiction to painkillers and his depression had gone completely.

He resigned from his post as anaesthetist, downsized from a large house to a modest house, changed his car from a Mercedes to a smaller eco-friendly hybrid car, began voluntary work and sought out opportunities to serve others.

He now considers himself to be more caring and loving and has sympathy for others and is overwhelmed by the desire to help others with their own healing process. Through the insights he gained during his NDE he has been inspired to write about and undertake workshops and seminars on spiritual wellness. He ended his email to me with the following sentence: 'In my old life, I used to put people to sleep. Now I wake them up. And I have woken up too.'

## Electrical Sensitivity and Inability to Wear a Wrist Watch

A lesser-known after effect is that NDErs can develop sensitivity to electricity and also find that wrist watches will not work for them. In some cases the wrist watch will completely stop working when they wear it, even though it functions normally when others put it on; in other cases the watch cannot keep accurate time. Sometimes they don't even connect this to their NDE. This has been reported by other researchers in the field,[17] which intrigued me, so I started asking the people I was researching if they experienced this and I found that many of them did. In fact, in most cases it was only when I raised the subject that they then traced the start of their sensitivity back to the time of the NDE.

While chatting with my colleague whose NDE is described in Chapter 1, I noticed that she was not wearing a wrist watch. I asked her why this was so and she replied that she stopped wearing watches years ago as they never worked for her. Then she thought about it and was quite surprised when she realized that this problem began after her NDE. Her mother had bought her an expensive watch but it wouldn't work for her and she never understood why as there was nothing wrong with the watch and it worked when anyone else wore it. All watches worked for a while then stopped or 'broke' and it wasn't until I'd mentioned this as an after effect of an NDE that it all made sense to her.

More recent research[18] concluded that NDErs were more likely to report changes in electromagnetic fields than those who had a close brush with death but did not report an NDE. Those who reported deeper NDEs had greater problems with electromagnetic fields.

One lady who works in a high-tech environment contacted me after she saw an article I had published in the media. She had had an NDE during childhood and she reported that all types of electrical items malfunction in her presence and she cannot wear a wrist watch as they all just stop working. In fact, she needs to monitor time as part of her job and has resorted to wearing an alarm clock on a string around her neck. Kettles in particular cause great problems as they usually stop working immediately or even blow up in her presence. She had never associated this with her NDE, but when I talked to her about this effect, she traced the start of these problems back to just after her NDE.

The following is from a lady who had an NDE during childhood (read her experience on pages 61–2):

*Just read the second article in the newspaper. The part about electrical-sensitivity syndrome struck home to me and was quite a shock (sorry for the pun) as I had never heard of this being connected to NDE.*

*After my experience at age ten my parents gave me my first wrist watch as a birthday gift that year. I was, of course, delighted as I had always wanted my own watch but dismayed to find that it kept stopping when I wore it. It ran fine when I did not wear it or anyone else wore it, though. Until a few years ago I still could not get a watch to run properly when I wore it. Also I had problems with switching on lights and electrical appliances in that I used to get small shocks from them when either switching them on or touching them when they were switched on – ditto with motor vehicles whether running or standing and not switched on. I could and still do blow light bulbs regularly when switching them on. It became a standing joke that I could not go near anything electrical. My mother used to say I had too much static in my body and I had just put it down to that and thought no more about it and never connected it to NDE.*

*When I began work (in an old-style office in the mid-1960s) I was banned from going near or touching the photocopier as it would cease working or run erratically if I did so. I have also been thrown backwards and right across a room several times when using or touching electrical appliances. I can feel a slight surge through my body when I am within a few millimetres or touching the switch or appliance and know whether there is going to be any problem or not there and then. I can also feel a slight surge when passing or being near small electrical substations (the small ones about the size of a car or smaller which are dotted around towns). When I first started using a computer I had horrendous problems and almost gave up trying to use it, thinking I was the problem once again, but they found that the computer was at fault and it was replaced. No further problems regarding that as long as I use wired and not radio-controlled mouse and keyboard, etc. The remote radio-controlled keyboard and mouse and I were not compatible!*

The following NDE is interesting because it left Julie, from Llanelli, with quite a few after effects:

*It happened in 1996 after I had a haemorrhage following a tonsillectomy. I'd gone home then had to go back to hospital because I had started bleeding. I was admitted to a ward then I started haemorrhaging really badly. Blood was gushing from my mouth like a waterfall. I pressed the buzzer and a nurse came in, then there were nurses and doctors from everywhere. One of them held my hand while the others rushed around. They put me on a heart monitor. Then I got weaker and I heard the nurses and doctors say, 'Quick, we're losing her.'*

*The next thing I knew I was in some kind of . . . all I can describe it as is . . . like a big kaleidoscope. It was as if I was conscious but in this big kaleidoscope with white, silver and purple circles. It was weird. Then I saw a slide show of the whole of my life played before my eyes. Everything that had happened in my life from childhood to present was just played before my eyes. It wasn't fast but very slow and once one image was shown then another one would appear. The last image I saw was one of my mother's face (she's still alive). But it was all as if I was very much awake; it's hard to describe.*

*Then after the image of my mother's face I just saw like orbs of light – purple and silver orbs of light floating in front of me. Then a bright light appeared, it was a very bright light that got brighter and brighter. Then it started to dim as if it was like a dimmer switch and then it got really dim. I was just surrounded by this dim light for the next ten minutes or so, I would think. I can't really put a time on it. It was as if I was just suspended there in this dim light and then I started to hear the nurses calling my name and I woke up in the recovery room.*

*The funny thing is that I wasn't scared; in fact it was a fabulous experience. I was really comfortable and I was enjoying it.*

*Since the experience I've had some weird things happen. It was as if I was picking up on everyone's feelings. I seemed to know what people around me were feeling and thinking. Even complete strangers I'd never met before. Once I was on holiday in Spain and I was sitting by the pool reading a book. I glanced over and saw a man and woman also reading. Then all of a sudden it was as if I engaged with his thoughts, I knew what he was thinking. The words 'I hope she will be happy with this, I miss her. Why did she have to die? . . . cancer . . .' then that was it. I thought I was going mad. When I went to bed that night I said to my partner, 'I feel really sorry for that man by the pool, he's lost someone close to cancer.' Then we went off to sleep. The next day my partner went down to the pool before me and got talking to the lady who I'd seen with the man. She told my partner that they'd just got married and his previous wife was her best friend and she'd died of cancer. I arrived at the pool about an hour later and my partner told me – then teased me that I was a freak!*

*I used to get that quite a lot. I would be in board meetings at work and I could just look up and tap into people's thoughts. It was like an empathy . . . I knew what they were thinking . . . that's all I can describe it as. It lasted for about five years or so and was very powerful at first but then gradually got less and less and it's gone now. I'm still empathetic and pick up on people's feeling but I can't read their thoughts any more. It used to freak me out and I thought I was going mad.*

*Another thing is that I couldn't wear a watch for about three years after the NDE. I've got a nice expensive watch but it would just go haywire. I bought new watches but they would just not work for me; it was really frustrating and used to really annoy me. I can wear one again now but it will lose time now and again but only ten to fifteen minutes, nothing like it used to be.*

*Then, whenever I was around electrical items, things just went haywire too. I would walk into a room and the TV would switch itself off. I could walk into a room and the hi-fi would switch itself on. The most noticeable was when I went to the dentist – every time I sat in the chair the equipment stopped working. The dentist had to take me into the other room; it was only with me that it happened!*

*These things used to happen but they've stopped now and I'm glad – I didn't want those abilities! One thing that has stayed with me since the experience is that I'm not afraid of dying any more. Whenever I talk about it with friends and they say they are afraid of it, I'm not. I'm definitely not afraid of dying.*

The following account was sent in response to a newspaper article. The gentleman prefers to remain anonymous:

*I am writing following the recent newspaper in which you mentioned some features that you are investigating related to NDE. I was most interested in your revelation that NDE subjects seem to have a distorted electrical system because it appears that I have a similar problem that is most obvious in that I cannot wear a wrist watch – and I have never understood why. Your suspicions that it could be related to NDEs has made a connection with NDE that might be of interest to your researches and I have detailed this.*

*During the 1950s, when my parents lived in Edinburgh, it was common for us to visit the beaches on the East Coast before continuing to Kirkcaldy, where we would catch a train back to Edinburgh. On one such visit, when I was aged four, I was running down the beach to the sea when I was bowled over by a breaker and, as far as I was concerned, drowned. I say 'as far as I know' because I have retained a strong memory of looking down on the scene and seeing a crowd of people around whilst clearly thinking, 'That's me down there,' yet feeling totally dispassionate as I also looked around the bay at Kinghorn where the incident happened.*

*The next thing I was aware of was water being forced out of my lungs as I began choking and gasping as, presumably, someone had resuscitated me and I regained consciousness.*

*After that there is little to recall as I was led up the beach and remember little other about the rest of the day, which would have followed the normal mix of activities.*

*As you can understand, even after 50+ years this event has forged a strong impression in my memory, and although I have always connected this to my abiding fear of water, I had never thought to connect the 'drowning' to my electrical problems.*

This African nurse's NDE is reported in Chapter 4:

*When you mentioned that people can't wear watches or get problems with electrical equipment after their NDE, that's when I realized my problem with wearing a watch began. After my NDE I wasn't able to wear a watch – it would work for a few days then just stop. My father bought me several watches but the same thing happened: after a few days they'd just stop – they were always new watches. My brother-in-law had bought my sister a very expensive watch and when I began my nurse training she gave it to me as a gift as she was so excited for me. It worked for a month then it stopped. I gave it back to my sister and she wore it and it worked for her. It was a big family joke that I was unable to wear watches. I couldn't even wear a nurse's fob watch as they would stop too. I didn't bother trying to wear a watch for many years, maybe 15 years after that. I can wear them now and they work but I'm so used to not wearing one that I seldom put a watch on my wrist.*

*I'm not sure if this is connected to the electrical disturbance but my older brother used to regularly take me to the cinema to watch a film. After the experience I no longer enjoyed going to the cinema. Everything seemed imbalanced when I was looking at the screen; it was like a 3D effect as if the actors were coming out of the screen towards me. I was sitting in the audience but I kept jumping back in my seat. Also, I could no longer stand the lights there and the flashing lights would make me sick whereas this had never happened before. I stopped going until after I was married about 12 years later. I still didn't enjoy it, the effects weren't quite so bad but the picture seemed to be jumping so I didn't go again. Even when watching TV, if there are flashing lights I can't stand it.*

Ken Ebert[19] from Taos, New Mexico had an NDE 27 years ago. His full experience can be read in his book *Theater of Clouds: A Near Death Memoir*. Ken contacted me and was kind enough to answer many of my questions. Below are some of the after effects that Ken has been left with.

*I got a laugh when you asked about the watches – haven't worn one since 1985. Those first few years after the NDE I also sometimes blew out light bulbs just being near them. The other thing was that I could 'feel' light as a **texture**, i.e. passing by a lamp would sometimes feel as if brushing a woolly substance. I still get that to some degree, but only when I am fatigued. Another unusual phenomenon was that my hearing became very acute. I first verified this by turning on and off a motion detector silent alarm. I could hear the transmitter in the thing. This still sometimes happens, but not often.*

*But I also could pick out conversations in a noisy room. Still can, but I do not like the aural sensitivity. The store where I work is a 10,000-square-foot room and I can, if I try, pick out conversation on the far side of the store, but I keep my filters up because I get overwhelmed by sound if I do not squelch it with my mind. The useful part of this sensitivity is that if something is relevant to me but is spoken below my range of hearing I can hear it anyway, almost as if it was spoken right in my ear.*

## Develop Psychic Tendencies/Premonitions/ Enhanced Intuitive Perception

Some people develop such highly sensitive intuitive abilities that they often become reclusive as a result. One lady contacted me in response to a newspaper article and described being 'able to read other people's minds'. This became very disturbing for her as very often she was able to foresee people's deaths or foretell that 'bad things' were going to happen to them. She could not go out where there were crowds of people as she could somehow pick up on people who had things wrong with them or were about to experience misfortune. The lady now seldom ventures outside as a result and when she does have to go outside she always wears headphones and has music playing loudly to distract her.

A similar ability was also reported by a colleague who had an NDE at nine years of age. She explained that she has the ability to 'read other people's minds', which she does not like as she feels it to be morally wrong. In fact she really has to concentrate hard to block this ability.

Shortly after her NDE in 1979, Dr Yvonne Kason[20] had her first psychic experience where a vision she experienced prompted her to advise her friend to visit her doctor. Her friend was subsequently diagnosed with meningitis. Her speedy diagnosis and treatment resulted in a good recovery.

## Develop a Healing Ability or Being Healed

Sutherland[21] reported cases of healing ability following an NDE. Morse and Perry[22] reported the case of Kathy, who had an NDE and found that her cancer had totally disappeared after the NDE. Similar cases of healing from a brain tumour and Hodgkin's lymphoma were reported by Dr Larry Dossey.[23] A most remarkable case of a congenital abnormality was that of patient 10 from my own research, which will be discussed later in the book. Below are two cases where a person discovered that they had healing abilities following an NDE.

The following example was sent from a lady in France:

*I read your article and am glad that someone is taking this as a true experience. When I was in Turkey working about 20 years ago I had an ectopic pregnancy. I managed to be taken to a women's hospital by one of my English students. They operated on me without any anaesthetic but gave me blood and fluids. During the operation I died, travelled the tunnel, found my grandmother and was told, 'This is not the right time, you must go back.' I re-entered my body with a thud, all the pain and responsibilities returned.*

*The experience changed my life. For many years, I had no wish to be here as this life appeared to have no advantages, being a constant struggle. But now I realize that there is a reason, as I have some sort of gift and find that I can 'tune in' to people's feelings, which makes my work with babies understandably easier. I also attract sick or injured cats that stay for a while then move on.*

The following was emailed by a 38-year-old man:

*Date of experience 1984. I was in bed with the only dose of real flu I have ever had. Completely exhausted, I felt as if I was dying. I do not really know what happened to me but can only relay the crystal-clear memories. At some point, I was outside of my parent's house, on the roof, looking at a velux window with ice on it. The lead around the top of the window was very curled and I looked at it, thinking it was amazing that water had not entered my bedroom. I was so excited about being out on the roof that I went off to look around the other rooftops of houses nearby. I could see people walking in the snowy streets below, but could not smell or touch anything. I was just seeing the most amazing views.*

*It was a timeless experience, which led me to my grandmother's grave in a nearby cemetery. She stood there clear as day, much younger than when she had died and told me I had to go home immediately. Still in a sense of euphoria at feeling so free, I found myself looking down through the velux window, and was quite shocked to see myself in bed, white and motionless. It was so shocking that I wanted to get back into my body as quickly as I could. It was only when I saw myself lying there that I realized what was happening and wanted to get back into my body.*

*I knew when I woke it was not a normal dream, since I felt my heart start beating again and, a short while after, I began to breathe. I knew I had been outside, but my initial excitement had now turned to immense relief.*

*I was in bed for a few more days, and relayed the experience to my parents. My father decided to look at the lead on the roof and assumed I must have been able to see it from my room. He could see none of the lead. A few months passed, when having some slates replaced, the roofer told my parents the lead around the top of the velux window needed replacing because it had curled up and cracked.*

*I have to say that I have never experienced the more extreme electrical malfunctions you mentioned, but have experienced and continue to experience unusual feeling and symptoms which I can only attribute to a heightened sensitivity to electricity. The main one that is constant is my discomfort in environments where there are lots of electrical systems in use around me, mainly in department stores and large shopping centres. I feel a sense of confusion and interference with my thoughts in such places and it sometimes gets so bad that I have to leave the buildings despite the fact that I really enjoy being in a retail environment.*

*The other one is at home, where I find that long periods in front of the computer screen or television leave me feeling really drained regardless of the entertainment value of what is on the screen. It has reached the point where I prefer not to watch television and use the computer only for short periods. I rarely use my mobile phone for the same reason. I find that one particularly unpleasant and feel a dull, hot pain in my head after a call lasting more than ten minutes. The heat is totally real. Most noticeably, in open air spaces where there are lots of people or no people at all, none of these symptoms occur, and in the countryside I feel as if I have been released from something, and have often thought that this is because of the reduction in electrical fields in such places.*

*I consider the work you are doing to be enormously comforting and at long last feel understood after years of not telling many people about what happened in case they thought I was mad for believing it was more than a dream or coincidence. I hope it never happens again, because the next time I may not be so lucky, despite the initial feelings being really beautiful.*

*The healing ability came to light when I was 18 years old, which was four years after my experience on the roof. It was something I discovered by accident and then gradually became aware of the effect it had on people both spiritually and physically. One really amazing incident occurred in my mid-twenties when I was walking through Boots the chemist, and amidst the hustle and bustle I clearly heard an assistant on a beauty counter telling her friend about her sore hand that she thought had a trapped nerve in it. Without hesitation, and pleased it was in public so as not to look weird, I went straight over to her and told her I could sort it out. Within a couple of minutes she was stunned that her hand that had bothered her for weeks was better. I quickly disappeared in the crowds as I did not want to draw too much attention to what had happened, nor did I want praise. As far as I was concerned I had just channelled a higher energy. I still believe it is not me doing the healing directly. It seems like a force for good that I somehow connect with which in turn acts as a catalyst for people to heal themselves. But that's only what I think. I do not know, but that is my explanation. I often think I would like to do the rounds on a hospital ward, before and after operations, to give people the strength to get through what must be quite scary. I believe that modern medicine and human healing could be combined. I suspect it won't happen that often in busy hospitals where government targets need to be met.*

*I would love to get the chance to help someone who was seriously ill but always feel afraid to offer if I do not know them well enough. I worry they may find it odd and I would not want to upset anyone who is under conventional medicine and feels it is the only way. I do know, however, that one day the chance will come and I will take it and do what I can, with no promises.*

## Huge Psychological Boost

'Sally's' NDE was so profound that it left her with one of the most remarkable after effects I have come across. The experience is deeply personal and sacred to Sally and it is so ineffable that the interview took a long time. It was very difficult to find the words, for what she experienced was beyond normal human understanding. As Sally recalled the experience her eyes were closed and she seemed to be actually reliving it, constantly being overcome with emotion. Although I cannot convey much of her actual NDE, the after effects that she lives with every day of her life I find truly inspiring.

Sally was an amateur athlete and suffered severe head injuries following a cycling accident 30 years ago. Four days after the accident, while Sally was unconscious in hospital, the doctor prepared her husband for the worst and said that he was unsure whether she would pull through. If she did, she would have to retrain her memory and learn to walk again and would never run again as she would most likely be severely debilitated.

Sally recalls it taking a long time for her to realize who and where she was. She had to rebuild herself gradually, all the while *knowing* that everything was going to be wonderful. She recalled the following, which occurred during unconsciousness:

*This is difficult for me to put into words . . . there are no words . . . what I'm saying is not doing it justice . . . I feel so lucky to have been given this yet I can't describe it. There was more beauty . . . more than the greatest thing you can ever experience in life. I can always call on it **always**.*

*There was the voice . . . it said, 'If you choose to come back you will be stronger.' I'll never forget it; it's always with me . . . I've never told anyone this part – ever – you are the only one who knows this next part.*

[I have omitted the next part as this was so deeply personal to Sally. Although she gave me permission to use it, I think it's best withheld due to its sacred nature.]

*As I'm telling you this now, I can see the image of me. Until it happens again, it will do just to be able to have the image of it. It must be difficult for you to believe . . . Not one NDE can be the same. That's why it's so difficult . . . it's so personal . . . I always cry about it, I always get emotional. I can't tell you what it's like to me . . . They are tears of happiness, as if it jogs something in my mind. I can't talk about it with anyone, not even with my family . . . I just can't describe it. Other than yourself, I don't tell anyone – people will think I'm absolutely barmy.*

*I'll never forget the voice saying, 'If you choose to come back you'll be stronger.' That strength never leaves me and I can tune into it every day. If ever I feel down I just tune into it. Not only does it give me physical strength but also mental strength.*

*When I first came to I couldn't work out why I was here* [this refers to the sacred aspect of the experience] *. . . does that make sense? I didn't know if I'd decided to go back or stay where I was . . . where was I? Had I made the right decision? Was I meant to be this side or that side [of life]? It was problematic being in the real world again – maybe I should have gone on? The voice must have thought I was strong before because it said I would be stronger . . . for the minutest second something told me I was strong before . . . It is so difficult to put all of those feelings into words . . . That strength never leaves, though; it's with me every day.*

50

*This doesn't seem fair to say . . . if I didn't wake up . . . my family would be devastated, I know . . . I feel so guilty for thinking that but I know I'd go back to that place. I love life and I really like living life – it's like a real gift to live your life, why let things get you down? I know I will also love the other life. I have absolutely no fear of death.*

*It's given me strength in all situations in my life. I am now a carer for my parents and some people can't be a carer but I don't get phased by it. Nothing bothers me; I have great joy doing it and feel privileged to be a part of it.*

*'If you decide to go back you'll be stronger' – nothing is ever too much for me. It gives me great mental and physical strength. Be true to yourself, have faith in your experience. There is nothing greater than living every day . . . I am so lucky . . . so happy . . . so happy . . . I **adore** life, I love waking up. The voice is coming back right now; I can't explain it, I always get flashbacks of it. It's a wonderful feeling; I get it so much, an awful lot. In my life there are no boundaries, nothing will worry me. I feel really blessed, every day. I can't wait to go back but I am also so happy to live my life here. In reality I want to make the most of things. I don't doubt, I just go ahead and do things. I don't have any fear of death because I know God is going to look after me. There are no inhibitions in my life – no doubt. You've got to be true to yourself and live your life.*

*I'm not religious as such but I am spiritual and have a faith in Christianity. I rarely go to church . . . once in a while if I'm out running and pass a church I'll pop in. Since my NDE I've never been able to go into a church without a huge release of emotion. I always end up in floods of tears. My faith . . . whether it's religious or not, I can't separate it.*

*My body seems to have a lot of static. If I'm in the supermarket and touch the trolleys I get an electric shock. Also when I worked if I touched the metal plaque on the door to my office I'd get a shock – I had to go through doors but touching them with my elbow first.*

Perhaps most remarkable of all was the effect the voice had on Sally's life. Incredibly, after being told by the doctor that she'd have to learn to walk again and would probably never run again, she ran a ten-kilometre race a month after she was discharged from hospital! However, this was just a minor feat in comparison with what Sally went on to accomplish.

In the 1980s she earned places in the Guinness Book of World Records for her remarkably fast times of long-distance running. The first race was a distance of 100 miles in just over 15 hours. Following this, Sally became an ultra-distance runner. She ran 420 miles in six days, but her greatest achievement was running the phenomenal distance of 625 miles from Sydney to Melbourne in just eight days non-stop – with no sleep! Now in her sixties, Sally continues to run for miles daily. She recently did a 'short' run of 40 miles to raise money for charity.

> *Whenever I run I just tune into my experience, it's always with me. After the first few miles I just tune in and I can run forever and ever. When I ran from Sydney to Melbourne I did it without any sleep. I ate and drank as I ran; the toughest time was in the night, and one night it was so cold that I almost became hypothermic. I had such a good backup team following me. Before I started the run I weighed about 9 stone and when I finished I was 6 stone 13. It was all the fluid I lost. I knew I'd do it. I never doubt anything. The voice is always with me.*

I wanted to include Sally's experience because I think it really highlights the impact that such an experience can have on a person's life and how it can motivate people to achieve incredible feats.

As this chapter has highlighted, the NDE is far more than a mere hallucination and there are many resultant after effects which can greatly affect a person's life in many positive and negative ways.

NDEs can occur at any age and throughout different cultures, as the following chapters show.

# 3

# Childhood NDEs

NDEs that occurred in childhood are particularly interesting because at such a young age we don't expect children – during a time when they are unconscious – to be able to construct an elaborate sequence of events that seem beyond their understanding. Children NDErs are less likely to be culturally and socially influenced in comparison to adult NDErs.[1] Many accounts in the literature of childhood NDEs were retold when the person was in adult life. Investigation of this aspect showed that the NDEs recalled retrospectively were not embellished with time and the memory remained vivid.[2]

Dr Melvin Morse conducted a study of 121 children who had been patients in intensive care and been subjected to the fear and psychological trauma associated with intensive care. He found that 118 of these had no recollection of their hospital stay, and three recalled vivid dreams, though nothing resembling an NDE. He also interviewed 37 children who had been treated with mind-altering medication and found that none of them reported anything similar to an NDE. However, when he interviewed 12 children who had survived cardiac arrest he found almost every one of them reported at least one component of NDE.[3]

It has been suggested that NDEs are due to cultural conditioning and expectation. However, several NDErs have emphasized how different their experience was to their cultural and religious background.[4] Following the NDE some children are left with a renewed spiritual understanding which contradicts the religious views they were brought up with.[5] In fact, many childhood NDErs have been considered disruptive by their church leaders as, in all innocence, they have asked questions which the ministers have been unable to answer.[6] Katie, one of the NDErs in Morse's study, was brought up as a Mormon. Her grandfather had died a few years previous to her NDE and she was told that death was like sending someone on a boat ride. However, Katie did not report any such imagery during her NDE.[7] Similarly, hospice consultant John Lerma[8] reported the case of a young Muslim girl who saw Jesus, as opposed to Allah.

The NDEs of children are similar in content to those of adults and the components experienced by adults are also reported by children,[9] except children may report more rainbow colours and some may report living relatives, not deceased ones.

One example from someone who emailed me:

> I thought that I was one of very few people that have had this experience. I was six years old when I had my experience and I am 70 years old now. I was living in London. I fell out of bed onto a jug and this brought on meningitis of the spine. I was taken to hospital late in the evening. By now I was in a coma but all of my nerves were alive. I was put into a bath of ice to try to stop the poison going to my heart. This in turn stopped my heart.
>
> This is when I floated out of my body and looked down at myself. Then I went down a tunnel but the lights I saw were coloured. When I was young there was no such thing as psychedelic or strobe lights and it took me years to try to explain to my mum what the colours were like. I still haven't seen it. I got nearly to the end of the tunnel where all of these beautiful colours were when I heard my mum calling me back. So, reluctantly I turned around and came back. The next thing I remembered was lying in a pure white bed in a bright room.

The structure of the NDE is the same as adult NDEs but the interpretation and descriptions are less likely to be due to cultural or social expectation.[10] Children experience powerful feelings, knowing, a sense of presence and a protective, all-knowing, loving darkness that leave lasting impressions.[11] They too report deceased relatives or friends, animals and departed pets, religious figures, God – experienced as a male figure – and sometimes brief appearances of people who are still alive. In many cases the child is given the option of returning to life and they often return so that their families will not be upset, as is highlighted by the case below.

*I spent my tenth birthday in hospital; I had what I believe was hepatitis. I had been ill for a few months when I was rushed into hospital with a high temperature and yellowing skin. I have got vague memories of going in an ambulance with the lights and sirens going. The next thing I remember is what I can only call a dream.*

*I was looking down on my living room from the ceiling. There was a small white coffin on a trolley; there was no other furniture in the room. The curtains were drawn and my mother was crying, dressed in black with a veil and she was smoking. I distinctly remember thinking that she shouldn't smoke, that it was bad for her. There was a light behind me and a voice told me this is what could happen, it was up to me whether I wanted to go back. I decided to go back. I woke up and there was a nurse at my bedside, who looked very happy to see me awake, even though I was sick all over the bed. The feeling I had was one of absolute peace and it is something I have never experienced since, even though I am happily married with two boys. I have no fear of dying; my only fear now is dying too soon and leaving my husband and children alone.*

*This all happened in 1967 and as far as I know I was not aware that children were buried in white coffins or that my mother's family would follow the tradition of drawing the curtains when there is a death in the family. I have also found out that the doctor told the medical team that if my temperature hadn't started to drop within a few hours to call my parents in because I wouldn't make it through the night.*

On initial investigation of childhood NDEs it appeared that the life review was absent.[12] However, subsequent research[13] has uncovered more cases of life reviews in childhood NDEs. It has been suggested that the older a child was at the time of the experience the more aspects of the life review were experienced.[14] Below is a case reported to me by Natasha, 33, from Cardiff, that has the life review and life's purpose components:

*I had whooping cough when I was eight or nine. The doctor did home visits since I was too infectious to be taken to hospital. There was one particular night where I was at the worst of it because I was still coughing and very weak and when the doctor visited in the evening apparently he told my parents that he didn't expect me to survive the night and there wasn't anything more that he could do to help.*

*My parents put me in their bed (I had a cabin bed that was too high) and they slept in the spare room. I 'woke' during the night because there was a bright light spilling into the room around the edge of the door and I could hear my name being called. I'm profoundly deaf and can't hear anything at all without a hearing aid in. I got up out of bed to see what the light was and turned round to see myself still in the bed, asleep. But the voice kept calling me and the light was really bright so I opened the bedroom door and it was just this pure brilliant white light, and I stepped into it and kept walking towards the voice. I was just walking in the light; there wasn't anything else.*

*Then I was in a room and saw my life playing in front of me and I realized there was a presence behind me and he put a hand on my shoulder but told me not to turn around because the light would blind me. Then he said that I had to go back because I was important and I had a job to do. It went white again and I walked back and saw myself on the bed again and climbed back in.*

*I don't remember waking up or the recovery, etc., but apparently that day I was better. I was still very weak and the residual cough was there but I had more or less recovered overnight. I didn't tell anyone for many years about it. I thought they'd think I was lying or crazy. I'd lost my faith as a child when I was around seven so I wasn't religious but still didn't know if God was real or not. I still don't believe in God even though I think that if someone were to ask for a sign of God's existence that would be about as much as he could possibly give!*

*It did change my life because it gave me inner strength and self-belief that I am here for a reason. I knew I was important or special. Given that I had a really difficult childhood especially as a teenager, and having been born deaf, there was a lot to keep fighting through. I still don't know what I am meant to do but I make sure I live as full a life as possible and give as much as I can through that.*

The most remarkable difference between adult and childhood NDEs is the children's reactions to them.[15] Children have no reason to question their experience – to them it is nothing out of the ordinary. They are far more accepting of the experience and many don't mention it because they think this happens to everyone. Following a retreat attended by 25 NDErs it was concluded that the *needs* of childhood, teenage and adult NDEs are very different but the authors didn't elaborate on the ways in which the needs differed.[16]

Even if the NDE was experienced at a very young pre-linguistic age, it was recalled in great detail yet its expression may remain childlike.[17] Some cases in the literature on this subject emphasize this point – a young child who underwent an NDE at the age of six months[18] developed an anxiety when crawling through a tunnel with his siblings. Three years after the NDE, while it was being explained that his grandmother was dying, he asked if she had to go through the tunnel to meet God.

It is common to undergo more than one NDE if the first occurred during childhood.[19] However, in multiple NDEs differences have been noted between the NDEs and each was unique.[20] In many cases the later NDE clarified the confusion of the first NDE.[21] Different researchers have found different associations between the NDE and mode of near-death. All of Morse's patients were in intensive care and had undergone cardiac arrest. Below is a case reported to me by a man who as a child had a cardiac arrest, during which he had an NDE:

*I have two things that may be of interest. I was 11 years old and in hospital in London having my squint corrected. The operation was going fine when for no accountable reason I suffered a cardiac arrest. I found myself floating up in a corner of the theatre watching the staff trying to resuscitate me. A metal kidney bowl fell on the floor and the surgeon kicked it away. It rebounded across the floor and hit a nurse on the ankle. The anaesthetist tried electric shocks and injections and then said, 'Got him'. At this point I passed out and woke up in the ward. I had a number of puncture wounds to my arms and my chest hurt. The next morning the surgeons made their rounds and the consultant said, 'You gave us some entertainment yesterday, how do you feel now?' I replied that my eye hurt and also my chest. He said that it was to be expected but it would all calm down in a couple of days. Did I have any questions? I said that when he kicked the kidney bowl across the theatre, and hit the nurse, did it hurt her? He asked how I knew about that and I told him that I was up in the corner of the theatre and saw it happen. He turned to the rest of the staff and said, 'Interesting', before moving away. The staff never mentioned the*

*incident and when I brought it up they said that I was dreaming;
anaesthetics do funny things.*

*The second incident concerned my four-year-old son. I was in
the army at the time, based at the military hospital in Berlin. For
a number of days he had suffered with projectile vomiting and
a barium enema suggested that he had some form of intestinal
blockage. He was taken to theatre immediately. As it was a small
hospital, it was the path lab! Getting on with my work, the tannoy
system burst into life announcing a cardiac arrest in theatre. As
normal, I got two pints of O negative out of the blood bank and ran
to the theatre. I was met at the door by one of the technicians, who
took the blood off me and closed the door in my face. I suddenly
realized that my son was still in theatre and so I sat down on the
floor outside the theatre. About 40 minutes later the surgeon came
out and, seeing me there, said, 'It was touch and go at one point,
but he is all right now. You can see him up on the ward.' He was to
make a full recovery.*

*A few months later a relief came to Berlin so that I could have a
few days off. I asked the boys where they would like to go and my
son said that he would like to go to that park again. We asked him
which park, as we had never been able to get away until this relief
arrived. 'The one through the tunnel.' We asked him which tunnel.
'The one I went to when I was in the hospital. There was a park with
lots of children and swings and things, with a white fence around it.
I tried to climb over the fence but this man stopped me and said that
I wasn't to come yet and he sent me back down the tunnel and I was
back in the hospital again.'*

*I have spoken to my son again about this but he has no recollection
of it now. As he was only four at the time I cannot believe that he
could make this story up.*

One researcher has found drowning to be the most common cause
of NDEs, followed by suffocation, surgery, tonsillectomies and child
abuse.[22] Interestingly, I have received many reports of childhood
NDEs that, similar to tonsillectomies, occurred while having gas at the
dentist. Other research shows the most common causes of childhood
NDEs to be associated with illness such as pneumonia, asthma and
cardiomyopathy, followed by drowning, then as a result of violence or

child abuse.[23] Below are some examples reported to me of childhood NDEs occurring in such circumstances.

In response to a newspaper article in 2006, Steve Rushton reported:

*It was a Sunday afternoon in October 1967; I was nine years old and had gone fishing in the local canal, with some friends. I was leaning over the water, attempting to catch a large snail with my fishing net, when I suddenly fell into the water, which was around 12 feet deep. At the time I was unable to swim, though I learned soon after. I started to throw my arms about instinctively, but this only sent me further away from the tow path.*

*The first time I went under, I managed to get back to the surface but then total panic set in. The second time I went under, I still somehow managed to get back up but by now my strength was sapping away and I grew extremely weak, and was starting to swallow a lot of the dirty water. The third and final time I went under, well that was that; at first everything went black and I now realize that I was drowning. After a while the initial panic began to ebb away, and a very strange sense of calm set in. I felt at peace.*

*This was the point when I was being drawn into the white tunnel. It was a very bright light in there. As I moved further up this tunnel I approached what appeared to be two arched, brown, church-like wooden gates. On the left-hand side at the entrance, I saw a figure, dressed in a brown-coloured cowl, resembling a monk's habit. This was when I heard the immortal words, 'Go back, it is not your time.' It was a woman's voice but I could not see her face. It was a very comforting voice. The next thing I remember was coming back around on the canal bank, having had the kiss of life four times. The man who saved my life had been working at a nearby factory, on his first Sunday shift for eight weeks. How lucky was that?*

*I was told afterwards that I had been underwater for about six minutes. He said he thought I was dead when he first pulled me out as I was totally lifeless and my skin had turned grey. I was rushed to hospital, where they pumped the dirty water and some tadpoles from my stomach. I remained hospitalized for a week. I have not had any other effects, but it left me thinking there must be a reason why the lady in brown turned me back. I honestly believe that I died for some minutes but came back. The experience will be with me until I do actually pop my clogs. Perhaps that is when I get to see her face? The point of no return? Back then I knew nothing whatsoever about NDE. Since then I have read many things, which confirm what I saw that day. It still makes me go cold whenever I recall those events. I definitely do not believe the cynical explanations of the so-called scientists. I have been there. I often wonder why I was given a second chance. Please believe me, there is truly some place else, out there.*

Another lady emailed me in response to a newspaper article:

*I read your article in the newspaper about near-death experiences with great interest.*

*Everybody pooh-poohs my story because when mine happened I was only a child of six, that was in 1948. The experience is as clear today as it was then. I was very ill with pneumonia and apparently there is a time of crisis when you either come through or you die. I remember being in bed, with my mum by my side and suddenly looking up at the window and on the window sill there was something I can only explain as looking like the Sindy dolls of today and she was beckoning to me. I followed her and we were in a very bright beautiful tunnel and at the end all I could see was either sunshine or a brilliant light.*

*Suddenly I could hear my mum calling me not to go and I came back and obviously recovered. This experience has given me some comfort when recently my mother died suddenly and I just hope she had the same feelings. If that is dying then I certainly have no fear of it. I hope this is of some interest to you.*

Another example:

*I am in my sixty-sixth year and I had an NDE when I was 14 years of age. It started when I caught what was thought of as a cold and very quickly turned to pneumonia overnight, when I became unconscious. When I was in hospital it was 'touch and go', as was the expression then. I experienced a bright light all the way up a staircase which I had started climbing. I climbed and climbed and found it hard work. When I reached the top there were gates – I held the down prongs in my hands. Then I looked up to see a man, I knew it was Peter. He said to me, 'It's not your time – go back.'*

*From that time I became slowly better but it was a long time before I became conscious and then better. I was in the hospital for five months before going for a month's convalescence. People always put this down to my dreaming it happened, but to me it was very real. The bright light had continued until I was sent back. I have always had religious beliefs, going to Sunday school as a child (Methodist Church). I changed my religion after marriage because my husband was a churchgoer.*

The following was sent in response to a newspaper article:

*1957 (aged ten) I had a reaction to penicillin – my parents were advised by the doctors and specialists that I would not survive many hours and certainly not the night after hospital admission, and they were told to go home and get some sleep. I can remember everything vividly up to the point where my father lifted me out of my bed to carry me to the ambulance that took me to hospital. I blacked out with the pain of the large blisters bursting on my back when he lifted me and I drifted in and out of this as they wheeled me on a trolley into a ward and placed me on a bed, then I knew nothing for some time. Shortly after being admitted to hospital I can remember, in this half-haze of blackout/coma that doctors and nurses were in the room tending to me and trying to get something put in my mouth (I later discovered it was a thin tube which they wanted to insert to help with my breathing as my throat and airway had blistered and swollen). I can very clearly remember what happened next and later drew many pictures of it for my mother to try and describe what happened.*

*While the doctors and nurses were dealing with me shortly after admission to hospital, everything went black, then I was suddenly at the foot of a very large and tall staircase looking upwards. The stairway would have been about 10 to 12 foot across, quite steep and it seemed to go upwards forever – to me as a young child. The steps were either lit up or white and on either side, standing on each step, were people looking and smiling at me. They were all ages, old and young and children and dressed in all sorts of clothes. I had no idea who they were, being a young child. They held out their hands towards me and motioned, silently, for me to climb the stairs, which I did. The stairs were difficult to climb as they were a bit high for a young child to step up onto each step.*

*The whole place was very brightly lit from somewhere and was brighter the higher up the stairs you looked. The top of the stairway was almost too bright to look at as it hurt my eyes. I climbed quite a way up those stairs and the people were still silently encouraging me to climb further up. I reckon I got about two-thirds of the way up the stairs and could see a tall thin figure of a man standing at the top. He wore a long white coat or robe and had his hands stretched out towards me and was smiling. The bright light surrounding him and the whole area made it almost impossible to see much. I wanted to climb further but was too tired and sat for a while before trying to climb further. Then suddenly it was all gone and I was 'frozen' in the coma, unable to communicate or move. I have no idea how long this experience lasted but my mother said that the doctors thought I would not last more than an hour after admission to hospital and were amazed that I survived a few hours. They had thought I had gone late in the evening/early morning but were again amazed that my condition started to stabilize, although I was in a coma.*

This letter was sent in response to an article in a magazine:

*I was very interested in your article because I believe I had an NDE but mine happened to me when I was only five years old, which was 51 years ago! The story was related to me by my mum, who was obviously quite shocked to hear what I had to say at such a young age. Apparently, I was very ill with complications of scarlet fever. I was unconscious at the time. When I regained consciousness I said to Mum that I had seen a beautiful lady dressed in a long white dress who was floating in front of a very bright 'sunshine' light. She beckoned me with her finger and I was just about to go with her, as asked, when my granddad (who died while I was ill and they hadn't told me because I was so ill) sharply told me to go back. I didn't **see** him, he was beyond the light and I **heard** him. He sounded very stern (which was unusual for him to speak to me like that) so I did as I was told and didn't go. My mum was obviously very upset at this story as she had just lost her father and I was very ill.*

The following case is from a nurse from the Philippines. Although she originally told me about her NDE approximately ten years ago, it is only recently that she has given the full details, along with the after effects. The NDE occurred at the age of nine when the bike she was riding was involved in a collision with a car.

*The car was behind me and it clipped the end of my bike and I somersaulted backwards onto the windscreen, which smashed as my head hit it. All I could see was just . . . I didn't see stars . . . but just small lights. I could see people from one place to another but I don't know if they were real people or not. I could hear people talking but I couldn't remember who it was but they were calling me. When I heard people calling my name I was pain free and I thought I was floating. It was like a free feeling . . . freedom, it didn't even occur to me what was going to happen. It was . . . like fresh, it came to me that I may have been dying. Then I 'woke up' and all I could see was light. It was a bright light straight ahead in the distance. I was trying to get near it but it seemed to be getting further away. There was a big, long, long staircase to get to the light. It was long, I was tired but I wanted to get to the light. There were shadows in the light and I wanted to get near them. It was all black, like the feeling like being in a pitch-black, blackest black cave so I just wanted to get into the light . . . I just wanted to be in the light. I felt frightened then that I couldn't get to the light. I was running, trying to get to the light, thinking I don't want to be alone. I was so frightened I just wanted to be in the light. (As I am telling you this the hairs on my arms are standing up – I've got goose bumps just thinking about it.) I tried again to climb the stairs – they were small stairs but there were so many of them. I was tired but I persevered to get to the light. As I was about to get to the light somebody called my name. I thought the voice was in the light and I was about to go in.*

*My father told me that I was dead, because in A&E all of the alarms went off. I had stopped breathing and I had had a cardiac arrest.*

*I woke up in the hospital and all I can remember is that I was thirsty but there was something in my mouth. I could see my dad, there were a lot of people around me. There was blood because I had a suture in my head, I had sticky things on my chest. I couldn't move. Then all I could see is my dad; the other people were unrecognizable. My dad started crying because he thought I wasn't going to breathe again. Then I was kept in the hospital for two days to monitor my head injury.*

This next bit was not mentioned on previous occasions. Initially she was very reluctant to discuss this aspect as it is something she cannot understand or explain and as a result is concerned that others will consider her crazy.

*Then I went home and I started dreaming of this old woman walking down the street but she's got a big, big, net bag that I am always curious about for some reason. I want to know what she's got in that bag. She's got white hair that is tied up and wears a white dress. It's as if I am trying to peek at her through net curtains. I am frightened of her so just try to sneak a peek at her but she looks at me like she's seen me. Then she walks away and fades, then she's gone. Whenever I have those dreams of her the next day someone I know dies. This has happened since the accident and continues to this day.*

*For instance, shortly after the accident, a lot of people from the same family died and I dreamed of the woman before each one died. I told my mum because they were family friends who died. It became worse because when we went to visit the family members of the people who died I could see 'other people' in the room (that no one else could see) but I don't know if they're dead or not. They were just there watching me, they were amongst the other people. They looked at me, they smiled at me but it's just blank. It's as if they are just watchers or spirits – they just watch you. They know I saw them but they were just watching. I think they could be angels. I was young, I didn't have a clue what was happening; it frightened me. I see these watchers still but I tend to block them, I've got a headache now actually just talking about it. When I block them I get a headache. That's why I came here to Wales to get away from it all and then I meet you!*

*I know when a patient is dying or not. When I walk into the room, I feel heavy. I feel their suffering and when they are suffering too much I mention to the doctors that it seems that the patient has had enough and maybe it's time to talk to the family.*

*I also get electrical sensitivity. In work the non-invasive blood pressure cuff will just start working for no reason, even when it's not connected to a patient. The ventilator at an empty bedside will switch itself on. I get a lot of radio static and light bulbs just explode around me – I switch it on and it just explodes. The intravenous drug pumps will be working fine all day then will start alarming for me. Radios play up for me and computers will just switch themselves on and off when I'm around. We recently had a death when I was working and all of the electric bulbs and all the electricity went off; the backup generator took over. When the engineers came, everything just switched back on and they couldn't find out what was wrong. It was my patient who died and I knew he was going to die.*

*The NDE happened 31 years ago and it's still as vivid in my mind but I try to block it out. I don't want to remember it while I'm here in Wales. I've tried to forget it. I came to Wales to forget the experience and the after effects that it had on me. But then I met you and heard you speak about your research and it's brought it all back for me so there is no escaping it!*

I have also received reports of NDEs that occurred during unexpected, traumatic or accidental circumstances. Christine Stewart emailed me in response to an article of mine on the internet a few years ago:

*I was 11 years old when it happened. I am now a grandmother of 52 and the experience I had has never left me. It was the most profound thing that has ever happened to me and, what is more, it still affects me. I have no fear of death and I do not grieve for the dead or dying because I know they have gone on to another dimension.*

*Briefly, I was like most kids of 11, mucking about on the way home from school that day. I stepped off the pavement without looking, into the path of an oncoming car, which hit me in the back. I was thrown across the road and remember thinking that it was going to hurt when I landed. I heard a loud 'snap' and saw a flash, at which moment I was rising out of my body at rapid speed. I felt no pain as I seemed to lift higher and higher, it became dark and I was still travelling rapidly. There was an overwhelming sense of being loved, like the whole universe loved me. I came to a stop in front of some sort of barrier which looked like a privet hedge. There were flowers growing in the hedge which were huge, much bigger than my head! Beyond the hedge there were people looking out at me; they all seemed very interested. Then there was the lady. I call her 'the shining one'. She was so beautiful. I knew immediately that she was hundreds of years old but had the face of someone perhaps in their thirties. I was happy to be there, the feeling of love and peace was beautiful. 'You must return,' the lady said, although I never once saw her mouth move. I went to object, at which moment I found myself in a great deal of pain back on the side of the road with ambulance men and a huge crowd of people around me. I learned quickly that my experience was something I should keep quiet about, as folk looked at me strangely if I spoke about it. But I won't ever forget it and as I grew older I realized that many more folk than myself had had a similar experience. That experience has helped me through some of the darkest times in my life. Death is not the end!*

## The After Effects of Childhood NDEs

Connecting with unconditional transcendent love, then returning to life was confusing for many childhood NDErs.[24] Many children reported that they wanted to return to where they were and would even attempt suicide to get there. Suicide in this case is not a means of self-harm but a means to return to that wonderful place of love. Consequently, Atwater found that over half of her sample had severe episodes of depression and 21 per cent attempted suicide, in contrast to less than 4 per cent of adult NDErs.[25] She also found that a third abused alcohol, which contradicts Dr Melvin Morse's findings.[26] Out of his sample of 30 child NDErs, none of them had turned to drugs or alcohol. However, this may be due to the fact that Morse had followed up all of the NDErs from the time of their NDE. The fact that he acknowledged their NDE and validated it for them shortly after it occurred may have made it easier for them to understand and integrate it into their lives. Integrating the NDE experienced during childhood is a very sensitive issue and must be taken seriously, yet child NDErs are less likely to see a counsellor.[27]

Some NDErs become shy and stop talking about the NDE,[28] whereas some are viewed as disruptive or withdrawn.[29] Some take up meditation following their childhood NDE.[30] There is an increased propensity to gain knowledge and learn, with the children often excelling in their school work and creative skills. They often surpass their school friends and may be found to have a very high IQ. Many child NDErs are adept at computers, may become inventors, physicists, excel in arts and humanities.[31] Those who experience teenage NDEs are most likely to undertake counselling, healing or ministering roles.

According to the research of Atwater, child NDErs are likely to have long-lasting relationships when older, in contrast to the high divorce rate amongst adult NDErs. Electrical sensitivity is higher in adults than children. Parent–sibling relationships may be strained following the NDE. For example, following her childhood NDE, Nadia asked her grandmother about the beautiful lady she had met during her NDE. Her gran told her not to ask such questions and from then on believed the young girl to be possessed and always reminded her of it.

Some research has shown that in the adult lives of child NDErs money and salary are not important factors but stability appears to be very significant: 80 per cent reported job satisfaction and 68 per cent owned their own homes.[32]

A high percentage of childhood NDErs claimed their excellent health was attributable to a spiritual attitude to life and complimentary therapies. Interestingly, the tolerance for pharmaceuticals decreased as they got older. Other health-related issues appear to be lower blood pressure and sensitivity to light and sound.[33]

Martine Alexis from Swansea had a childhood NDE:

*Please forgive the length of this, but it's the only way I can articulate it! This has been very healing to write, so thank you for letting me!*

*Back in 1967, I was four years old and was admitted to hospital with a serious cerebral viral illness. I had basically lost the use of my limbs and speech functions. My parents had been prepared for 'the worst'. My NDE only really made sense to me in hindsight, at a much later age, but it was so real that I recall every detail, even now, at the age of 49. Here's a description of my experience exactly as it happened:*

*During the night, all visitors had long since departed, and the ward was quiet with only a few child patients and night staff. I was in bed, unable to move any of my limbs or speak. I did not feel good at all, I was frightened, and I would perhaps describe myself as 'slipping away'. The next thing I experienced was being up on my feet and running from the ward, along an upward-sloping corridor. Another child was beside me, running with me and holding my hand. I remember feeling excited and joyful. I can still feel and see the green linoleum floor of the corridor!*

We continued to run, and I vividly recall waving goodbye to all the other children on the ward, who were in side rooms, on the corridor itself. Many were crying, and they seemed so sad and miserable to be there. I was just very glad to be getting away! We made it as far as the end of the uphill corridor, the other child still held my hand. There was a door at the end, with light coming from the door jambs, both upper and lower. I really wanted to get to that door! I remember looking back down the corridor, and whilst I really felt I wanted to go forward, at that point I started to think of and miss my mother (alive both then and now, and very close to me). I felt a dreadful panic, it overwhelmed me. I suppose I would describe my emotions then by using the the analogy of desperately wanting to go to a party to which I had been invited and was excited about, but not being able to go in case my mother didn't know where I was. I remember dropping the hand of the other child and apologizing to her. I never saw the face of the other child clearly, but I knew it was another little girl and I knew 100 per cent that I loved her. In the background, a 'grown-up' voice was saying something like 'It's ok, let her go, she can go.' The next thing I physically experienced was the physical waking in bed and being coaxed into taking a very bitter tasting 'medicine'.

I would like to add that the experience did not frighten me in any way, then or now. In fact, I find it 'comforting' in a really visceral way. I have had no fear at all of 'death' since, and never have. The legacy of the experience, however, has had a tendency to make me less 'involved' in life, as if I am only 'marking time'. Not in a sad way, but I am quite detached, happy to be solitary and I resist most attempts to keep me in 'permanent' situations which might 'anchor' me to the earth, emotionally and practically (like parenthood, long-term relationships).

Following the experience, I developed the ability to see, hear and feel things that were beyond physical. In short – psychic ability. I know many people are sceptical about these abilities (which I find insulting and upsetting). However, time has proved me right on more occasions than I can count! In fact, I have worked as a professional psychic for more than ten years now. It is a huge relief and brings me great joy to use my abilities, after quite a varied career path, which included university and a secondary (high *school) teaching post, none of which made me happy at all. I've found a place of peace – or the nearest I can get to it – until I can really 'go home' and finally get to the end of the corridor I ran along over forty years ago.*

Clearly NDEs occur at all ages but those that occur during childhood appear to be more readily accepted by the experiencer. When I read these cases it strikes me how consistent childhood NDEs are with what is reported by adults who have an NDE. None of these accounts appears to have been exaggerated and all seem to be accepted as normal events by those who experienced them.

# 4

# The Cultural Variations
# of the NDE

NDEs and similar altered states of consciousness occur in all cultures. A survey by George Gallup and William Proctor undertaken in 1980–81 estimated that eight million Americans had experienced an NDE.[1] Since then, with advances in medical technology, that figure has probably markedly increased as more people are surviving critical illness. A survey published in 2005[2] estimated that 8 per cent of the Australian population has experienced an NDE. Australian NDEs are consistent with other Western NDEs. A study conducted in 2001 showed that 4 per cent of a sample of German people reported an NDE, which gives an estimate of three million Germans who have experienced an NDE.[3]

In Western NDE literature only small numbers of cases have been published from other cultures. There may be far more reports of NDEs within different cultures which are not written in English, hence the readership is usually restricted to the language in which it was written; unless there is enough interest to provide translations for these cases, they remain within their cultural context.

This chapter will summarize some cases from other cultures already reported in the literature. Unfortunately, studying NDEs from other cultures and time periods is laden with problems and there are many points to be aware of when comparing the various reports. In many of the accounts there is no way of ascertaining how close to death the person came. It must also be borne in mind that different cultures have differing definitions of death and in some cultures a person may be considered dead from the moment of loss of consciousness – for example, in Melanesia. Another factor which may influence content of the NDE is the varying life expectancy between cultures. Some cultures do not have access to healthcare, and death at a young age is common. Therefore, people are more likely to confront their own mortality and pay attention to cultural stories passed on by tribal elders and also acknowledge experiences described to them by those who approach death.

As mentioned, there are far fewer reports in English from other cultures so the ones reported may not be a true representation of NDEs within individual cultures. Many of the reports are historical,[4] not always first-person accounts[5] and some of the accounts are from transcribes and not original interviews.[6] Some may be derived from an oral tradition and have been passed down over many years and are therefore subject to embellishment or loss of meaning. Most reports in the literature were compiled by early explorers and anthropologists, all of whom had different interests and recorded the accounts for different purposes; some are autobiographical accounts. Current methodological concerns were not considered by early investigators and the interview protocols were not consistent: the cases were not randomly selected and none used tools, such as the Greyson NDE Scale, to assess if an NDE had occurred. There is also the language barrier: things inevitably get lost in translation. Due to the ineffability of the NDE, the accounts are open to misinterpretation, especially when translated from another language.

The time period during which the NDE was experienced can greatly influence its content as the work of Carol Zaleski[7] has shown. The medieval otherworld journeys highlight the historical and cultural differences between NDEs 14 centuries apart. There were many consistencies, such as the barrier/point of no return and the journey itself, but they appear to have been interpreted in a different way. Medieval NDEs were associated with torturous scenes and torment in contrast to the pleasant, beautifully coloured garden scenes of contemporary NDEs.

However, the reports give an insight into how NDEs are interpreted through the filter of different cultural conditioning. Each culture has slightly differing views and influences regarding death. It is beyond the scope of this book to include a thorough examination of each of the cultural beliefs so all I will do is briefly describe the NDEs reported in the literature.

## Indian NDEs

In 1977 the first cross-cultural study of Indian and American deathbed visions was undertaken.[8] Nurses and doctors who had observed dying patients were surveyed by means of a questionnaire and over 1,000 cases of people close to death were reported. As death approached, many patients were witnessed communicating with unseen 'people' or reported visions or meeting spirits. The Indians reported seeing religious figures of the Hindu culture such as Yamraj, the god of death, and his messengers, 'yamdoots', whose purpose was to take the person away.

A prevalent feature of Indian NDEs is a man called Chitragupta. He has a book which lists all of the actions of the person. The fate of the person is decided by their actions in life. Those who have performed favourable deeds will proceed to heaven, whereas those who have behaved in an unfavourable way will be sent to hell.[9] Mistaken identity or clerical errors are commonly reported where the wrong person had been brought for judgement. It has even been claimed that the person who was initially intended to be brought before Yamraj or Chitragupta actually did die after the other person revived, as in the case of Srinivasa Reddy reported by Indian researcher Dr Satwant Pasricha.[10]

In Indian cases the life review appears to have been replaced by the book of deeds. Other differences between Indian and Western NDEs are the absence of some components such as loved ones sending the person back to life, tunnel and light and OBE. On return to life there are also reports of marks on the body which were injuries sustained during the NDE.

## Thai NDEs

Out of the ten Thai cases reported by Todd Murphy,[11] nine reported encounters with yamatoots, messengers sent from (the god of the dead) Yama's office to take the dying person to hell. Yamatoots could be considered as comparable to angels that feature in Western traditions. Their appearance varied in the cases reported by Murphy but their role was to guide the person to Yama. Similar to Indian cases, there were five instances of mistaken identity, where the yamatoots had taken the wrong person – the person subsequently revived. In one of the reports of mistaken identity Yama's book contained the name of another person in the village, whose date of death was three days later – the person returned to life and apparently three days later the other person, whose name was in the book, died.

Again, the fate of the experiencer was decided according to good or bad deeds accumulated during their lifetime which were recorded in a book. Yama's record keepers had the role of accountant of merits. Good karma cancelled the negative karma.

One of the examples described a tour of hell where there were scenes of torture.[12] People were forced to walk over hot coals, prisoners' tongues were held with red hot pincers and they were forced to drink acid.

There were both similarities and differences between Western and Thai NDEs. The tunnel was absent in Thai NDEs, as were feelings of bliss and ecstasy. Whereas in the West dead relatives are prevalent, in Thai NDEs they only featured in four cases and their purpose was to inform the NDEr of the rules of the afterlife. Thai NDEs were mainly distressing in nature and depicted scenes of hell and torture. The dying person was forced to observe the tortures but did not experience them. There was only one case of an encounter with heaven.

Again the life review appears to have been replaced by a book of deeds which are reviewed in order to seal the fate of the person. Clerical errors are also reported in Thai NDEs and Thai NDEs featured Yama as opposed to a 'being of light'.

## Tibetan Delogs

Tibetan delogs are predominantly women who, during a period of unconsciousness or when near death, report journeying to the afterlife with a personal deity.[13] It must be noted that the concept of death varies amongst cultures so not all delogs may have been close to death: some may just have been unconscious or briefly fainted or been in a state of exhaustion. Some delogs have also been considered to be epileptic. However, French ethno-historian and Tibetologist Francoise Pommaret investigated ten historical cases and interviewed at least four living delogs and was convinced of their authenticity.

It is common for delogs to leave their body and view their body below. The delog is taken to the Lord of Death and guided through hell, where they witness the torture of other sinful people. These people ask the delog to convey messages to their family, asking them to perform rituals to absolve their suffering and urge others to live in a moralistic way. They may meet their own deceased relatives then go to paradise and return to the Lord of Death. A judgement of souls with a bridge, weighing scales or a mirror is observed and then the delog is judged. If enough good karma has been accrued they are sent back to life and given a message to tell others. When they revive, the message is passed on and everyone is encouraged to practise faithfully their Tibetan religion. Often the delogs are considered to be reincarnations of previous delogs.

Interestingly, to enter into the other world, delogs may traverse a large bridge that spans an enormous river but this is not a point of no return as in the Western NDEs. As a result of their tour of the land of the dead they understand the karmic tortures.

## Japanese NDEs

Until recently there were very few reports in Western literature of NDEs in Japan. Of the few accounts, long dark rivers and beautiful flowers appear to be prominent features.[14] During an illness and acute fever, Matsunojo Kikuchi of Iide[15] appears to have had an NDE. He travelled through a field of poppies towards the family temple. Components of the NDE that he described were an OBE, nice feelings, a temple gate that enclosed a crowd of people and dead relatives who told him he had to return. With much sorrow and disappointment he decided to go back. He regained consciousness and found his relatives throwing water over him to revive him.

More recent work on NDEs in Japan has been undertaken by Dr Ornella Corazza.[16] She reported three cases of Japanese NDEs. There were themes of rivers, dead relatives, noisy children dressed as monks, a rainbow bridge, being sent back to life by a dead relative, time distortion and a wall of golden light that had to be crossed.

All three denied that their experience was a dream and were insistent that it was a real experience. The experience was pleasant and there was no pain or suffering.

Dr Corazza also drew attention to the work of Yoshia Hata, who interviewed 17 patients who had come close to death. Nine had no memories of the experience but eight recalled visions of rivers or ponds. However, five of the eight memories were unpleasant, with themes of fear, suffering or pain.[17]

I met a Japanese doctor at an NDE conference and he told me a really interesting account of his grandfather's NDE that had occurred in Japan many years previously. He had been pronounced dead and sent to the mortuary, where he later revived. He described going on a journey to his new house but it was still in the process of being built. He was told to go back and that it would be ready for him in a month's time. He died a month after he had revived.

## Chinese NDEs

Initial accounts of Chinese NDEs were described by monks who were seriously ill but recovered. During their illness they underwent deeply subjective experiences that motivated them to convert to Pure Land Buddhist religion.[18] In one account the monk had a vision of himself holding a candle and moving into a void where the Buddha Amitabha placed him on the palm of his hand and the light of the candle spread throughout the universe. He woke up and reported his vision, which had a consoling effect on those grieving around him. His body appeared to have recovered and no signs of illness were apparent. Later he put on his clothes and sandals and stood looking, as if he could see something. He said the Buddha was coming, and then he died.

A later analysis of approximately 120 deathbed visions showed both similarities and differences to Western cases.[19]

There is an interesting case of the wife of a Confucian scholar that was reported nearly a century ago.[20] Mrs Jang had twice attended lessons in the Christian faith and had supposedly been converted to Christianity. Following a long illness she apparently died. Her body was prepared for her funeral but a few hours later her family heard a noise coming from her room. They found her sitting up in bed and she had removed her funeral clothes and was in her usual clothes.

She reported walking with Jesus to gates of pearl which were opened by angels that let them in. She saw beautifully coloured houses and walked with Jesus along golden streets. She saw thousands of angels encircling a throne on which the Heavenly Father sat and he told her that she may go back for a while but must return on the twelfth of the month. A few days passed and on the twelfth of the month she dressed in her funeral clothes, lay down on the bed and died.

Apparently the woman had only received two lessons in Christianity and had not been taught any of the things she described when she revived. According to the author, many people travelled to hear her experience. There may be a slight exaggeration as the author was also a missionary intent on converting the Chinese to Christianity.

Another text, from Chinese literature, which describes experiences that parallel NDEs, is the Chinese writer Pu Songling's *Strange Tales from the Liaozhai Studio*.[21]

Eleven years after the 1976 earthquake in Tangshan, China, 40 per cent of 81 survivors reported an NDE.[22] There were reports of accelerated thoughts, euphoric feelings of peace, panoramic memory and a life review. There were no reports of being sent back to life and no 'being of light'. Some described the experience as dreamlike and having a lack of identification with their body and some felt as if the end of the world had come.

## NDEs in the Philippines

In 2000 many nurses from the Philippines were recruited to work at the hospital where I worked. Consequently I came across some who had previously undergone an NDE. I have two first-hand accounts and one told by the granddaughter of the experiencer. The predominant religion in the Philippines is Catholicism and the accounts were all similar to those reported in the West.

The first NDE has been reported on pages 63–5 and occurred when the girl had an accident when playing on her bike.

'Esther' had her NDE during complications of childbirth, where the baby died. She found herself floating outside of her body, wondering what was happening. She worked at the hospital where she was now a patient and she knew some of the staff in attendance and was trying to tap them on the shoulder to communicate with them. Each time she attempted to touch them her hand would just pass straight through their bodies. She tried to call out to them but still there was no response – no one could hear her or feel her touching them. Then everything became black and she could see a small speck of light in the distance. She began gently floating towards this bright light at the end of a tunnel. While inside the tunnel she had a conversation with a male person and although she could not see him she believed it was Jesus. Although they had a long conversation she could not recall any of it. Thoughts of her other two young children came into her mind and she wanted to go back to them. As soon as she thought about her children she found herself back in her body. The experience remained vivid in her mind even though it occurred over 17 years previous to when she told me about it.

Another colleague reported the experience of her grandmother, the story of which she often heard while growing up. Approximately 60 years ago her grandmother, who lived in the remote countryside, was unwell and became unconscious secondary to exhaustion. She stopped breathing and was not responding to any external stimuli and all of the witnesses believed her to be dead. On regaining consciousness she recalled seeing a vast mountain which had the sea on one side below it. She knew she had to climb to the top of the mountain. She was frightened at this and was very anxious because she was afraid of water and if she fell down the mountain she would end up in the water. The journey up the mountain was very long and arduous but she eventually got to the top. At the summit was a house and she met a man with a beard, wearing a long white robe. She thought he was Jesus. He resolutely told her she had to go back. She was very upset by this as her journey had been so difficult and had taken a great deal of effort and she begged him to let her stay. He told her that she had to go back as she still had a job to do.

## Aborigine NDEs

There is an historical account of an Aboriginal NDE that is part of a long oral tradition has been cited by many sources.[23]

After reviving on his funeral pyre, the man described travelling to the land of the dead by canoe. There he met deceased relatives and the Turtle Man Spirit. He knew that he had to return to life. The spirits danced for him and showered him with gifts and told him he was not dead yet as he still had bones but he could go back to them when he had died properly. He revived and told of his journey but died three days later.

## Maori NDEs

A Maori woman was believed to be dead and her body was laid out and people gathered for her funeral. She revived with her grieving relatives around her.

She told them that she felt as though her spirit had left her body and hovered above her head then travelled north over various landmarks. She arrived at Te Rerenga Wairua – the leaping-off place of the spirits.[24]

She performed some rituals expected of the dead and prepared to leap off a ledge into the underworld or realm of the spirits. A voice told her that it was not her time, that she must return but would be called again.

## Guam NDEs

Four NDE cases of the Chammorro people described 'flying' through the air and visiting living relatives in far-off countries, meeting deceased beings and relatives and walking along a road.[25] Themes of walking along a road, travelling through clouds and meeting others and being sent back to life were described. One lady even found herself in her son's house in America but no one there paid attention to her, although her niece claimed to have seen her. She then travelled to her brother's house and watched him.

## NDEs in Melanesia/Western New Britain

Due to the limited availability of modern medicine, life expectancy is short in Melanesia. Heaven to the Melanesians consists of an industrialized, high-technology environment.

In the three cases documented by Dorothy Counts,[26] there were apparent differences between them and Western NDEs. Most noticeable was that scenes of beautiful gardens appear to have been replaced with scenes of factories, motorways and industry. There were reports of dead relatives or a religious figure and one report of a white robed, bearded man. They were reluctant to return to their bodies; one reported no fear of death as a result of what they had experienced. Many features such as the OBE, peacefulness, joy and tunnels were absent. Scenes of judgement were also prevalent and the punishment of sorcerers was witnessed.

## African NDEs

Dr Nsama Mumbwe from Zambia[27] described 15 cases of African NDEs. Common themes included being sent back to life, meeting people dressed in white robes, moving into darkness and being stopped by a barrier. The experience appears to have been interpreted in a superstitious way and it was considered to be a foreboding of evil or a bad omen.

More recently, eight Central African Kongo NDEs were compared with two Southern African Basuto NDEs.[28]

The Christian Kongo NDE[29] described themes of walking towards a destination with others also walking on the path. Difficulty was encountered at the foot of a big mountain but through calling Jesus the obstacle was easily overcome. The man found himself faced with a group of people holding the book of life and, although his name was on the book, it was not his time. He returned to life and found himself surrounded by grieving family and friends.

The Basuto cases were slightly different.[30] A man living in a remote village apparently died and revived. While dead, he described being on an unknown road, which he walked along for some time. The road forked but he was unsure as to which road to take. He encountered two men and one tried to lead him to hell and the other, who had a cross on his forehead, rescued him. He was instructed to return and find a teacher. The man revived and sent for a catechist, who marked his forehead with a cross. The man lay down and apparently died again, as his coffin was made, his grave was dug and the catechist was sent for to bury him. He revived again to say that the cross had disappeared and his Christian guide had told him to be baptized. After his baptism he died.

The following example was told to me by an African nurse who had heard a talk I had given on my research. She was very reluctant to talk about her NDE at first. After a few months she reported:

> I had not been well for about two days. It was nothing specific, just unwell, a bit of a headache. On the day that it happened my mother said that I looked tired and I should go and lie down. She told me not to lock the door of my room. I had my own bedroom and usually I locked the door when I went to bed. I went to lie down and drifted into a nice sleep. I don't know how long I slept for but I woke up and my mother, father and sister were all in my room crying.
>
> I'd been in a very nice sleep, very comfortable. I could hear my mother's voice very far away. It was almost like a whisper but I could tell it was my mother's voice . . . like she was calling. There was an image and I knew this was my mother but it wasn't a full image. I could see her figure but it was blurry and I couldn't make out any features – I just knew it was my mother. I couldn't wake up; I couldn't

respond to her calling, I was trying but I couldn't. I was thinking to myself, 'I need to wake up but my body won't move.' My whole body was too heavy for me and I couldn't move it. Then suddenly I was floating but floating towards my mother, where her voice was. It took a long time, the whole process was in slow motion.

On the opposite side to where my mother's voice was, I could hear my grandmother's voice. I could see her face but not her body – she looked younger than when she died. She was smiling. It was my mother's face that looked upset. I could see her face but not her body. When I looked at both my grandmother and mother I went towards my mother as she was crying and calling me but my grandmother was smiling. I went to my mother as she was distressed and seemed to need me more. My body was struggling to wake and move; I needed to go to my mother, then I had the floating feeling and I was going to where my mother was. I don't recall making contact, just floating towards her.

I can't remember anything else, just waking up with my father leaning over me. My father had been shaking me for a very long time to wake me up. To my family I had been completely unconscious. I was not making any movement at all but in my mind I felt that I had made some movements. They all thought that I was dead.

I later learned that my mother was the first to come and check on me, she called me and started shaking me but there was no response. She called my father; they were both shaking and calling me but there was no response and I didn't make any movement.

When I woke up I felt really tired and just wanted to go back to sleep again. They wouldn't let me go back to sleep – they were too scared. For the next three nights my mother slept in my room and my mother woke me up each night because I had gone into a very deep sleep. Every time she woke me she could tell by my breathing that I was going into a very deep sleep. I don't know if these are connected to that experience but I was having very strange dreams at the point of waking. The first time I was in a deep ditch and my mother was trying to get me out, then I was trapped in a car and my mother was trying to get me out; I can't remember the third dream now. Every time she woke me it was taking a long time for me to wake, much longer than usual.

*I didn't think anything about it until I heard you talk about them. My mother always stopped me talking about that time because it frightened her so much; I was never allowed to talk about it. The only other person I told about it was my sister but that was years later. We were talking about the time I wouldn't wake up and she said that I'd scared the whole family and then I told her about what I remembered. I never attached any significance to it; I just put it down to an odd experience.*

Interestingly the same nurse told me of a patient that she had resuscitated while working as a nurse in Africa.

*When the man revived he heaved a big sigh of relief. I asked him if he was ok and he told me that he'd been in a strange place and was surrounded by taxis. There were taxis of all different colours but there was a red taxi amongst them. People were trying to force him into the red taxi. He didn't want to go into the red one, as to him red symbolized danger. He wanted to go in another colour taxi. Eventually he was pushed into the red taxi. Inside the car was all red and he was being taken to a place that was all red. He was struggling to get out of the car. When he came round, to him, he felt that people had pushed him out of the red taxi. When he revived there was a big sigh of relief then, 'What was that? I was in a red car! Oh . . . oh . . . I was really in a red car. I really fought hard to get out of that car.'*

*It brought back memories of my own experience but I didn't tell him about it, I just said that some people have these kinds of experiences.*

## Native American NDEs

The main source of accounts from Native Americans are from early explorers, ethnographic accounts and some autobiographical accounts.[31] It is customary for the dead to be buried in their best clothes and as the family are making preparations they continue to talk to the dead as if they are still alive. (This is common amongst nurses whilst laying out a dead body.) The dead are warned of dangers they may encounter such as dark, rapid-flowing rivers.

A lengthy case of an NDE that occurred sometime between 1900 and 1910 is described by Hopi Indian Don Talayesva.[32] Components of the NDE that he described included leaving his body, being pain free, seeing his relatives but they couldn't see him, meeting a man who guided him to the place of the dead, entering into a tunnel-like hole, a reassuring voice, a place of judgement and seeing Masau'u, the god of death. He was confronted by naked witches and clowns with painted bodies. The village was guarded by a spirit man who led the dead in – those who were virtuous were guided along an easy path whereas bad people endured rough terrain. He was told to return to his body before his coffin was closed. He awoke and the head nurse told him that he had died during the night but his body did not cool so they did not bury him.

A popularly cited case is that of Black Elk,[33] who had an NDE during a childhood illness from which he nearly died. Another 11 accounts were described[34] and included two reports of people who had apparently revived after they had been buried. Components that were commonly reported were observing and trying to communicate with living relatives, travelling along paths which could be arduous or easy, and densely populated settlements with beautiful scenery with large animals. There was no life review, the experience wasn't reported as being pleasurable, there was no 'being of light' and no OBE comparable to Western OBEs. Darkness was not a prevalent component and a tunnel-like hole and subterranean passage were mentioned in a few cases. Guides with a protective function were reported. Some were sent back to their bodies with the purpose of telling others how to live.

## Hawaiian NDEs

This is a single report which was documented in the 1907 edition of *Hawaiian Folk Tales* by Thomas Thrum.[35] Following apparent death, the lady's body had been laid out and she revived during her funeral and described an NDE. Components that she experienced included an OBE, walking along a path towards a volcano, meeting people she knew were dead and being sent back to life.

## NDEs of the Mapuche People of Chile

Chile is inhabited by the Mapuche people or 'land people'. A Mapuche man was considered dead for two days then revived and reported an

NDE.[36] He described a journey to a volcano where only dead souls go. Other components of the NDE that he described were meeting dead relatives, encountering a barrier (going through a series of gates) and being sent back to life. He told everyone that all of the dead people were together and in a very happy place.

## Muslim NDEs

Initial study of Muslim NDEs seemed to indicate that, despite many months of investigation and hard work, no such cases could be found.[37] However, subsequent research has confirmed that NDEs do occur in a Muslim population and a total of 27 cases have so far been reported.[38]

A 12-year-old boy called Muktar lost consciousness after he fell out of a tree. On regaining consciousness he reported an NDE that had scenes of green grasslands (uncharacteristic of his sandy environment), hearing unusual music, seeing a bright light that didn't hurt his eyes and meeting dead relatives and communicating with them telepathically.[39]

Mustafa fell into the ocean while taking a pilgrimage to Mecca and apparently drowned. He recalled seeing a bright light that was not blinding, travelling through a tunnel and having a highly detailed panoramic life review.[40]

## Summary

There are many other reports of NDEs from different cultures posted on the internet; a particularly informative resource is the Near-Death Experience Research Foundation (NDERF) website set up and maintained by Dr Jeffery Long and Jodie Long, at www.nderf.org.

It is evident that NDEs are worldwide phenomena and it has therefore been suggested that they are merely the effects of a dying brain.[41] However, some cultures report components that are not present in other cultures, which would rule out some materialist explanations.[42] As some components are interpreted according to culture then it is reasonable to construe that the components may be interpreted symbolically through each individual's cultural filter. This could suggest an underlying collective consciousness, as discussed by Dr Carl Jung.[43] Therefore there would not be physiological causes of the experience as they are psychological interpretations of symbols.

Although this chapter has given examples of the sorts of things that people in other cultures experience it must be reiterated that these are only a small number of cases and may not be a true representation of all the NDEs within a particular culture. Until a thorough multi-cultural survey is conducted using the same research and interview protocols no firm conclusions can be drawn and the cases in the literature can act only as a guide. However, this chapter has confirmed that subjective experiences during a close brush with death or during a period of unconsciousness associated with illness occur throughout different cultures, although the content of the experience varies.

# 5

# End-of-Life Experiences and After-Death Communication

'. . . and on to the next section. 'Billy' in bed six is on his way, he'll be gone by the end of the morning. He's been talking to his dead mother since three o'clock this morning.' I looked up from my notepad. Were the other nurses trying to shock me or play some sort of joke on me because it was my first day on the ward as a student nurse? Everyone else was carrying on as if nothing out of the ordinary had been said. No one even looked at me.

After the hand over had finished I approached Billy's bed; he was lying down and looked as if he was sleeping. After a few minutes I saw him raise his arm as if he was calling out to someone. I got closer and heard him whisper something to someone not visible to me then he put his head back on the pillow and closed his eyes. I was called to assist the staff nurse with another patient. Throughout the course of the morning I continued to observe Billy making gestures to someone not visible and he began calling his mother. He then began smiling, put his head back on the pillow and closed his eyes for the last time. As predicted by the nurse on the night shift, he had died before the morning was through.

This was my first encounter with death as a young nurse and I couldn't quite get my head around how matter of factly the staff nurse on the night shift had predicted Billy's death. I thought about that a lot when I finished my shift that day. That event stayed in my mind but it wasn't until a few years later that I gave death any real consideration. As my nursing career progressed I realized that patients calling out or talking and gesturing to unseen people symbolized fast-approaching death and was commonly accepted by many nurses that I worked with.

Deathbed visions were documented in the 1800s by members of the Society for Psychical Research (SPR),[1] in 1908 by James Hyslop and in 1926 Sir William Barrett wrote a book, *Death Bed Visions*, inspired by a vision experienced by one of his obstetrician wife's patients. A large cross-cultural survey of deathbed visions was undertaken in the USA and India in the 1970s which showed that patients reported deceased relatives, friends or pets coming to meet them with the purpose of leading them into death. It was noted that patients usually died within two to five days of the onset of such visions.[2] Similar experiences have been reported by young children.[3] There have been more recent publications on this phenomenon[4] and research to investigate it has been undertaken in palliative-care hospices and nursing homes in the UK.[5]

At the end of life, vivid dreams of dead relatives[6] or the use of symbolic language or talk of going on a journey or packing a case[7] are common. Patients often appear to be communicating with an unseen person as the end of their life becomes imminent. People who have witnessed or undergone deathbed experiences are often reluctant to discuss them for fear of being considered crazy or weird[8] and patients are more likely to report them to nurses than to doctors.[9] Although they have been considered as hallucinations, caregivers argue that these experiences are different from drug-induced hallucinations and occur during clear consciousness.[10] Deathbed visions result in a peaceful acceptance of death whereas hallucinations can result in anxiety or confusion.[11]

Two types of deathbed visions (or ELEs – end-of-life experiences) have been noted by Brayne and Fenwick:[12] transpersonal and final meaning. Transpersonal ELEs reported by healthcare workers and relatives who have been in the presence of dying patients include:

- A change in temperature at the bedside of the dying patient
- Seeing patients have conversations with dead family members
- Seeing light around the body just before death
- The appearance of the dying person to a relative who is not present at the deathbed
- Malfunctioning of electrical equipment
- Clocks stopping at the time of death.

Sometimes there are reports of other disturbances such as glasses smashing at the time of death or birds in the vicinity of the dying person.[13]

Final-meaning ELEs are related to the motivation of the dying person to complete unfinished business and resolve family issues. Sometimes a confused patient has a moment of lucidity that enables them to say farewells to relatives – this is becoming more apparent from reports of people suffering from Alzheimer's disease.[14]

I helped my grandmother nurse my paternal grandfather at home 18 years ago. In the days leading up to his death I remember he often used to point to the doorway and in a whisper say, 'Look who's here, they're at the door.' My grandmother didn't like him saying this and always walked out of the room when he acted like that. He told her that her deceased father was there with him. At the time I'd never really heard of deathbed visions so didn't think to explore his visions further.

The following two cases were reported to me by a hospice nurse:

*A few weeks ago while on a night shift I was nursing a lady on the 'end-of-life care pathway'. She was unconscious and comfortable by then. She had been on the care pathway for about five days and her family had stayed all that time with hardly any sleep. I was talking to the son-in-law during a night shift and he told me that a week before, the patient had been staring at a point on the ceiling and said she could see her brother and her husband, both of whom had died, sitting in a pub, holding out drinks and calling her. She told them she wasn't ready yet. At around that time she also called out a name and looked over to the curtains by the door. The brother-in-law reassured her that he was there as it was his name she had called. The patient told him it was her brother (who had the same name) who she was calling. She said her brother was standing by the curtains.*

*Back in the summer I was nursing a man in his early sixties. While talking to the patient and his wife I found out that they used to attend a spiritualist church. The patient was getting more poorly and began to have vivid images of people coming up to his bed. The medical team put this down to hallucinations and began reducing his MST, even though he didn't show any other signs of opioid toxicity. While showering the man one morning I broached the subject of his spirituality. He told me that his father used to be able to communicate with the dead and he also used to have the ability, although it lessened and he had stopped going to the spiritualist church for years. When asked about the figures at the bedside he admitted that it was the same experience as when he used to communicate with the dead. He wasn't afraid of the figures but saw it as a sign that his life was coming to an end. He appeared to have relief that someone was listening and not putting his experience down to medication.*

Fourteen-year-old Tamsin was approaching death after a serious illness. This is what her mum reported:

*On one occasion Tamsin described how she had felt that she was dying (weeks before her actual death) and her (deceased) nana was showing her heaven and she said it was a wonderful place where she felt so happy. Tamsin said that there was a well, which was very deep, and she could sit at the top and communicate with us down on earth from heaven. Tamsin drew pictures of this vision, which had an African theme.*

*On another occasion Tamsin said that she had felt that she was letting go of life and started to go into this amazing light where she felt wonderful and happy, but came back from it. One of these visions took place in hospital where she was very ill and just wanted to return home as she did not want to die in hospital.*

## Lights Around the Body as Death Approaches

Some people have reported seeing lights or a mist around the dying person at the time of death. This was told to me by Hazel Cornwell, the experience is her gran's and has been published in a small booklet.[15]

*My dad sadly died of cancer in 1934, but when he passed away something wonderful happened. Mum and I went up to see him in an old-fashioned hospital in Fulham where they put the patients in big cots, and over Dad's cot was a small window. I've always felt it was a miracle because we were sat there, and his face was really drawn with pain, when all of a sudden I saw a light go from his chest, over his head and up through the window. When I looked back at his face it was beautiful – all his lines had gone. When we got back home that night I said to my mum, 'That was a strange thing with Dad today', and before I could go any further she said, 'I know what you're going to tell me, because I saw it too.'*

Hazel continues:

*My nan was full of stories like this. I remember her telling me that she was there when another member of her family was in bed dying. I think it was her mum. Her mum had suddenly started to sing, despite being very ill and near to death. When her family asked her why she was singing, she said that she was singing with the angels that were at the foot of her bed.*

## Premonition of Death

One lady wrote:

*This happened in 1966. I'd gone to see my grandmother, as I did every day when I walked the dogs. This particular morning she was quite upset by what had occurred during the night. She said it was like a dream but it wasn't a dream – that's how she explained it.*

*She said she was in a place where there was a bridge and at one side of the bridge was 'the dad' – that was what she always called my grandfather, who had died in the 1950s. She started to walk over the bridge towards him but he held up his hand and said, 'No, not you. Go back.' She was upset about this but I made light of it and in fact made some remark like: 'You've been eating something for your supper that has upset you.'*

*What happened later that night was devastating. My mother, who was 61 and in fairly good health, and had that day been to town and down to see her sister, had a massive stroke. She was unconscious and by three in the morning had two more strokes and died. My grandmother said it was my mother who he was calling over that night. My grandmother was 86 and in very good health and certainly not given to fanciful thoughts. I will always believe there was something there. Incidentally, she lived until she was 97.*

Tamsin, whose deathbed visions have been described above, also appeared to her sister after she had died; this is what her mum reported:

*When our younger daughter was 11 years old she was sitting beside the TV chatting to me about everyday things when she stopped in her tracks, looked startled and could see someone in the study through the door, which was ajar. Then she smiled and said, 'Oh it's Tamsin, she's floating toward the gerbil cage,' and described her as having 'no gravity'. This only seemed to last a moment and then the vision had gone.*

*I asked her to describe further what she had seen and she said that Tamsin had looked misty and floaty but was wearing a long, very light-pink dress and seemed taller than usual. Half an hour later, my husband came out of the bath and into the room and asked us if we had noticed that Tamsin's gerbil had died in its cage. It had been alive earlier in the day, but had not been well. Putting the two events together, it seemed as if Tamsin had been there when her gerbil died as if to take its spirit with her. It sounds so completely bizarre but had I not seen my younger daughter's face as she was watching this, I might have doubted what she had described as Tamsin.*

Another:

*Almost ten years ago I was in the USA, staying with friends in Virginia. In the middle of the night I was woken and in my room appeared my old nanny, who I had not seen for several years, although we corresponded on birthdays, etc.*

*In real life she was well over 80 but in the vision she was ageless and surrounded by an immensely bright light. She smiled at me, put her hand out and telepathically told me all was well. I was shocked and stayed wide awake. The next morning I told my hosts I thought my old nanny had died. The same day I returned to my house in Florida and told my family. Later that day a cousin of mine called from England to tell me she had died. It was totally amazing. I don't dream to any extent. I can only tell you it has given me so much confidence for the future. She left me some money but her telepathic message was the real legacy.*

Children's author, 39-year-old Shelley E. Parker, contacted me following a newspaper article. Shelley is very interesting as she has experienced premonitions since her childhood and also recently had an NDE – she has never discussed these before for fear of being thought crazy or disbelieved. She was diagnosed with Burkett's lymphoma and has been treated with chemotherapy. Following one particular chemotherapy treatment Shelley came close to death and had an NDE. She also had a premonition when she was 19 years old that she would get cancer in her mid-thirties.

*The dream I had at 19 about getting cancer in my mid-thirties featured a young registrar who subsequently was my registrar for real when I was having cancer treatment. Part of the dream was of him carrying out a medical procedure where he drew blood from my right wrist – a procedure I didn't even know was performed in reality. This procedure was then carried out for real during my cancer treatment: same registrar, same procedure. The procedure is where they remove oxygenated blood from an artery to assess oxygen levels in the blood and he removed it from my right wrist, just in the way he had done in my dream, almost 20 years earlier.*

*The reason I knew I'd get cancer in my thirties was by assessing his age in the dream – he seemed around 23, so I figured from this that I'd be 35. In fact, he was 25, so I was two years out and was diagnosed at 37. I knew, however, from the dream, that I was definitely going to get cancer – I don't know how I knew but it was a certainty from that point on that I'd recover from it. Knowing this made it a little easier to deal with when I was diagnosed. Hearing a disembodied voice shout, 'NO!' in my head when I asked one of my consultants if I'd die, when I was diagnosed, also reassured me.*

The profound impact that these types of experiences have is highlighted by how much the following premonition has helped Shelley to cope with the loss of her fiancé. To be left with such devastation, yet cope so well, is testimony to how powerful the effect that these experiences can have:

*My fiancé Steven and I had been together for 24 years. We were childhood sweethearts. I knew we would only be together for a specific length of time, due to something that happened (a premonition) when we first met. A week before the crash, I was very ill with pneumonia, as a result of my chemotherapy treatment. As I recovered, I 'sensed' death and assumed it was for me. I started to get my things in order but the day later, it began to move and the sense of death moved to Steven. I disregarded it but it wouldn't leave.*

*The night before the crash, I had the dream. I dreamed I was in a beautiful house and walked into a room to the right of the hall. Inside the room was actually the altar of my local church. Steven was standing next to me but it was as though he was in a dream state and didn't play any part in the dream. To the left of the altar was God (I know that sounds insane but it's true). He was human up to his neck, and his head was a mass of moving grey and silver scribbles – how I saw God when I was much younger. God told me that, as I knew, Steven would die before me and it was time. I protested and asked if I could go instead – I had cancer, so it made sense. He refused, saying I had more to do here and was very stern with me. He seemed very disappointed in me – which I now have more understanding of.*

*God said Steven would die the next day, or the following, depending on what happened in his life. He said it was ok as, every time I was in this dream state, time would go quickly and He said I already knew there was an afterlife where Steven was going. At the back of the room, a door opened and a beautiful blue sky was reflected through. This made me feel better and I agreed to let Steven go, on the understanding I'd see him soon and he'd be close to me all the time. I knew I wouldn't be allowed to tell Steven he'd die and I didn't. I now wonder whether I could have stopped him dying had I told him but I don't think I could have done.*

*They showed me how he'd die. I felt a rush and felt as though I dropped to the floor. I remember feeling offended they'd shown me, as I knew he'd die in a helicopter crash anyway. I feel, had he not done, it would have been in a car crash but he would have died somehow. I think this is where free will comes from. The next morning when I saw him, it was very hard to let him go. I took a plastic bag he'd been holding into the hospital with me (I'd been home for the weekend) just to have something he'd recently been in contact with. He died around noon that day.*

*I know this may sound unbelievable. It's true and I can't explain it but I've gained such strength from it. I feel there's a reason I'm prepared for these big things in my life. I hope you believe me. I'm a published children's author, as I've already mentioned, and I could come up with something far more dramatic than this if I wanted to lie about the afterlife! I really hope these experiences do help people to come to terms with death and perhaps see that, as far as I'm concerned, there's definitely an afterlife because I've seen it. I personally think it's something everyone can experience for themselves and I wonder if it's because I was so close to death myself that it was as vivid and prophetic as it was. I really do mean it when I say I wouldn't be here but for that dream about Steven – there's absolutely no way I could have lived without him had I not been prepared for his death and been promised I'd see him again.*

Following a further conversation it transpired that Shelley had previously experienced something similar:

*I had another dream of a little girl about ten years ago. She was the daughter of someone I knew and was almost three years old when it happened. She was a lovely, pretty, happy little girl, fit and healthy. I didn't know her well but I'd seen her on a few occasions. I'd been away living in the USA for about five months and when I came back I had this very vivid dream. In the dream I was in Bala, in North Wales (yet I knew in my mind it was 'the outskirts of heaven') and I was walking along this path and in front of me was this little girl and she was with her aunty. I'm not sure how accurate the image of the aunty was as I'd never met her or seen photographs of her – I just knew that she'd died about 20 years previously. I didn't look behind me because I 'knew' there would be just space there. The aunt said she was there to take the little girl to heaven. The girl was dressed in pink and had a pink bucket and spade and glitter makeup on the side of her face. She was very happy and excited to get to heaven and was frustrated that they hadn't got there already. She was dancing around expectantly. The aunt said that she'd been with the little girl all day and was exhausted looking after her. The little girl had to go first and the aunt would be with her. I knew they were both going to heaven but they had to go in one by one. There were mountains in the background, while I could smell the loam in the soil; it was a really overpowering smell of soil. Then the dream ended.*

*I woke up the next day and felt really unsettled. I thought about phoning the little girl's father but then thought better of it, trying to rationalize to myself that it was just a dream. That feeling of anxiety lasted all day, I just couldn't shake it. I went out to dinner with the family and then in the restaurant I looked at my watch – it was 10.10pm and all of a sudden all of the unsettled feeling and anxiety just fell away and I thought at last I'm starting to relax. The next day my mum got a phone call to say that the little girl had died unexpectedly the night before. She wasn't pronounced dead for some time after because the hospital staff worked on her but I sensed the release at 10.10pm.*

## The Empathic or Shared Death Experience

A less-reported phenomenon is that of the shared death experience or empathic death experience.[16] A case in the literature describes how Louisa was at the bedside of her dying husband.[17] She suddenly felt herself rise out of her body and saw that she was accompanied by her husband, who looked much younger and radiant. They travelled towards a dark tunnel but she was prevented from going any further by a wall of light. Her husband briefly looked back at her then proceeded into the light. She felt herself fall back into her body and realized she was holding the hand of her dead husband. Despite his death causing great sorrow this experience helped her through the grieving process – something that was also described to me in the following situations.

Two separate cases of shared death experiences were reported to me by relatives present at the deathbed of a dying person, as well as one case where a daughter experienced feelings of bliss while her mother died hundreds of miles away and the unusual experience reported by a doctor present as her patient died. In the first two the family members also experienced visions and participated in part of the journey of the dying patient. In the visions the relatives were only allowed so far; then the patient went on alone into the light, which coincided with the time of death. The family members reported that they were left with feelings of bliss, elation and happiness at knowing that their loved one was at peace.

Accounts of empathic experiences remain sparse. This first example was given to me by a man who contacted me after reading a newspaper article about my research. The following is from two independent phone conversations I had, with him and his daughter.

**Husband:** *This is a very strange event that I find difficult to describe. I'm not even sure exactly what happened, but it was something very 'unusual' – for want of a better word. My wife died in 2004. I was with her, as were our son and daughter; we'd been with her 24 hours a day. The day of her death I knew it was close. Myself and my son were holding her hand and my daughter had her hand on my wife's forehead.*

*My daughter said, 'Mum is walking with a group of people. No, she's stopped, she's going back; no, she's going to the people . . .' then I saw this very bright light and a tall person stepped forward out of the light. I was watching this as if from my wife's eyes. This tall person was holding his arms outstretched as if to greet my wife and welcome her. She walked further along this path until she reached this tall man. He was waiting there as if to give her a welcoming hug; there was a sense of peace and love. There had been such sadness leading up to my wife's death then this happened and we were left almost elated. I can't explain it. In fact the nurses and ward sister must have thought we were very insensitive because we all felt this sense of elation and happiness. What should have been a sad event for us all left us with big smiles on our faces and a sense of happiness, knowing that she had gone on to something else, if you like. Don't get me wrong, we were all upset that she'd died but that experience just took all of that sadness away and replaced it with an inexpressible feeling of ecstasy and joy.*

**Daughter:** *We both had a slightly different experience of it. Dad 'saw' it as if through Mum's eyes but I'm not exactly sure what I experienced. Whether I saw this or it was a picture of it in my head I don't know. Mum was unconscious and I had my hand on her head. My brother and I were willing her to go. All of a sudden I could see her walking into the distance on a path. She was right in the middle of this path. It was like a summer's evening and around her head was like a sun. On her right-hand side I could see the silhouette of* *some people. Her eyes were closed during all of this. Dad sobbed and I looked around and saw this tall person – I don't know who he was. She walked towards him on the path. When she reached him he took her into his arms as if in a warm welcoming embrace that was full of love. Mum's breaths got shallower and then there were no further breaths and the image or scene disappeared. I don't know what it was but Dad saw it too; my brother didn't see anything, though. It was all very vivid. I was left feeling calm and more accepting of Mum's death. I'm not as frightened of death as a result of what I experienced.*

I received a letter from a lady who had been present at her dying mother's bedside.

*I read your article in the magazine. I had an experience just before my mum died. Three days before Mum died she slipped into a coma. I was very close to my mum. It's what happened as my mum went into the coma that shocked me. All my family were in my mum's room, I was sitting next to her bed, holding her hand, I held her hand next to my cheek. Then she was walking a foot pace in front of me, Mum turned around and she looked so happy and well. Then she said, 'Go back now, it's not your turn.' As Mum let go of my hand I seemed to jolt back to reality. My mum had slipped into a coma. I spoke to a medium, as I was very confused by why it had happened; I thought it only happened to someone who was passing over. The medium said I was honoured to have it happen to me, that my mum was showing me she was safe. I would be grateful if you could explain what happened.*

In September 2011 I spoke at the British Psychological Society Transpersonal Section Annual Conference. Over breakfast I was discussing my research with some of the participants, and transpersonal psychologist, Hara Willow, mentioned an experience she had on the day that her mother died. This is what she had to say:

*Twenty years ago last April at 6.45am I suddenly awoke from a deep sleep. That in itself was unusual, as I had moved two months before to the Welsh hills, just under 1,000 feet above sea level, from the seaside town of Hoylake in Merseyside. I didn't think you can actually get altitude effects from a rise of 1,000 feet, but it seems that for my fiancé and I, the move from a town by the sea to a farm in the mountains knocked us out completely. We slept each night for about 12 hours, for nearly a year, before we acclimatized to the mountain air and the physical work of running a smallholding. We were usually in bed by eight or nine at night and rarely awoke before 8.30am.*

*That morning, it was 27 April 1991, I just found myself awake much earlier than usual. I sat up and looked at the clock and then at my sleeping fiancé and the sun streaming across the leaves of the beech trees outside the window, and I felt so good. Then the feeling of wellbeing just deepened into an unimaginable sense of peace and love and rightness. I remember being swept up in the feeling and not being present in the room any more, simply lost in the experience. I suddenly just knew that there was not ever anything to worry about; I was surrounded by and filled with the most profound, pure, ecstatic, unconditional love, love like I have never felt before. It was total, it infused every bit of me, filled me with joy. I knew that I was, always had been and always would be totally safe; that everything was just as it should be; there was never any reason to feel fear; that everything was PERFECT and could never be anything but perfect. That the universe was unfolding exactly as it should. It felt as if I was seeing life, the universe and everything from a distant, clear perspective, from outside myself, and that this perspective was the TRUTH, and it was familiar to me. Although I never recall feeling anything like this before. (I have, however, since then, a very few precious times during deep, deep meditation, reached that place again.)*

*The feeling gradually faded back to a normal feeling of wellbeing and the room coalesced around me and, smiling, I lay down and went back to sleep cuddled up with my soon-to-be husband. At 8 o'clock that morning the phone rang. It was my sister calling to tell me that at 6.45am our mother had suddenly and unexpectedly died.*

*It was a few months later, when I was still stuck in the middle of grieving for my mother, that I finally connected her death with the wonderful experience I'd had. I was sitting in the garden listening to a lecture by Elisabeth Kübler-Ross, at that time the world's expert on death, dying and transition. During the lecture she shared the stories of various people who had had similar experiences. They were just a small example of the many people whose experiences had been recorded. Each of them had felt a variation of that pure love, peace, joy and perfection at the moment of death of a very close loved one. Usually they were very close, such as parent–child or husband–wife relationships that had come to a sudden end with the loved one dying elsewhere. While I listened I cried my heart out and felt some stirrings within me of the possibility of moving through my grief. I remembered the knowing that I had felt, that there was nothing to fear or worry about and that all was well, and I knew that she was in that place herself and that she had shared it with me. I was so moved and grateful that my mother had shared that with me and the healing of my grief really began there.*

Hara also seems to have been changed by that experience in the same way as NDErs have:

*Since that time I have never felt any fear around death or dying. I know from that time and from other experiences I have had since then that death is not the end of our consciousness. I have had countless experiences that have proved that to me. For example, I have sometimes been aware of spirits around me, including my mother a few times, and my grandmother at various times, whom I also saw in spirit when I was at a retreat in the USA, on my birthday. I have even seen the spirit of a child who was the twin of a living girl I know, walking behind the mother. I saw this child so clearly I thought it was the living twin, who was actually 200 miles away. I didn't know until I told the mother what I had seen, that she had given birth to twins and one had died. That's when I knew that the child I had seen was in spirit and that she had grown up and was the same age as her living sibling. I have also had a dream about the funeral of a neighbour I had known for over 35 years, before I had been informed that he was dead.*

*I need to add here that I have regularly meditated, chanted, done yoga and other spiritual practices with great commitment since the death of my mother and I was told by a much-loved teacher that perhaps the psychic experiences I have are siddhis – the well-known side effects of spiritual practice. However, since they really began in earnest after my mother's death, I wonder if that experience is what opened me up to a deeper spiritual connection and faith and that it is connected to my very profound and frequent experiences since.*

*There have been very many wonderful and amazing occurrences over the last 20 years, but the most beautiful of all my, I suppose you would call them 'psychic', experiences was during my pregnancy. I was about 12 weeks pregnant at the time. I hadn't long discovered my pregnancy. One night I had a dream and in it I saw the face of the most beautiful boy. He was around three or four years old, and somewhat resembled my mother and maternal grandfather. He spoke to me and said, 'Mum, there's two of us in here.' When I awoke, I remembered the dream as if it were a waking experience and just knew that it was a genuine conversation with the spirit of my, as yet, unborn child. I went for my first check-up at the maternity clinic a few days later and told them I thought I may be having twins. They gave me a scan and I was pregnant with twins. They are now 19 years old. Both boys. One of them, Kris, was the child who communicated with me. He grew into the face that I saw in my dream when he was around three years old. He looks like my mum and grandfather. We still have psychic moments together.*

*When my boys turned two years old I began training as a spiritual healer at the College of Healing in Malvern, and I found that I have a natural affinity for it. Kris was born a healer too, and does it naturally. I channel energy from that source that I touched at the moment of my mother's death. I love my life and I love living, but I'm also looking forward with trust, faith and openness to being fully immersed once more in that pure, joyful, peaceful place, and to be back again with my mother.*

I often find that once people know about my research they tell me about experiences they have had. I was recently chatting to a doctor who had this to say:

*One of the patients in my GP practice was a lady who was dying of cancer. Over the months I made several home visits and I got to know her and her husband well. One day her husband showed me a photograph of his wife when she was about nine years old and standing next to her was her father and a big black dog; it was a very old photograph.*

*On the day that the lady died, I was present. As she died, I had an overwhelming feeling that everything was going to be all right, I just **knew** that her father and the black dog had come to meet her. It was a very strange experience for me that I just can't explain. I have over 18 years' experience of being a doctor and have looked after many dying patients. I have never before or since had such an overwhelming feeling with any other patient. It was a nice feeling – as if the lady was safe and that she was being happily reunited with her father and her childhood pet dog.*

These experiences are much harder to explain or dismiss as the production of a malfunctioning brain as they happen to people who are not close to death. These experiences clearly have a very overwhelming effect on those who have experienced them yet they cannot be explained by our current scientific beliefs.

## Terminal Lucidity: End-of-Life Experiences of People with Alzheimer's Disease

Another area of interest is the experiences of some people with Alzheimer's disease as they approach death. Although it is a new research topic, there have been recent publications that suggest a return to lucidity as people with Alzheimer's approach death.[18]

Several cases of people suffering mental disability recorded in historical English and German literature have been discussed by Michael Nahm.[19] The cases highlighted how people with such afflictions as dementia and other forms of mental illness became lucid and coherent in the short time just before their death, which was a great surprise to those treating them.

I have two very interesting examples related to me by different friends. The first is from Lyon White from Sussex:

*My mother Peggy, whilst in the latter stages of Alzheimer's disease was no longer able to converse with any coherency at all. Her conversation consisted of what could only be described as 'gobble-de-gook'. She had a spell in hospital. On one particular visit she was lying on the bed with her back facing towards the door. As I slowly entered the room I could hear her speaking very clearly with her eyes closed . . . Listening carefully, she was having a conversation with her father, who had passed over many years previously. He had been a much-loved policeman in Kent and had been murdered on duty; Mum had been devastated as they were very close. I heard her say, 'Yes, Dad, I know how much my Bobby loved me' – Bobby was my father, who had passed away about six months before. It was then that mum realized there was someone in the room with her, opened her eyes and reverted to her state of being unable to communicate with words of understanding.*

*I may be making assumptions but it was clear to me that she was in another dimension with my grandfather. Mum used to say to me that she could 'go' if I went with her. When she talked about going home I knew it was not to bricks and mortar that she meant!*

A good friend, Dr Ayesha Ahmad, reported the following account of something she witnessed:

*Agatha suffered with Alzheimer's disease and was over 70 years of age. In her final years, Agatha's children had attended to her in ways not too dissimilar from the maternal experience of their early years. Every day, Agatha would adorn herself with beautiful pearl necklaces and wander through the nursing home, chatting to staff and residents alike with her usual sweet demeanour. After some years of relatively stable health, Agatha changed. The transition was rapid. Within a few days, Agatha's body was manifested by weight-loss, fatigue, and it was apparent she was dying.*

*Agatha spent her final hours in a peaceful state, with her family holding her hands. Occasionally Agatha awoke, and attempted to express some of the last words she would ever utter. During one of these episodes, Agatha began repeating the name 'Jane'. To the staff who had nursed Agatha for many years and who had become familiar with the names and references that Agatha would precipitate into her flurry of conversations, the name 'Jane' bore no meaning. However, the sentiments that accompanied 'Jane' were wholly evident to be of meaning to Agatha.*

*On witnessing Agatha's repeating of 'Jane', her family became startled. Somehow this name also connected to a shared sentiment, a meaning that related to all of their experiences. Her daughter quietly*

101

*explained: Jane was the first-born daughter of Agatha. Sadly, Jane died during her first year of life and had left a legacy of grief so strong that Agatha had not said her name since.*

*However, in this setting of Agatha's home, although not the home she had made with her family, and the body dying – not flourishing as it once did, when it flourished so much she gave life to four children – Agatha felt the memory, felt her daughter's birth and her daughter's death. She brought her into the room to be alongside the rest of her siblings, so that the unity of the brothers and sisters was complete, under the watchful gaze of their mother – the gaze that greeted them upon life and the gaze that helped and enabled their mother to fall through to her death whilst supported by their love, a memory that could never be forgotten.*

## Control Over the Time of Death

During the course of my career it has become apparent that patients actually have more control over the time of their death than we realize. The first time I noticed this was when I reflected on a case that had particularly upset my colleagues and I.

It was a Sunday morning and the cardiac monitor attached to a young female patient began to alarm because her blood pressure had dropped. 'Jean' had been chronically ill for the past ten years and had been cared for at home by her husband. She had been admitted to ITU the previous week and we had got to know her and her family quite well and we were in awe of the way that she was so well cared for at home. Not being used to being away from Jean, her husband found it difficult to adjust to having time alone. Jean's condition was stable so with a bit of persuasion from friends and family he decided to relax a little and accompany his elderly mother on a day trip that had been planned by her local church. The morning of the trip he phoned to check on Jean's condition. We reassured him that Jean's condition was stable and that she was doing well and for him to go and enjoy the day with his mother.

An hour later Jean's blood pressure suddenly began to drop and, despite treatment, within 30 minutes Jean had become very unstable. We called her husband to report the sudden deterioration and advised him to return to the hospital. Every half-hour her husband phoned on his journey back to the hospital. Then suddenly Jean's heart rate slowed down and stopped. Thirty minutes later her husband ran into the unit in a terrible state: he was inconsolable and blamed himself for not being there for her. It was awful for us to watch and we all blamed ourselves for encouraging him to go on the day trip. He spent time at her bedside and then left in a very distraught state with the rest of the family. This situation affected the whole team that day and when the afternoon shift arrived on duty they instinctively knew that something was wrong.

I considered other patients I had looked after who had also died while their family was absent and then looked at the whole situation. The way I rationalized it in my mind was that the family being away from the patient may have made it easier for the patient to make their transition into death. It appears to me that the love of the family is what keeps them alive and the fact the family were not physically present made it much easier for the patient to let go.

Over the years I've noticed many other patients who have died while their families have taken a quick break. 'Sam' was in his eighties and at the end stage of his illness. His family had been with him almost constantly throughout the week. As I attended to Sam I could see how tired his family were and suggested that they may want to go and have a break in the canteen – it was 2pm and they had been at the bedside since 8am. They were grateful for the suggestion and left the bedside. I continued with Sam's care when I noticed, on his cardiac monitor, his heart rate slow down. It did not recover and continued at a slow pace so my colleague attended to him while I ran to the canteen to find his family. By the time we returned to ITU Sam had died, much to the distress of the family. This is not uncommon and I have witnessed it on several occasions. Similar experiences have been reported elsewhere.[20]

Hospice and palliative-care consultant Dr John Lerma has reported that 70 to 80 per cent of his patients waited for loved ones to leave the room before dying.[21] He also remarked that he had witnessed patients who had been certified dead return to life as the pain of their loved ones had pulled them back from a place of peace and love.[22]

Some patients on the other hand appear to wait until an estranged family member arrives at the bedside or for a special event such as a wedding or birthday. There was one case reported where a male patient remained unconscious for days longer than his expected death. He died on the day that an insurance policy became valid, thus ensuring his wife was financially secure.[23]

## After-Death Communication

An often-reported phenomenon is that known as after-death communication (ADC).[24] In the days, weeks or months following the death of a loved one it is not uncommon for people to report seeing them, feeling them or smelling the perfume of their loved one. Sometimes they may have a very vivid, lucid dream. These experiences ease feelings of loss and help the person through the grieving process. Although this was recognized in the medical literature in 1971,[25] it remains predominantly ignored.

In recent years techniques have been developed to induce ADCs[26] and further techniques were discovered during grief therapy.[27] While treating patients for post-traumatic stress disorder, psychologist Allan Botkin discovered by accident that some patients had reported meeting deceased loved ones. Using the eye movement desensitization and reprocessing (EMDR) technique it was reported that patients underwent a complete psychological resolution with their deceased loved ones by experiencing a reconnection with them.

Hazel Cornwell, whose grandmother's experience was described previously in this book, reported:

*My mum had called to let me know that my nan had passed away peacefully. It was July 2008 and Nan had been very ill for a month, at 95 she kept telling everyone that she had had enough and she was ready to go.*

*After my mum had called I didn't want to be alone so I met with a friend and we went for coffee. I was sitting quietly reading a magazine and I was very relaxed, although I was conscious that I was upset at my nan's passing. I sensed a small ball of energy to my right, it was about a foot off the floor, and it was about the size of a grapefruit. Its energy was extremely strong (I am a reiki practitioner and psychic so I am used to sensing energy) and it slowly began to grow until it reached a certain point and stopped. I couldn't concentrate on anything else while this was happening, and the only way I can explain it is that it was a human aura without the person at the centre of it . . . It was pure energy! I felt overwhelmed with love and happiness, and I knew instantly that it was my nan. In my mind I could see her turning cartwheels, she was so happy and saying to me, 'Don't be sad, I'm home!' The energy stayed beside me for a short while then it slowly came towards me and sat within me. The energy of my hands was pulsating, and my hands felt huge. I had to go to the cafe toilet as I felt that I needed to be alone. My nan loved reiki and always asked me to give her some whenever I saw her; I felt this was an unspoken confirmation of her presence.*

*It's hard to say how long this experience lasted but it would probably only have been for a few minutes, although it felt a lot longer. My nan was a strong believer in the afterlife and I felt this was her way of saying goodbye. It was a beautiful experience and I will never forget it. My mum, aunt and uncle were with my nan when she passed and my mum said that just before my nan passed away the room became very still and peaceful, and she knew that my granddad was there . . .*

Tamsin also seemed to communicate with her family after her death. Her dad said:

*Tamsin died in the early hours of Monday 8 August 2008. On the Wednesday, we went for a walk after visiting her body in the chapel of rest and Tamsin's sister lagged behind us. Then my wife heard footsteps running behind her and turned round expecting to see Tamsin's sister but she was dawdling still some way back. The footsteps sounded like the way Tamsin used to run in her trainers with her typical solid pace, but on turning round there was no one in sight.*

Her mum reported:

*Sometime on a later dog walk, my husband was walking alone when he saw a lovely light through the trees and heard the sound of Tamsin's giggle. It isn't something he can logically explain and he is very sceptical of any afterlife explanations, but felt it was Tamsin's voice that he heard in the light.*

Shelley's account of the premonition of her fiancé's death is described earlier. A short while after his death Shelley reported the following:

*What happened to me is quite lengthy. It happened around 12 days after Steven's crash. Steven and I frequently texted one another during the day and my mobile was always close by. I was in hospital, it was a Sunday night and* Dirty Dancing *had been on TV. Watching their relationship in the film caused me to get almost hysterical with grief and I became worried, as I couldn't control the emotion. I was lucky as, being on a cancer ward, I was surrounded by women who were far older (and deafer) than me and I was crying and left on my own. The nurses were aware of my crying but I told them I'd be ok and they were busy with other patients.*

*I was saying over and over, 'I love you.' As I got to the point that I really thought I was going to go mad with grief, as people always say, my phone beeped three times, something it had never done before. The noise it made wasn't the familiar text alert but it shocked me out of my grief for a second and I checked the phone but hadn't received a text or phone call. I started crying again and saying, 'I love you.' Each time I said it, the phone beeped three times. I didn't realize for a while, as I'd have breaks from crying and then the emotion would well up again. By the time I realized what was happening, this had been going on for around 15 minutes. The phone only beeped when I said, 'I love you.' I started talking to the phone as it was lying on my bedside table. I didn't ask if it was Steven.*

*This started to calm me down and after a while longer, I started to feel tired. I remember saying to the phone that I was getting sleepy now and that no doubt he was, too. I said, 'I love you' one more time. The phone bleeped three more times and then went silent. It never did this again and, around three weeks after I left hospital, it fell apart in my hands as I was talking to Steven's brother. I've still got the phone, though. There are other parts to this but I'd be writing all night, so, if it is something you're interested in, I'll elaborate another time.*

Shelley discussed this with one of Steven's cousins:

*Strangely, I told one of Steven's cousins about the 'phone call' I had from Steven and she said that, since his crash, her lights have been flashing on and off, particularly her bedroom light and only when she's reading scary vampire books and gets to a frightening bit! This made me laugh, as I've always had a terrible vampire phobia (sad but true! Very few people are aware of this – three, in fact, and now you, so four – and certainly none of Steven's family), which Steven always found hilarious, so it's odd that her lights flicker when she reads this kind of book. She and her son even shout 'Steven, stop it!' when they flicker, as they've been in their house for around ten years and this has only happened since the crash. I'd never really seen much of Steven's cousin until after the crash and we're only just getting to know one another now, so I'm only just hearing about her experiences.*

*She and her mum (Steven's aunt) have both experienced their mobile phones playing tunes that aren't even programmed into their phones at inappropriate moments, since his death – it actually happened during my friend's father's funeral last week. As his coffin was going down the aisle, Steven's auntie was outside the church when her phone began playing a sea shanty, which she found hugely embarrassing. She's tried to replicate this and can't even find it on her phone. Fortunately, everyone thought it was part of the funeral service, as it was really loud and it was a while before she could get it to stop! The man whose funeral it was, was a sea cadet for most of his life, which was why everyone thought it was part of the funeral. Steven would have thought that was hilarious, which is why they're all convinced it was his work!*

*Steven had a wicked sense of humour and they're convinced it's him. His brother's phone played 'Mr Blue Sky' at his dad's birthday dinner last year, as he was sitting next to me. Steven always liked that song and his brother was astonished as his phone wasn't set to play anything. They're all convinced it's Steven. The book I published, which was dedicated to Steven, as he helped me to come up with ideas, used to fall off his parents' bookshelves, too, which it had never done before his death.*

These experiences appear to be far more common than is realized. I was discussing my NDE research with a colleague, a nurse from Nigeria:

*Oh, that is so interesting because a similar thing happened when my father died in Nigeria. My eldest sister had moved further north and the day that he died he appeared to her. He was well dressed as if he was dressed to go on a journey. He smiled at her and looked much younger and very healthy; he was surrounded by a bright light. At the time my sister didn't even know he was unwell. The time that she saw him was about the time that he died; now how do you explain that?*

In 2006 Bev Newcombe emailed me in response to a newspaper article:

*I am 48 years of age and this happened when I was 22. My mother had suffered many years with awful bowel cancer. When she left this world she always promised me that, if there was some way she could let me know that life still went on after death, she would show me. A week or so after her death I went to bed one evening and had a vision I went on a journey (and please, before anyone says I was dreaming, I was not!).*

*Down a long white tunnel I approached this wonderful warm bright light and felt peace I have never experienced in this world. I found myself in this white, bright room, and in this room was a long table like the kind at the last supper, at the end of the table standing looking and smiling at me with rosy cheeks and lovely golden hair was my mum (so different to how she left this world, as you can imagine) – she looked so well and happy we communicated with our minds and all I could say was, 'Are you ok, Mum?'*

*She said, 'Oh yes, I am very well and happy, but you have to go now, you can't stay.'*

*'But Mum, I want to stay here with you.'*

*She said, 'No, you can't, you have to go,' and with that I gradually pulled backwards back into my awakened state.*

*Not long after this event, one evening I was woken by 'something' and as I slowly opened my eyes I witnessed something that was about to change the rest of my life and lead me on a journey that even to this day fascinates and excites.*

*There in front of me was this bright yet not blinding light of sheer-like gossamer cascading down from the height of my ceiling. The power, THIS thing, was telling me that we/us/the human race are but grains of sand compared to the strength and power of this image; it went as quick as it came and I never really knew why it appeared to me, to give me strength for my years ahead, because I certainly needed it – I have never experienced it since, but I know what I saw and felt – since then I have witnessed several spiritual beings but I don't profess to be a medium by any means.*

*All I do know is that none of these experiences are by chance or because of medications, etc. I was a young healthy 22 year old with an outgoing attitude to life – Do I have a fear of dying? No is the answer because I know that there is something out there much bigger than we can ever know or imagine – I don't believe we will ever be allowed to find out either, before our time is ready!*

Another common phenomenon is seeing deceased spouses after their death.[28] In fact my paternal grandmother often used to sense my grandfather at night when she was in bed. She described physically feeling him lying in the bed next to her; this gave her great comfort during the many years it took her to get over his death.

Another example:

*My wife died two and a half years ago aged 76 years; I am 78. During the night whilst in bed she has appeared on numerous occasions by the bed and even lying in the bed next to me where she used to sleep. The thing is my eyes are open, I am not asleep – is there any explanation for such occurrences?*

## Summary

From these accounts it is apparent that many people undergo pleasant experiences as they approach death. By paying attention to what the dying are trying to communicate to us in subtle ways we can help to meet their spiritual needs and to ensure they have a peaceful death. Dismissal of such transcendent, spiritual experiences by those who have not experienced such a state could be detrimental to them and could even make their dying process more traumatic. It is important to allow the dying to express their experiences and give them the validation they need by reassuring them that such experiences are common, whatever the belief of the caregiver. Deathbed visions have a healing quality,[29] bring comfort, allow people time to review their life and give great meaning at the end of life. Patients who experience visions usually have a peaceful transition into death.[30] A few years ago I had a conversation with a hospice consultant who had counselled many dying patients during the course of her career. She believed that the patients who had the most peaceful deaths were those who had previously experienced an NDE.

Caring for dying patients often causes anxiety for inexperienced staff. Looking after a dying person is not something that can be learned in college or from a textbook. Valuable insight may be gained through these means, but it is not until one actually cares for the dying that one really begin to learn. Hence it is important for all carers and healthcare workers to be prepared for things they may encounter in the course of their work.

Deathbed visions are a common phenomenon but as a society we seem not to talk much about them. This is not because they are not a part of the dying process but because we are not exposed to them as much as we would have been years ago. Dying people were cared for more at home and death was a social event with family, friends, neighbours and children all being present at the deathbed. In the 1880s visits to doctors and advances in surgical techniques started, resulting in the deathbed moving from the home to the hospital sometime in the 1930s.[31] Since then we have become more shielded from death and it is not such an expected part of life. Further advances in technology have resulted in many more patients being treated in intensive-care units than ever before. Most patients who die in intensive care are usually hooked up to various different machines and in drug-induced comas, which leaves no room for deathbed visions. Even patients who die on a hospital ward or in a hospice are not observed by their family 24 hours a day so family members are not always present if deathbed visions occur. So it is not that they don't occur – we are simply not exposed to them as frequently any more.

# 6

# Proposed Physiological and Psychological Explanations for the NDE

*A new scientific truth does not triumph by convincing its opponents and making them see the light, but rather because its opponents eventually die, and a new generation grows up that is familiar with it.*

Max Planck[1]

Below are a few very brief discussions of popular materialist theories proposed to explain the NDE. There have been many other theories put forward to explain the NDE, such as the NMDA receptor within the brain, neurobiological processes, temporal lobe epilepsy, psychosis, schizophrenia, defence mechanism, depersonalization, multiple personality disorder and reminiscence of birth. I have selected only the most popular due to the scope of this book. These explanations are a logical way to try to explain what causes NDEs but on deeper investigation they do not sufficiently explain many aspects of the experiences. The NDE is a highly complex multi-factor phenomenon, which makes it incredibly difficult to find an adequate explanation for such experiences.

## Anoxia and Hypoxia

One of the most popular materialist explanations for the NDE is that it is due to anoxia or hypoxia. Anoxia is when there is no oxygen getting to the brain at all and hypoxia is a reduction of the oxygen levels in the blood.

Early studies on the effects of hypoxia showed reduction in both physical and mental function, irritability, lack of concentration and difficulty in remembering.[2] Near death, hypoxia can be of gradual onset and the body can compensate for the gradual loss of oxygen, or it can be sudden, depending on the circumstances. For example, in cardiac arrest there would be immediate cessation of blood flow to the brain whereas in a person experiencing breathing difficulties the body may compensate while becoming increasingly hypoxic. When blood flow to the brain stops, consciousness is lost within ten to twenty seconds.[3] Brain damage is irreversible when blood flow has stopped for more than five to ten minutes.[4]

As hypoxia progresses, brain function becomes increasingly disorientated, confused and disorganized, resulting in unconsciousness. I have witnessed this many times when working as a nurse.

NDEs are reported with great clarity of thought: they are lucid, structured experiences, people report a heightened sense of consciousness and the recall of them remains vivid in their minds for the rest of their lives in many cases. This is not what one would expect from a disorganized brain with no or greatly reduced blood flow. I have nursed hundreds of unconscious patients (who did not report an NDE) and as they regain consciousness it is a gradual process and they are usually dazed and bewildered as they come to.

Gravitational-induced loss of consciousness (G-LOC) is a recognized phenomenon that can be experienced by pilots exposed to high levels of acceleration.[5] During training procedures some pilots have become unconscious as their heart has been unable to pump blood effectively around the body. These have been compared with NDEs as some components appear to be the same, such as visions, feelings of euphoria, positive emotions and OBEs. However, there are also differences – these experiences were difficult to recall and were quite random and none of the pilots appeared to have any of the life changes reported by NDErs. There is also the case of an NDEr who was a pilot who had also experienced hypoxia at high altitude and he believed the two experiences to be totally different.[6]

It has been suggested that the tunnel and light components are due to hypoxia and drugs administered during resuscitation.[7] When adrenaline or atropine is administered the pupils dilate, which is believed to account for the tunnel and the bright light.[8] If anyone has ever tried shining a pupil torch in their eyes the first reaction is to close the eyes because it hurts. The light reported during NDEs does not hurt the eyes. Pupils are dilated when in a dim room so when exposed to a bright light, the eyes close in response. If the pupils are dilated because of the drugs then they cannot contract in response to light. It is unlikely that the light reported would be described as bright but not hurting the eyes. Also this does not account for NDEs that occurred where these drugs were not administered and no resuscitation procedures were undertaken. Not all cultures report the tunnel component of the NDE and it is been argued that it is only a symbolic representation of Western NDEs,[9] which would also invalidate this theory. If the NDE is due to anoxia then all patients who have a cardiac arrest should report an NDE but approximately 80 per cent of cardiac arrest survivors do not report an NDE. Throughout the course of my career, I have nursed hundreds of patients who have been hypoxic but very few of these have reported an NDE. If the NDE is due to lack of oxygen then I would expect the majority of these patients to report an NDE.

## Hypercarbia

The side effects of high levels of carbon dioxide in the blood were first discovered by American psychiatrist Charles Meduna,[10] who experimented with carbon dioxide to treat psychiatric disorders. Side effects include OBEs, past memories, bright colours, wonderful feelings, real dreams, geometric patterns and feelings of discovery, and some of the experiences were frightening. Although some of these appear to be characteristic of the NDE, Meduna's patients also displayed neurological dysfunction and none had the after effects characteristic of NDEs.

Again I have nursed many patients who have been hypercarbic and their muscles twitch and jerk spasmodically, this doesn't occur during an NDE. If hypercarbia was the cause of the NDE then I would expect NDEs to be more frequently reported.

## Drugs

Euphoric, blissful, hallucinatory states can result from the ingestion of recreational drugs such as LSD (lysergic acid diethylamide), psilocybin, DMT (N,N-dimethyltryptamine-130), ketamine, cannabis and mescaline. While under the influence of such psychotropic drugs people have reported an expansion of consciousness, feelings of serenity and cosmic insights.[11] However, drug experiences can be random as opposed to the set pattern of the NDE. Although people claimed to be transformed by their drug experience, it was found that they did not display such behaviour to support those claims[12] as people do who have had an NDE.

When such drugs are ingested it is usually with the intention of inducing a mind-altering experience. Thus the psychological set, setting and context must also be taken into consideration. The set refers to the person's individual characteristics, such as mood, past experience, personality and expectations. The setting refers to the environment and people present. The context refers to the experiences in which the experience occurred – was it with a guide? Was it to escape from problems? Was it to experiment? All of these factors can influence how the experience develops. Whereas drugs are taken with intent, the NDE is unexpected and sudden, and therefore experienced in a very different context. In both types of experience the individual may be accessing the same state of consciousness but it is interpreted according to the circumstances in which it occurred.

A recent study comparing the similarities between NDEs and ketamine experiences[13] highlighted many similarities between both types of experience. Those who took ketamine also reported the main features of NDEs (as defined by the Greyson NDE Scale[14]), such as meeting deceased relatives and friends, feelings of peace, seeing a light, flashes of their life and entering into another realm.

There were some differences between the NDE group and the ketamine group. A much higher percentage of the NDE group reported deceased relatives and visions of religious figures, especially Jesus. The ketamine group merely reported a presence or being of light that wasn't recognizable. A much higher percentage of the NDE group reported a bright light. However, a higher percentage of the ketamine group reported a feeling of being at one with the universe or a sense of harmony. Very few of the ketamine group reported a barrier or point of no return whereas this was reported by the majority of the NDE group.

As pointed out by the author of the study, Dr Ornella Corazza, not all ketamine experiences resemble NDEs. The NDE-type experience was most noticeable the first time ketamine was used and the experience diminished as ketamine use increased. Of course, all who took the ketamine did so with intent and some form of expectation.

DMT occurs naturally within the body and it has been suggested that this can play a part in the NDE.[15] However, controlled experiments with this drug revealed that the experiences reported were a little different from NDEs: many reports were of encounters with alien-like beings. One subject reported an experience which did have themes of the NDE, such as a tunnel or channel of light that was bright and pulsating. The tunnel was very big and the subject encountered beings in the tunnel that looked like small gremlins with wings and tails.[16] It is apparent that there were similarities to an NDE but it must also be taken into account that the subject was also reading books of NDEs by Betty Eadie[17] and Dannion Brinkley,[18] both with prolific accounts laden with such imagery.

It is well known that anaesthetic agents and analgesic drugs such as morphine can induce hallucinatory experiences. However, drug-induced experiences can be both subjective and objective. I have witnessed many patients who have hallucinated following the administration of such drugs; their inappropriate behaviour is clearly observable. They may become irrational, paranoid and try to remove drips or try to get out of bed; they may even become aggressive towards staff. In contrast, NDEs occur when the patient is usually unconscious and unresponsive.

It may take some time for the effects of anaesthetics to wear off and patients are usually sleepy for some hours post-operatively. When I followed up patients in my study, most patients had very little or no recall of being in intensive care. This again is a complete contrast to the vividly recalled NDEs. Also, there were NDEs reported in the absence of drugs being administered.

## Endorphins

The body can manufacture its own opiates and these are called endorphins. Their function is to reduce pain, induce peace, pleasure and calm, and aid survival by responding in times of stress. Endorphins are released during conditions in which an NDE can occur and have been shown to be released in the brains and body fluids of dogs that were conscious at the time of death.[19] However, if endorphins are released at the point of death then it does not explain why not all people report an NDE when they survive a close brush with death.

However, it has been argued[20] that high levels of endorphins would be expected in long-distance runners but they do not report NDEs. It has also been suggested that endorphins are not strong enough hallucinogens.[21] The effects of endorphins can last for up to 22 hours[22] yet the NDE is very brief and pain returns as soon as the person regains consciousness.

Endorphin release is followed by sleepy, dreamlike states.[23] There is a release of endorphins during a grand mal seizure but the person is usually dazed and fatigued[24] after the seizure. Both are the opposite of the hyper-alert state of the NDE.

## Neurobiological Processes

Neurological processes have been suggested to be the cause of the NDE and there are several theories describing these processes in detail.[25] Most of these theories have been proposed from the premise that the brain creates consciousness. However, it remains unexplained how conscious experience can arise from neurological structures and accompany the neurological processing.[26] In light of more research in the clinical area it would seem that, rather than these neurological processes being responsible for *creating* consciousness, it would appear more plausible that the processes are merely *mediating* the consciousness. More research into NDEs may provide further support for these neurological processes being correlates as opposed to the popular materialist belief that they are causations. This in itself would completely revolutionize the way in which consciousness is understood.

## The OBE

Verification of the OBE component of the NDE in my research was suggested by Paul and Linda Badham.[27] Inspiration for verifying the OBE component of the NDE came from experiments conducted in the 1960s and 1970s.[28] Subjects who claimed to be adept at leaving their bodies also successfully projected into experimentation rooms where their pet animals were resting. At the time of the claimed projection, the animals became restless and acted as if their owner was present. One lady correctly reported a number that was placed in a box above the bed where she slept in the laboratory.[29] Objects hidden in suspended boxes were also correctly identified.[30] However, these are only a few studies and they have not been replicated.

## Autoscopy and Heautoscopy

Autoscopic experiences[31] are where a second body is seen without changes in bodily self-consciousness. The mind remains identified with the body, which is not typical of the altered body/mind perception reported during an OBE.[32] Heautoscopic experiences[33] are when people see a phantom of themselves while their mind and body remain identified with each other. During heautoscopic experiences there is an identification with the phantom body and often the person describes perceiving and existing in two different places at the same time. The phantom seen is usually actively moving, transparent and only the face or part of the body is visible In contrast, during the OBE in an NDE context, the mind exists completely apart from the physical body and recognizes it as separate as opposed to an image.

## The OBE with Seizure/Epilepsy

OBEs have previously been reported during epileptic seizures, psychosis and temporal-lobe epilepsy.[34] Some cases may resemble NDE-type experiences but they also exhibited bizarre behaviour indicating that the individuals were out of touch with reality. Most of the similarities between the epileptic experiences were restricted to autoscopy,[35] which is very different to the clearly defined, precise and accurate OBEs reported in an NDE, where the person believes that they have existed apart from their body. Events were also discovered to be inaccurate on further investigation, whereas others described feeling detached as if in the movies or dreamlike.

Temporal-lobe seizures that have been induced by electrical stimulation of the brain are fragmentary and variable,[36] unlike the clear, integrated NDE. Many details of hallucinations are forgotten three to four minutes after the stimulus.[37] Despite having over 30 years of experience of treating temporal-lobe epileptics, Rodin[38] stated that he has never treated a patient who reported an experience that resembled an NDE during a seizure. Some seizures may result in alteration in body image, space, time and the experience of déjà vu, but they are very confusional.

Some NDE components may manifest in confusional, fragmentary form due to abnormal temporal-lobe discharges.[39] That such a devastating brain event that produced the seizures could evoke a highly structured NDE, however, is very unlikely. Whereas NDEs are life-enhancing, the experiences reported by epileptic and psychotic people can have the opposite effect.

## The OBE and Electrical Stimulation

In the 1980s Canadian neuroscientist Michael Persinger devised a 'God helmet', in which magnetic fields of varying strengths were passed through the helmet placed on the subject's head, with the intention of inducing mystical experiences. The helmet was used to induce minor seizures in the temporal lobes, which Persinger proposed would result in OBEs and religious/mystical experiences. The results of the experiments showed that two-thirds of the subjects reported the sense of a presence when the magnetic fields were activated but, interestingly, a third of the control group reported the same effect even though there were no magnetic fields activated.[40] None of the magnetic experiences resembled an NDE and there were inconsistent reports amongst subjects.

Replication of the same experiments revealed quite different results and the only two subjects to report strong spiritual experiences were in the control group and had not been exposed to the magnetic fields. The researchers concluded that Persinger's results were due to psychological suggestion.[41]

Out-of-body-type phenomena have also been evoked during experiments involving electrical stimulation of the brain.[42] When taken at face value these appear to be the same as OBEs reported in a near-death context, whereas in-depth scrutiny reveals many differences between the two types of experience. Some patients have described the experience as superimposed on their consciousness and out of context and place.[43] On examination of the research it is apparent to those familiar with OBEs that the reported experiences, although resembling OBEs, are very different to the accurate, precise OBEs reported in the NDE context.

In 2002 and 2004 research[44] was published which suggested that electrical stimulation of the angular gyrus within the brain could evoke OBEs, reinforcing the belief that OBEs are created by the brain.

I read the articles with interest. Unfortunately, the article was written with the a priori belief that consciousness is a by-product of the brain as the researchers believed the OBE to be generated by the brain. The authors provided the reports of their six research subjects – neurological patients, four of whom suffered from epileptic seizures, one who had arterial hypertension and one who suffered with hemiplegic migraine. All patients underwent neuroimaging and EEG recording and the focus was on the 'description of the OBE/autoscopic phenomena'.

What each patient reported was very different to the precise and clear OBEs reported in association with an NDE. The subjects in Blanke et al's study reported viewing unknown people, vague 'impressions of dreaming', viewing only the legs and lower trunk, being in two positions at once without feeling she had left her body, feelings of distortion of body movement, viewing only the upper torso and face and could give no details about the area around the body. These were not characteristic of the precise and clear details reported during an OBE associated with an NDE. For full details of what the subjects reported refer to both published papers.

Another case was reported to me (see also patient 10 from my study in Chapter 7). This lady reported an OBE during surgery:

*I am a mother and grandmother, I went on to university after my out-of-body experience, which I had approximately eight years ago. I have a degree in psychology and a masters in psychoanalytic studies, not bad for an olden and a dyslexic!*

*I was having problems and to cut a long story short it culminated in an operation. The private operation was to be finished by 4.30–5.00pm, my husband was told to phone the surgeon at 5.00pm and he would speak to him, telling him how it went.*

*The first thing that happened was that I was aware I was wide awake in a very bright yellow room; I felt the walls were covered in yellow tiles and the lights were very bright. I knew immediately that I was in hospital. I was very calm and felt really, really well; I looked to my left and saw the clock on the wall: it was showing the time as 6.50pm. I felt immediately sorry for my husband as I knew he would be panicking, not having been told all was well yet. I looked down and could see my arms, and lower body. In my left hand there was a double tap (allowing 2 points for drugs to enter). I was aware that there were people behind me, but I couldn't see them. I tried to look right but couldn't really see that side of the room.*

*There was a panic going on in the room, which surprisingly I wasn't at all worried about; I was more concerned about my husband. The person behind me on the right was a woman – she informed my surgeon, who I recognized (even though he was in greens, white Wellington boots, blue jay cloth type cap on his head and face mask dangling around his jaw line) that my blood pressure was dropping, she repeated this info at quite regular intervals. My surgeon was getting really cross and agitated, this surprised me as this was a side of him I'd never seen before. He began yelling at the man in a white coat who had come into view from the right, who I recognized as the person who had taken my blood tests earlier. He had a clip board in his hand which he was looking at; he was clearly shaken at the surgeon's tone with him. The surgeon demanded to know how many units of blood I'd been given, he answered two, at which the surgeon exploded: 'No you didn't, there was at least three empty on the floor.' He was pacing up and down, to my left, looking really concerned. Another man dressed in day clothes entered from the right, who I recognized as the anaesthetist. The surgeon was again very confrontational with him, demanding that he do something. The anaesthetist ignored the ranting and calmly spoke to the woman behind me, asking how low my blood pressure had dropped and then calmly looked at the clip board that the white coat man was holding; he returned it and walked around the foot of the bed. I watched as he lifted my left hand; he didn't acknowledge me. He was holding a syringe; he uncapped one of the taps and put the syringe into it.*

*Everything went black and I was back in my body and I felt very, very ill. I tried to sit up and speak to the surgeon and they restrained me and pulled out the throat 'thing'. I gagged, then started to say, 'Don't have a go at the others.' I wanted to say more but was overcome with nausea. I looked up at the clock, it was exactly where it was before, it was 6.50pm and I looked to the right and could now see the end of the room (only beds and a wall). I was checking for myself that I hadn't dreamed it. I definitely had not! The room was a recovery room and wasn't as bright or yellow somehow, but it was the same room. The surgeon was so relieved he kissed my cheek, he ripped from his head the blue cap and pulled his mask off and said,*

*'I can go home now.' I glanced down as he turned to walk away and there were the white wellies!*

*The next day the surgeon came to see me; he asked me if I remembered anything from the night before. I told him that they had had trouble with my blood pressure continually dropping. His jaw dropped – I think he was shocked. He went on to tell me that it had indeed dropped and adrenaline was administered, and then all was well. There had been complications and the op had taken longer than they expected.*

*I know without a doubt that the experience was real, the clock, the timing, the surgeon's attire and the things I'd seen did happen.*

There is a huge contrast between that experience and those induced by electrical stimulation. The cases reported during stimulation were very non-specific and not related to events going on in the room around them. For example, one of the reported OBEs related not to something that was going on in the room but to his wife and in his home. Although there were some vague similarities between an OBE during an NDE and those reported during stimulation this does not provide evidence that OBEs are generated by the brain. The areas of the brain associated with these experiences are just as likely to be correlates as opposed to causations. For a fuller response to the above research, see the article by Holden, Long and McClurg.[45] Clearly OBEs reported during near-death events are very different to those induced by electrical stimulation, suggesting that the authors are a little presumptive in their statement that: 'These observations indicate that OBEs and complex somatosensory illusions can be artificially induced by electrical stimulation of the cortex.'[46]

## The OBE in Prospective Research

There are reports in the literature of patients who had an OBE then correctly described seeing things they could not have from their field of vision during the emergency.[47]

Other studies have tried to establish veridicality of the OBE during an NDE.[48] Marker cards that could only be viewed from an out-of-body perspective were placed in the emergency room (A&E), intensive care and coronary care. These studies were replicated in my study and Dr

Sam Parnia's study.[49] None of these studies was conclusive but patient 10 in my study very accurately reported the actions of the nurse, doctor and physiotherapist who were present during his emergency situation.[50] I know his report was accurate as I was actually the nurse who was present at the time. The current AWARE[51] study is also conducting the same veridicality experiment.

## Hypnagogia and Hypnopompia, Dreams, REM Intrusion

Hypnagogia is the state at the onset of sleep and hypnopompia is the state on waking from sleep. During these states visual imagery can occur.[52] This is the state in which sudden insights can be 'acquired'. These states are considered conducive to inducing an OBE not in the context of near-death.[53] People experiencing this report feeling peaceful, calm, relaxed, indifferent and detached. However, those who report an OBE induced in the hypnagogic state feel like passive observers and don't have any analytical thought.

OBEs are frequently categorized as dreams but there are distinct differences.[54] Rapid eye movement (REM) sleep occurs during every 90-minute sleep cycle. This is accompanied by motor paralysis, muscle tension and periodic bursts of activity. The brief research on OBEs and EEGs[55] has shown differences between OBEs and REM sleep. Also, characteristic eye movements of REM sleep are absent from OBEs. There is clear recall of the OBE whereas REM recall is hazy, confused and very difficult. On waking, the person realizes they have been dreaming, whereas for OBErs its reality is emphasized. Whereas OBEs/NDEs are life changing, dreams don't invoke changes in personality and lifestyle.

REM intrusion has also been suggested as an explanation for NDEs. This is a condition associated with the REM sleep state, involving rapid eye movements, decreased muscle tone and dreaming. Occasionally the REM state can occur when someone is waking up or about to fall asleep. This is called REM intrusion and it can be experienced as hallucinations in the hypnagogic or hypnopompic states or it can manifest as sleep paralysis. In the latter case the person may be aware and feel wide awake but is unable to move or speak. In 2006 and 2007 two articles were published that concluded there was a relationship between NDEs and REM intrusion. Both articles were published in *Neurology*, one of the most prestigious medical journals devoted to the study of the nervous system.[56] There was extensive media coverage giving the impression that NDEs were attributable to these neurological processes. However, this claim was refuted in a 34-page response published in the *Journal of Near-Death Studies*.[57]

Further to that response I would just like to add the following in relation to my own findings. The researchers[58] discussed 'fight or flight' as a normal psychological response to danger or a life-threatening event. The neural pathways associated with 'fight or flight' are also associated with REM intrusion. They made the point that fear-related nerve pathways associated with REM intrusion could be evoked by a life-threatening event, as those reported in NDE. This would support a possible association between NDEs and REM intrusion. This did not seem to be the case in my study. During the first year I interviewed every patient who survived admission to ITU. All of these patients were in an enclosed critical-care environment and the majority of patients were in a life-threatening situation. Even those who were not close to death were within earshot of resuscitation scenarios and the treatment of critically ill patients in other bed areas close to theirs. I have witnessed patients become so frightened by what they have overheard or caught glimpses of in such situations that they have tried to jump out of bed and run away. The majority of the of patients interviewed during the first year of the study would have been privy to such situations yet fewer than 1 per cent of them reported an NDE. If it could be attributable to REM intrusion then I would expect a higher incidence of NDE reports.

## Life Review as a Psychological Process of Reminiscence

As people get older it is common to reminisce.[59] Reflection and revision of the past can reassure the person of a life well lived, it promotes wisdom and enhances understanding, therefore giving meaning to one's life as it helps prepare for death.[60] The life review appears to be an accelerated form of reminiscence and is an important psychological process.

Mountain climbers who have survived almost-fatal falls reported feelings of calm, peace, lucidity and seeing the whole of their life as they fell.[61] These climbers were not at the time actually dying but death was a real possibility. It appears that reminiscence is greatly accelerated when faced with unexpected near-death situations. It is unclear why it would be necessary to learn from our past actions if consciousness ends at death of the physical body. Indeed, following a systematic review of NDEs with life reviews, it was suggested that the life review is only comprehensible from the perspective of life continuing in some way as it has far-reaching consequences.[62]

## Psychological Defence Mechanisms

NDEs and OBEs have been compared to the psychological syndromes derealization, dissociation and depersonalization. Derealization is described as being dreamlike and not real. Dissociation has been defined as a structured separation of mental processes from the person's surroundings and in extreme cases detachment from physical and emotional experiences.[63] A life-threatening or frightening situation can trigger this syndrome, which has been shown to develop in childhood.[64] It is also common in people previously exposed to stress.[65] Any physical pain or anxiety is not experienced because the person has dissociated to another reality where they do not associate themselves with their body. Although some NDErs may have some tendencies of dissociation they are not pathological.[66]

Characteristics of depersonalization include a feeling of detachment, unreality and altered self-perception[67] and enhanced alertness.[68] The functioning self and observing self are experienced separately[69] but the person doesn't necessarily feel 'out of the body'[70] and they may feel numb. There is a dreamlike quality to the experience and a barrier between the observing and functioning self is often characteristic of depersonalization.

## Hallucinations

Many patients admitted to ITU hallucinate or develop ITU psychosis. The main reasons for this are sleep deprivation, increased sensory input, loss of circadian rhythm, noise levels and staff conversation, prolonged periods in a light environment, constant 'white noise' and drugs administered.[71]

Patients may report frightening, vivid imagery and bizarre, dreamlike experiences. Even when they appear to be coherent and respond appropriately it later transpires that they were hallucinating at the time.[72] Hallucinations are random and, on follow up, patients can rationalize that they have been hallucinating whereas NDEs are structured, follow a pattern and on follow up patients are adamant that they are real.

There are very interesting and important points made by Keith Augustine[73] suggesting OBEs to be hallucinatory, which have been responded to in counter-arguments. For the interested reader I would recommend reading the summer, fall and winter editions of the *Journal of Near-Death Studies* 2007 for the full arguments and responses.

## Wishful Thinking/Expectancy

It is logical to infer that as the majority of NDEs are pleasant they may simply be wishful thinking or what we would expect to happen when we die. Most NDEs occur in unexpected situations and the person does not have time to think about what is happening, let alone construct an elaborate scenario during a time when undergoing a severe assault to the brain. Many NDEs have been reported during childbirth or complications of childbirth – surely death would be the last thing on an expectant mother's mind? In my study I did not find that the NDEs were consistent with wish fulfilment – this will be discussed in the following chapter.

It has been argued that NDErs are fantasy prone.[74] However, Professor Bruce Greyson disagrees and highlights that there is no evidence to support this.[75] NDErs may score higher on standard measures of fantasy proneness than non-NDErs but scores are nowhere near sufficient for the people to be categorized as having fantasy-prone personalities.

Despite NDEs becoming popular in the media it was found that NDE accounts have remained the same before and after the publication of Moody's book in 1975. Accounts reported after 1975 were not embellished or different to those reported before.[76]

It is apparent that the materialist theories cannot account for the full range of complexities associated with the NDE. After over 30 years of research into the phenomenon of NDEs, not one of these proposed theories provides an adequate explanation. There are hundreds of NDE cases that have been reported anecdotally but have never been taken seriously, as it has been assumed that they can be explained by the above theories. Of course, another popular criticism is inaccurate reporting by the research team. However, it would take a major conspiracy of the medical staff, nursing team, patients and researchers to reach this conclusion and now that this research is being undertaken in clinical areas they are not so easy to dismiss.

So can these experiences be studied in the clinical environment? Does the data from prospective studies support the materialist argument that consciousness is a by-product of brain activity? The next chapter will briefly present the results of the five-year study that I undertook.

# 7

# A Five-Year Prospective Study of NDEs

In 1997 I was granted permission by the Local Research Ethics Committee to undertake a five-year research project to investigate NDEs at the ITU where I worked. The prior planning of the research protocol took approximately eighteen months. I was also given permission from my nurse manager and all of the consultants in the hospital (except for three from neurosurgery) to interview patients in their care. Each patient was invited to participate in the research and their written consent was obtained. No names were used and each patient was coded with a number.

There was no study leave or funding for the study: it was all undertaken in my own time and at my own expense. However, I was very fortunate and will always be very grateful to the Lifebridge Foundation in New York for funding my university fees for the duration of the eight years it took to complete my PhD. Although I approached many funding agencies in the UK, none was interested in funding the research.

Below is only a very brief summary of the study I undertook; a full description of the study has been written up in my previous book.[1]

## The Study

Having thoroughly reviewed the available literature prior to commencing the study, I wanted to investigate several aspects further and also add to previous research. There were ten specific research questions that I wanted to address, which included how common NDEs were, if they could be explained by abnormal blood results, if they were due to the drugs given, if they were wishful thinking or hallucinations and if NDEs only occurred during cardiac arrest. One component of the NDE which was potentially verifiable was the OBE.

## Can the OBE be Verified?

In order to investigate if the OBE component was veridical I decided to replicate previous research undertaken in the 1980s by Professor Janice Holden[2] and later by Dr Madeleine Lawrence.[3] I mounted random symbols onto Day-Glo paper to attract attention. These symbols were then laminated and placed on top of the cardiac monitor situated at each patient's bedside. The monitors were approximately seven foot off the ground. A ridge was placed around each symbol to ensure that the only way the symbol could be viewed was from an out-of-body perspective.

*The Pilot Study*
The pilot study was undertaken during the summer of 1997, this was really helpful as I was able to identify oversights from the planning process and modify the protocol accordingly. During the pilot study I found that my colleagues were very curious about the hidden symbols and in my absence some had actually climbed up on ladders to view them! The symbols were then shown to each member of staff and then replaced with a new set. It was reiterated to each member of staff the importance of not knowing what the symbols were; if they inadvertently spoke about the symbols at the bedside it could invalidate the research. I found that by the time the formal research began my colleagues were no longer curious about the symbols.

*The Study Begins*
During the first year I interviewed every patient admitted to intensive care irrespective of how close to death they had been. The reason for this was to establish how common NDEs are, which medical condition they are most prevalently associated with and to ensure that I didn't miss an NDE because it wasn't voluntarily reported. Interviewing all patients also helped investigate if NDEs could be evoked through psychological defence mechanisms if patients perceived themselves to be sicker than they were.

When I approached each patient I simply asked the question 'Do you remember anything about the time you were unconscious?' The research was explained and they were invited to participate. Their written consent was obtained and their case was coded with a number. Most patients didn't recall anything but if they did then they were interviewed further using the Greyson NDE Scale and an in-depth semi-structured questionnaire.

By the end of the first year I was exhausted and found it very difficult to sustain the practice of interviewing every patient. All of the patients were followed up in my own time, which meant that I had to go into work early, stay behind after my shifts had ended and even go in on my days off in order to keep track of the patients who were discharged to the wards when I wasn't on duty. I was spending more time in work than I was at home so I realized I had to modify the research as there was no way I could continue with that level of commitment for a further four years.

For the following four years I decided to follow up only the patients who had survived cardiac arrest and any patients who voluntarily reported an NDE associated with another medical condition. I also had no option other than to reduce my hours of working as a nurse and went part-time in order to commit more time to the research.

After the first year I had interviewed 243 patients but only two reported an NDE (0.8 per cent) and two reported an OBE (0.8 per cent). I had actually followed up many more patients than that but some were not suitable to include in the study for various reasons such as confusion, deterioration in medical condition etc. I hadn't expected to find many reports of NDEs as not many of those patients had come close to death.

What I found interesting was when I compared this sample with those who had undergone cardiac arrest. When cardiac arrest survivors were interviewed during the course of the following four years I found that, although the sample was much smaller, there was a much higher incidence of NDEs. So by the by the end of the five years, out of 39 patients who survived cardiac arrest, seven reported an NDE (17.9 per cent).

During the time when I was focusing only on survivors of cardiac arrest, a few patients with different medical conditions (not associated with cardiac arrest) also voluntarily reported an NDE. So in total, during the five years, 15 patients reported an NDE and there were eight reports of OBE-type experiences.

The most commonly reported component of the NDE was meeting deceased relatives; 11 out of the 15 patients reported this. Other prevalent features included entering another realm, seeing a bright light, feelings of joy, peace and calm, time distortion, vivid senses, being sent back to life, seeing a being of light and encountering a barrier. Interestingly, none of the patients reported a full panoramic life review and none reported visions of the future.

Two patients reported a distressing NDE, one was of the usual type but interpreted in a distressing way and the second was a hellish type experience. During the time she was unconscious as a result of a cardiac arrest, patient 4 believed she was looking into hell and was traumatized by the recall of it.

### An Interesting Case

There were 15 NDEs reported with many interesting aspects. However, patient 10 reported the deepest NDE in the study – an NDE which had many remarkable components. For a full examination of this case, see the 16-page article by Sartori, Badham and Fenwick.[4] This did not occur during a cardiac arrest but during a period of deep unconsciousness where he was not responding to verbal stimuli or painful stimuli. This is a very unique case and I was actually the nurse looking after him that day and was present during the time the whole sequence of events occurred.

The patient was making a good recovery from a critical illness and was still ventilated at the time of his experience. After we'd sat the patient in the bedside chair his condition rapidly deteriorated and he very quickly lost consciousness. In the summer of 2013 I once again interviewed patient 10 to investigate if his NDE had led to major changes in his life. This incident occurred in November 1999 yet despite a time lapse of more than 13 years, the experience remains vivid to the patient, as the following account shows:

> Oh yes, I still remember it. It's just as clear, I can see it in my mind very vividly. The first bit I remember is sitting in the chair. The next thing I was floating upwards to the top of the room. I looked down and I could see my body on the bed. It was lovely, so peaceful and no pain at all. All my pain had gone.
>
> I went into this pink room and I could see my father standing next to the man. I said it could have been Jesus but how would I have known because I've never met Jesus before. But his hair was scruffy, you know, like it needed to be combed. He had nice eyes, though; I can remember looking at his eyes. I can remember my

*father saying things but not with his mouth but we were talking, it's hard to explain.*

*Then I felt someone touching my eye, I looked down and saw my body and the doctor and I could see you, Penny. The doctor said something about my eye. Then after that you put that pink lollipop thing in my mouth to clean it. That other girl was there too, she was hiding outside the curtains, she was worried about me and kept looking to see how I was.*

*Then I heard someone say, 'He's got to go back.' The Jesus man said it. But I wanted to stay there, it was so nice, I was having a nice time. And then I was floating backwards and went back into my body. Oh and the pain when I got into my body was terrible, it was awful. I'll always remember that, it was all so clear. When I close my eyes, I can see it all again even though it happened all those years ago. I didn't see that thing you had hidden on the cupboard, though – just what was going on around my body on the bed.*

*It was very clear, not like those hallucinations I had when I was on morphine. Those hallucinations were terrible, I can't remember them so clearly now but I remember the room was spinning and spiders were running up and down the walls and it felt like the bed was moving and going through walls. No, the death experience was very different to that.*

There were some minor aspects that patient 10 had forgotten, such as the name of the physiotherapist, but the NDE appeared to be the same as when he first reported it. The NDE has had a lasting effect on patient 10 and has helped him cope with difficult situations he has faced, such as the death of his wife.

*Oh, the experience has had a big effect on my life. I believe in God and I definitely don't worry about death. If the doctor said to me I was going to die tomorrow then I would just sit back and enjoy it. I'm not saying I want to die but I'm saying I won't be afraid when I do go. I tell everyone I meet not to be afraid of dying.*

*When my wife died a few years ago I think that if I hadn't had that experience then I would have just wanted to die with her at the same time. I could never have imagined life without her before I had my experience. When she was dying I went up to see her in the nursing home; she opened her eyes and said, 'Thanks for coming to see me, I'm going to go with my mother now.' She died shortly after that and I know she's happy now and that she's with her mother. I cried, of course, when she died but I just know that wherever she is, she's happy.*

For me the most interesting aspect of this case was how a congenital abnormality appears to have spontaneously resolved following his NDE. Patient 10 has cerebral palsy so from birth his right hand was in a permanently contracted position. This was verified with the patient's sister, who has also signed a statement to verify this.

When I interviewed him he misunderstood my question and opened out his hand. At first I didn't realize the significance of this until I discussed this with the physiotherapists and the doctors. This should not be physiologically possible as the tendons are in a permanently contracted position so there is, as yet, no known mechanism to explain this aspect. If he had not misunderstood my question it is highly likely that this aspect would have been overlooked as I was not expecting to find it as part of my investigation. When I interviewed him again in 2013 I was curious to see if he could still open his hand.

*Well my hand still opens but not so much over the past year. I can't pick money up off the table any more. I can pick notes up and pens but it's not so easy any more, only this last year. It gets worse in the cold weather and I think I have arthritis in it now. I can still open it, though.*

This case was most interesting as he correctly identified which doctor had examined him, he correctly described the actions of the nurse and the physiotherapist that had occurred while he was unconscious. Everything that he reported actually did occur and he reported it with accuracy – I know because I was present for the whole duration but it wasn't until he regained consciousness that I realized he had been experiencing an NDE and OBE at the time.

*Other Interesting Cases*
During a night shift my colleagues and I witnessed a patient having a deathbed vision when his condition had deteriorated. Everyone who witnessed this remarked on how happy the patient appeared to be. His family had heard about my research so the next day they wanted to chat

to me because when they had visited the following morning the patient had told them that during the night he'd been visited not only by his deceased mother and grandmother but interestingly he also reported seeing his sister. Unbeknown to him, his sister had actually died the week before but the family had not told him because they did not want it to upset his recovery. He continued to have several visitations from his deceased family members in the days leading up to his death and each time these occurred he appeared to be very happy.

Another interesting case was reported to me by a relative of a patient who had a cardiac arrest at home. At a time that coincided with his cardiac arrest, the patient had appeared to his mother, who was also in hospital, 40 miles away. She described a 'funny dream' where her son had appeared at her bedside dressed in white and surrounded by a bright light. He was chatting to her and explaining that he was not well. She felt as if he was there to say goodbye. Cases like this have been reported elsewhere in the literature.[5]

Following his NDE, which occurred during a period of deep unconsciousness, patient 11 communicated with a dead relative who gave him a message for one of his living relatives. When he regained consciousness he gave this message to his living relative, who was absolutely astounded that he should know this information. During a time when he was deeply unconscious, this man gained knowledge of something he had not previously been aware of – how was this possible? According to the current explanation that consciousness is a by-product of the brain, this should not be possible. Yet it has clearly been captured during a prospective study.

*Verifying the OBE*
During the course of the five years there were eight reports of an OBE-type experience. However, none of the patients reported viewing the hidden symbol. Some of the patients did not rise high enough out of their body, some moved to positions in the room opposite to where the symbols were situated and two of the patients were so concerned with what was going on around their body that they were not looking on top of cardiac monitors for hidden symbols! One patient was so convinced of his experience that he remarked that if he knew there was a hidden symbol he would have looked at it and told me what it was.

Interestingly, one patient reported an OBE where she accurately described events that had occurred in the operating room. However, she also reported seeing a piece of jewellery pinned to her hospital gown – this was incorrect; no jewellery is allowed into the operating room and strict checks are undertaken to ensure this. This patient was also sedated for a few days after her operation and during that time also experienced hallucinations, so it can't be ruled out that the drugs may have affected her experience or the recall of her experience.

Undertaking this research in the hospital enabled thorough investigation of each NDE and OBE. One lady (patient 55) reported an experience that was more characteristic of an autoscopic experience.[6] On investigation it became apparent that what she had reported was a slightly confusional experience while recovering from the anaesthetic. A mind model was constructed from residual sight and tactile stimulation as she was regaining consciousness. She could feel and see some of the equipment that was being used to treat her at the time. No other components of the NDE were reported.

## OBE Control Group

Previous research used a control group of cardiac patients who were familiar with hospital procedures to investigate if the OBE was an imaginal experience or a mind model constructed from what the patients could hear going on around them.[7] Patients in that study were asked to guess what would be done to resuscitate them and it was found that the guesses were erroneous. This was criticized by Dr Susan Blackmore,[8] who correctly pointed out that not all of the patients had undergone cardiac arrest. Building on this research, I asked all of the patients in my research who had undergone cardiac arrest but did not report an OBE to guess what had been done to resuscitate them.

Most patients had no idea about how they had been resuscitated. The few patients in the control group in my study who were able to guess what had been done to resuscitate them made errors. A few assumed that a defibrillator had been used when in fact they had only had CPR and had drugs administered. The few patients who had been defibrillated did not point to the correct position of the paddles on the body. If the OBE was a creation of the brain in response to what they could hear was going on at the time and feel what was being done to them, then I would have expected the control group to have accurate reports of the actual procedures carried out during their resuscitation.

## *Quality of the OBE*

Caution has to be used when interpreting the reports of OBEs. Although there were eight OBEs, most were not of the same quality as those described in the literature. This is not to say that the reports in the literature are embellished in any way but it highlights that it is usually only OBEs that have sufficient impact and quality that are reported. By studying this phenomenon prospectively we gain a far more accurate indication of how frequent OBEs are and the different types of quality of the OBE.

The above also highlights the difficulties that arise when investigating OBEs. It appears that good-quality OBEs, where the patient clearly reports existing outside of the body and viewing the emergency situation, are very rare. As I discovered, even those who have good-quality OBEs are so concerned with what is going on around their body that they are not looking at the tops of monitors to view hidden symbols.

On the other hand it can't be ruled out that this type of research will yield positive results as there are cases reported where patients have been out of their body and have been able to see the lines and numbers on the screen of the cardiac monitor.[9] I received a letter from a lady who was herself a nurse and had had an NDE many years previously and reported to me that while out of her body she 'floated' to the front of the cardiac monitor but was unable to decipher anything on its screen.

Hence it is important to bear in mind that when this type of research is undertaken, especially with the AWARE project that is currently underway, just because the symbols are not identified doesn't necessarily mean that the OBE is not verifiable. It could merely be that the quality of the OBEs reported is not of the quality required to view the symbols – i.e. the patient has to rise high enough out of the body, be in the location of the symbol and have the presence of mind to look at things other than their body. It is a tall order but is something that may or may not be achievable with a lot of time and patience – only time will tell. If the research isn't undertaken then we may never know and, of course, I'm sure many people would criticize us for not doing so.

One thing to note is that some of the patients who reported the out-of-body-type experiences were sedated for a period of time following their emergency situation. It cannot be ruled out that the sedation may have in some way interfered with the recall of the experience. This has been noted by other researchers.[10] Later I will discuss the possibility that drugs may contribute to confusional experiences as opposed to creating the clear, lucid, well-structured NDE.

## Are NDEs Wishful Thinking?

It seems unlikely that the NDE is due to wishful thinking. Two patients reported distressing NDEs. The first was the usual type of NDE but it was interpreted in a distressing way. The second case was a hellish experience and in fact the recall of it was so terrifying for the patient that I had to terminate the interview. Such experiences are hardly the outcome of wish fulfilment. Further to this, some patients met dead relatives they did not expect to see and some had unexpected reactions from these relatives while others did not experience what they had expected. It seems that expectations were not met and some unexpected factors arose.

## Are NDEs the Same as Hallucinations?

Without doubt, many patients admitted to ITU suffer terrible hallucinations. In fact my reaction when the patient I was looking after reported her NDE to me when I was a very junior student nurse was that she had been hallucinating. However, having had the benefit of undertaking this research, coupled with a greater knowledge of NDEs and experience of caring for hallucinating patients and those who have reported an NDE, my views are now very different. When hallucinations and NDEs are both examined in depth and compared there are very big differences and they are clearly not the same type of experience.

During the first year of data collection I interviewed everyone who survived their admission to ITU. During this time I came across 12 cases of hallucinations, which I also investigated. Eleven of these patients had received large amounts of strong painkilling or sedative drugs (or a combination of both). One patient had hallucinations due to severe sleep deprivation. On further investigation it was established that experiences that had been reported by the hallucinating patients were actual occurrences: events that were going on in the background – the actual noises from all around them and staff conversation could be heard as their sedation was wearing off. Hence their brains created bizarre and confusional experiences as they were trying to make sense of the sensory input while regaining consciousness.

The following points briefly describe the sorts of random and bizarre things that were reported. Hallucinations jumped from one thing to another. The hallucinations reported included being:

- chased and stabbed with needles by drug dealers;
- taken to a prison in California by helicopter and the pilot of the helicopter was the ITU consultant;
- in Vietnam and then on a cruise liner having plastic surgery;
- on a train travelling through Bosnia with beautiful countryside scenery, then being in hospital in Palestine. There had been an accident and a woman had been killed and her husband and baby had been brought to the Palestinian hospital;
- in a fight and described being hit by balls of light which had a lot of force and were slamming their body against walls;
- back in the Blitz in Swansea then becoming an African explorer in the 1800s and convinced they was dead because African women were washing their body with grass;
- at their funeral, which was in a chapel that no longer exists, and at the back of the chapel was a corner shop – they could hear a ding, ding noise constantly (the cardiac monitor alarming). Then being convinced that the nurse looking after them was an American Indian in disguise and becoming suspicious of the nurses;
- amazed as he looked out of the window at his bedside to see a beautiful Welsh scene and a rope and cable bridge. As his nurse pulled the curtains around them to wash him he could see two huge French loaves and told the nurse that if she was hungry she could eat them.

A few cases demonstrate quite well how real events were perceived as confusional hallucinations:

One lady (patient 58) recalled very vivid hallucinations. One of the things she remembered was seeing curtains pulled around her and assuming it was because she was about to die. It was all very mixed up and it didn't make sense to her but she also recalled being in a theatre and her funeral was taking place, with her body lying on the stage. She also thought that she was on a ferry boat going to Ireland and could feel her body swaying as it dipped in and out of the waves.

On further investigation, this was clearly related to things which were actually happening as her sedation was wearing off and her nurse at the time had a thick Irish accent. For a fuller explanation, see my first book.[11]

While I was caring for one patient, although he was sedated he started to become quite agitated. He tried to jump out of bed and remove all the equipment attached to his body. Five of my colleagues immediately came to my assistance to stop him becoming a danger to himself.

When I interviewed this patient after he'd recovered he recalled terrifying nightmares. He repeated the actual words of the doctor who was trying to calm him down but the patient had mistakenly perceived the doctor's voice to be of someone who was trying to harm him.

There were also a few cases where some of the hallucinations reported could have been mistaken for an NDE, as the cases below demonstrate. This is why it is so important that anyone who undertakes research into these experiences investigates them all thoroughly and must have a good knowledge of NDEs and be able to distinguish between hallucinations and NDEs.

One patient recalled thinking he was in hell and being basted on a spit. My first reaction was that this may have been a distressing NDE. However, when I investigated it fully I realized it was due to what happened as he was regaining consciousness from anaesthetic. He had returned from the operating theatre and his body temperature was low so he was wrapped in a foil blanket and a hot-air blanket. His wounds were also leaking quite badly so the nurses had to frequently turn him from side to side to change his sheets. The nurse caring for him at the time recalled him suddenly waking up and being very frightened while this was occurring.

Amongst the hallucinations of another patient was one where she believed she was travelling through a tunnel towards a red light. I was alerted to this by my colleague who thought that she was reporting an NDE. However, when I investigated this I realized it was her actual experience of having a CT scan. The CT scanner looks like a big round polo mint and at the top of it, directly in her line of vision, is a red light. As the patient is moved through the CT scanner it can give the impression of moving through a tunnel.

When patients hallucinate they often display irrational behaviour. They may become incompliant with treatment, and can become aggressive towards nursing staff, trying to get out of bed and run away, and in extreme cases can even become a danger to themselves and others. Any intravenous infusions, wound drains, catheters or leads connecting them to the monitors are often pulled out or removed, usually resulting in blood and bodily fluids being sprayed around the vicinity and onto those trying to calm the patient down. Their bizarre behaviour is clearly observable and obviously confusional to the medical team, yet the patients are convinced of the reality of their subjective impressions. However, when they fully recover they either have no recall of their behaviour or they realize that they were hallucinating and are usually profoundly embarrassed.

Further investigation of reports of hallucinations showed that they were attributable to actual occurrences, background noise and staff conversation as the patient was waking up from sedation. On follow-up, patients could rationalize that they had been hallucinating whereas those who had had an NDE remained adamant that it was real. Further to that, people who hallucinate do not exhibit the same life changes as those of NDErs.

Some patients in the study experienced both hallucinations and an NDE and were able to distinguish between the two experiences. Patient 10 mentioned this earlier in the text. He described his hallucinations as not real and more like 'a bad dream gone wrong'.

It is interesting to note Professor Bruce Greyson's comment:[12]

*Why is it that scientists who have done the most near-death research believe the mind is not exclusively housed in the brain, whereas those who regard NDEs as hallucinations by and large have not conducted any studies of the phenomena at all?*

### Are NDEs due to Anoxia or Hypercarbia?

During the course of the research I realized there were many factors to take into consideration when examining the blood results as an explanation for NDEs. It was not always possible to verify during which part of the emergency situation that blood had been taken. Also, in many cases it was not possible to verify if the NDE had occurred at the time that blood was taken. Therefore, blood results must be treated with great caution as they can provide only a provisional estimate and guide.

However, there were two patients in my study (patients 11 and 17) who had blood extracted at the time of their NDE/OBE. Neither case was associated with a cardiac arrest and both patients were ventilated at the time and receiving oxygen. Their oxygen levels on the cardiac monitor had been normal and stable, as had all of their vital signs such as blood pressure and pulse. These two cases do not support the anoxia and hypercarbia theories but no firm conclusions can be drawn as the sample is too small. However, these results do suggest that abnormal blood results cannot fully explain NDEs.

### Are NDEs due to the Drugs Administered?

For a full examination of drugs administered, see my first book. In brief summary, however, the majority of the patients who were interviewed during the first year of the study were given strong painkilling or sedative drugs yet very few reported an NDE. If drugs were the cause of the NDE then I would have expected a higher incidence in this sample.

In the patients who underwent cardiac arrest, many were given painkilling and sedative drugs but did not report an NDE. There were also patients in this group who reported an NDE but were not given any drugs at the time.

Out of the 15 patients who reported an NDE, 20 per cent did not have any painkilling or sedative drugs administered. Patient 10, who reported the NDE with an accurate OBE, had not been given any drugs.

One patient reported to his visitors that he had seen angels at his bedside while he was unconscious. His condition deteriorated after this and he required further sedation. However, when he recovered a second time he had no recollection of seeing angels or telling his relatives about them. It seems that the sedative drugs given had an amnesic effect.

Interestingly, when drug administration is considered in the hallucination group, out of the 12 patients who reported bizarre hallucinations, 11 (almost 92 per cent) of them received both painkilling and sedative drugs. This appears to suggest that drugs greatly contribute to confusional, bizarre hallucinations which are in stark contrast to the clear, lucid, well-structured NDEs that were reported.

## Other Interesting Findings

The closest a person comes to death, the more likely they are to report an NDE. Those who had a cardiac arrest reported a greater incidence of NDEs.

The NDE is an under-reported phenomenon. Out of the 15 patients who reported an NDE, only two of them volunteered the information.

NDEs are rare. Approximately 3,000 patients were admitted to ITU during the five years of data collection but in that time only 15 NDEs were discovered and of these only two were deep NDEs similar to those described in the previous literature on the subject.

Endorphins have been commonly cited as a cause of the NDE. In the case of patient 10 he was pain free during the NDE, yet as soon as he returned to his body he was in excruciating pain. Endorphins have a long-lasting effect,[13] so if the NDE was due to endorphins then a gradual onset of pain would be expected as opposed to the immediate pain described.

NDEs do not appear to be a response to the psychological threat of death.[14] The ITU where the research was conducted is an open-plan design with patients in close proximity to each other. Often, emergency situations can be overheard by surrounding patients. If it was a psychological response then a higher frequency would be expected.

Those who reported the deepest NDEs had absolutely no fear of death after the experience.

Not all of the NDEs in this study had the story-like quality similar to those in the literature. Some were just fragmentary components of the NDE which the patients did not understand or pay attention to. This suggests the possibility of a subset of NDEs that don't have sufficient significance to motivate the experiencer to report them.

## Limitations of the Study

As with all research there were some limitations. The greatest difficulty was the unpredictability of when an NDE would occur. Emergency situations and cardiac arrests usually occur with very little forewarning.

As an enthusiastic researcher I would have loved to have spent more time interviewing the patients but the reality of the situation was that very often the patients were too tired to participate in a lengthy interview. Luckily my nursing experience prevailed and I terminated the interview if it was apparent it was too tiring for the patient.

I learned early in the study that it was essential that I get as much information from the patient as soon as possible because in a few cases the patient's condition deteriorated and they died before I could conduct a full in-depth interview. This has been reported by other researchers and is unavoidable.[15] Conducting the interviews was also frustrating as sometimes it would be interrupted by visiting relatives.

The hardest thing to do was to follow up the patients, especially when they had been discharged home. It is possible that long-term follow-up of all of the NDErs would have elicited further information. However, it was very difficult to follow up patients, predominantly because I had to do all of the work myself and I simply couldn't collect the data, analyse them, write it all up and do a full-time nursing job while also trying to follow up patients who had been discharged home. I did try to follow up patients but found that many died following discharge home, some simply didn't want to be contacted again and some had moved house and I lost touch with them. However, I have managed to maintain contact with patient 10.

## Recommendations for Future Research

Future research would benefit from a team of people who have a good knowledge and understanding of NDEs to collect the data as opposed to one person. Once I had completed my research I realized that it was a huge task that I had undertaken and as a result I was totally exhausted and burned out at the end of the PhD.

Ideally this sort of research would benefit from being conducted by a group of people working in shifts in a coronary-care unit or intensive-care unit around the clock to ensure that all potential cases of NDEs are captured. Thus all patients could be interviewed as soon as possible and prior to discharge to the ward, where they could be followed up a second time for a further interview. This would help reduce memory fallibility and ensure that any reports of OBEs could be double checked as soon as possible with members of staff present at the time.

It is also essential that future researchers have a good knowledge of NDEs. During the course of my research several of my colleagues had alerted me to patients who they thought had reported an NDE but when I investigated these cases it was apparent that they were not NDEs but a misinterpretation of actual events that had occurred.

It would also be important to include people who are highly sceptical of NDEs on the research team. This would ensure that every possible aspect could be scrutinized and all possible explanations could be thoroughly investigated. Rather than NDE researchers and sceptics working against each other it would make far more sense to put our heads together and come up with an airtight protocol which could further our understanding of consciousness.

There have been many people who dispute the validity of what is reported by the NDErs. When cases of NDEs have been reported anecdotally there is no way of ascertaining if these accounts are factual, particularly the OBE component. There is no way of knowing if the person really did come close to death, if their hearts had stopped, if they really were unconscious, what drugs had been given or if their blood levels were deranged. However, now that prospective hospital research is being conducted which is providing these details, it is far more difficult to dismiss NDEs and simply reduce them to materialist factors such as anoxia or drugs.

When the materialist theories are considered in relation to the research findings they do not offer a complete explanation for the fully structured, lucid, coherent NDE, which results, in many cases, in a transformation of the person's life and values. However, this is only a small study but it is in keeping with other prospective research of NDEs, which had similar results.[16] Having a thorough knowledge of NDEs and actually working in the environment where patients are most likely to report such experiences, as well as having conducted this research, it is apparent that materialist arguments simply do not suffice when trying to explain the very complex NDE. It is essential that future researchers keep an open mind and explore all avenues. It appears that there is no option but to consider these experiences from a different perspective and the most logical avenue of explanation would be that of consciousness being *mediated* through the brain as opposed to being *created* by it. If such research is conducted it may give us a completely different understanding of consciousness or it may well show that the materialist arguments are correct. Unless consciousness is explored from another perspective there will never be any adequate answers. Clearly, far more research needs to be conducted, as prospective research is highlighting that current scientific beliefs that consciousness is created by the brain are limited.[17]

# 8

# A Brief History of the Medicalization of Death

As our society has evolved, so too has the way in which death is viewed and understood. Once an expected part of life, death has now become ostracized in preference to more material aspects of life. By occupying ourselves with the material we detract from the fact that we will all eventually die. Consequently, what was once a social occasion, where all of the family and friends participated, death has now been relegated to a lonely side room or a high-technology critical-care area in a hospital, with the control of the mode of death being solely in the hands of the medical team.

Throughout the world various cultures have records of ancient texts referred to as 'Books of the Dead'[1] designed to assist the dying on their journey and help loved ones accept their loss. The Egyptian Book of the Dead is the oldest of such texts and comprises a collection of ancient papyri based on literature named *Pert em Hru*, which translates as 'Coming Forth by Day' or 'Manifestation in the Light'.[2] The text incorporates works from different eras covering a period of 5,000 years. A unique individualized collection was devised for each dying person from the large mass of funerary texts. This practice was initially exclusively for pharaohs but later became extended to other prominent members of society.

The most well-known Book of the Dead is the Tibetan version,[3] the *Bardo Thodol* or 'Liberation by Hearing on the Afterdeath Plane'. It was first put into writing in the eighth century AD. Although based on a much older oral tradition, it is attributed to the Great Guru Padmasambhava. It is a manual for the dying and the dead and serves as a guide, as is

144

consistent with Tibetan beliefs, through the different stages of the intermediate state between death and rebirth. Tibetan lamas recite the book out loud over the body of the dying person in order to prepare them for subjective experiences that may occur as they transition into death.

The Mayan civilization also had a great interest in death. Most of their ancient texts were destroyed by the Spanish invaders and by the climate. The *Popul Vuh*[4] was a Mayan epic based on an older oral tradition and features the story of 'hero twins' who ventured to the underworld, where they experienced many ordeals before experiencing death and rebirth. Another Book of the Dead is that of Nahuatl, which incorporates the myth of Quetzacoatl, a bearded man with a white complexion who founded their religion. The myth conveys the universal theme of death and resurrection, sin and redemption and the transfiguration of a human into a god.

In European countries there is the tradition of seeking a good death, depicted in the *Ars Moriendi* – 'The Art of Dying' – from the Middle Ages. During this era death was an everyday occurrence. Death and funeral rituals were part of life due to famines, wars, epidemics, public executions and the slaughter of alleged witches, heretics and Satanists.

There were two parts of the *Ars Moriendi* and they are not limited to the sick, the old or the dying, as they provided insight into life. Emphasis is on the attitude to death in life. The first part claims that materialistic attitudes are wrong as no possessions can go with the dying person at the point of death. The major point is that the awareness of death is the beginning of all wisdom – *mors certa, hora incerta* ('death is certain, its hour uncertain'). The main message is that we should live in the present, enjoy each day as if it is our last and that we shouldn't be concerned with prolonging life at all cost. Harmful behaviour should be avoided and life lived according to the law.

The second part concerns the experience of dying and the art of guiding the dying on their journey. The dying person was warned of states that would be encountered on the soul's journey. Great importance was placed on not introducing false hope and not denying death. The manual emphasized that it was more harmful to die unprepared than to anticipate death prematurely.

Historian of death Philippe Aries[5] described the history of death in the West from the Middle Ages to the twentieth century. During the Middle Ages death was always present so there was a great love for life, people appreciated their life – this concept can be difficult to grasp in modern times where death is denied.

The attitudes and concepts of death changed from the 'tame death' in the early Middle Ages, to 'one's own death' in the thirteenth century. Death had been a case of the dying person reminiscing, confessing their sins and begging God for forgiveness then being surrounded by family and friends following absolution. The dead were believed to reside in paradise with gardens of flowers and streams of light – all themes consistent with NDEs.

By the thirteenth century the artworks began to include scenes of judgement. Alongside the deathbed were images of Christ with a book of deeds in his hands, angelic beings and demonic beings. A life review began to feature as part of the dying process in the fourteenth century. The rituals remained under the control of the dying person, who was still the centre of attention.

The artwork changed to more macabre themes, and images of decaying cadavers were prevalent, in keeping with the increased incidence of death through disease and famine. Between the sixteenth and eighteenth centuries, the introduction of a last will and testament consisting of funeral instructions signified the control now being in the hands of those around the dying person. During the second part of the eighteenth century the will was reduced to a legal document concerning the distribution of possessions. It was during this time that the grief of the relatives/friends began to be suppressed.

Whereas mourning had protected genuinely grieving relatives/friends from excessive grief and allowed the family to express sorrow, by the nineteenth century mourning became exaggerated, signifying the fear of death. Funeral directors became prevalent in 1885 and their role took away duties which help the family to work through the grieving process. Funeral rituals also changed and the person was buried where they could be visited.

The next change of attitude resulted in death becoming shameful – the 'forbidden death' or the 'invisible death'. It became common practice to protect the dying person by lying about their impending death. Then the place of death began to change in 1930, when people were sent to hospital to die and all control was put in the hands of the doctor.

Deathbed scenes are a stark contrast to current hospital procedures. Medical advances have succeeded in separating pathological processes that are reversible from those that are not, favouring the sustenance of life. Physiological advances have resulted in more effective treatment and a greater number of people surviving to an older age. Resuscitation techniques now enable some people to be revived and those not so fortunate to undergo a gruesome, undignified death. Indeed, the intensive-care unit where I worked expanded from seven beds in 1993 to 12 beds in 1998 to 16 beds in 2003 to 17 ITU beds plus 12 high-dependency unit (HDU) beds in 2009. The intensive-care unit is bigger than some wards due to the constant demand for beds and there are still occasions where the demand is so high that patients have to be nursed in the recovery area of theatre.

There are often situations in which elderly people who are clearly at the end of their life are resuscitated. We may be technologically advanced but we have no understanding of death and we are taught to deny it.[6] We are educated in every subject except the one that holds the key to the meaning of life. Our current technology places the emphasis on cure not caring and to admit that treatment is no longer possible is to concede defeat.[7]

Death is not restricted to the elderly: it can occur at any age. Attempts to preserve life are a certainty today. A cacophony of treatment, usually causing great distress, is instigated in the hope of cheating death – surgery of uncertain benefit and prolonged stays in ITU when the situation is futile. Within our society we believe that if we err in the treatment of patients, it should be in doing too much for them rather than too little, therefore stripping the patient of their dignity.[8]

I witnessed a conversation between the ITU consultants and a young surgeon who was trying to arrange a bed for a patient he was planning to operate on. The lady was 87 years old, at the end stages of senile dementia; she was immobile and had several predisposing factors which did not make her a good candidate to survive a general anaesthetic. The surgeon was adamant that he was going to operate – his justification was that the family wanted him to proceed. Although this was the family's wishes I wonder how informed they had been regarding the outcomes. Had the young surgeon explained the intense post-operative care required and the likelihood of being in ITU for a few days/weeks and even then possibly not surviving? Were the family told that their loved one would probably be connected to a ventilator for a few days/weeks and would not be able to talk? Were they told that each hour the patient would have a suction catheter placed down the tube connecting them to the ventilator in order to remove the sputum from her lungs? Were they told how noisy ITU is and how little sleep and rest she would get? Were they told that their loved one would be turned every two to four hours, which can be very uncomfortable and even frightening for the patient? Were they told their loved one would be sedated? Were they told of the possibility of developing renal failure? Were they told that their loved one may be unrecognizable due to oedema from the fluids given to treat her? Were they told that even after such life-saving treatment there was still a very high chance of dying?

Further to that, in hospital, contact with loved ones is restricted. Visiting times are controlled by the routines of the hospitals and have little consideration of the probability that this will be the last opportunity for the patient to communicate with their loved ones.

Sometimes the inability to accept death causes family members to rely on the dying person for support, resulting in increased suffering for everyone.[9]

'Ann' had been admitted to ITU in a very unstable condition. She initially responded well to treatment but after a few days it was apparent that she was dying. She had a large family who stayed at her bedside for as long as possible. Ann knew she was dying and attempted to communicate this to her family – she was unable to talk because she was ventilated. She was obviously concerned about her wedding ring and tried to explain to her son and daughters who she wanted the ring to go to when she died. Several times I witnessed her family repeat to her that she was not going to die and not to communicate this because she *had* to get better, which left both Ann and the family even more distressed. After a further ten days in ITU, Ann died but unfortunately she never did manage to express her wishes for her wedding ring because her family couldn't accept her impending death. It is heartbreaking to witness such situations and the anguish that both patient and family go through.

Texts such as the Books of the Dead have many similarities to NDEs. For many thousands of years these have been reduced to myths but now they appear to be 'maps of the inner territories of the psyche encountered in profound non-ordinary states of consciousness'.[10] Maybe this is what is needed to reintegrate our spiritual roots with our huge advances in technology.

# 9

# Implications for a Greater Understanding and Acknowledgement of NDEs

*Western medicine itself, with all its materialist focus on the body and its insistence on ignoring the spirit, is literally making us sick – and then is making it virtually impossible for us to heal.*

Raphael Kellman[1]

## Implications for Healthcare

*Spiritual Aspects of Patient Care*

When spirituality is broached within the current healthcare system or everyday life it is given little attention for many reasons. It is difficult to define and is often seen as being the same as religion. However, spirituality is far more than just adhering to religious practice – it is something that gives meaning to one's life.

A recent survey of nurses showed that although spiritual care was deemed highly important only 5 per cent of respondents felt that they had met the spiritual needs of their patients.[2] Sadly, spiritual aspects of patient care are an area which is greatly lacking for many reasons, such as lack of confidence or experience, or lack of continuity of care, but probably the biggest factor is excessive workloads and resultant lack of time and nurses.[3]

When patients are admitted to hospital the predominant course of action is to treat the physical. However, addressing spiritual needs of patients and treating patients holistically has the potential to accelerate healing and recovery, reduce medication and resources required and so reduce the hospital stay – all of which would be welcomed in the current healthcare system, where hospitals are overcrowded. Finding meaning in their illness and feelings of wellbeing are essential for positive outcomes. Caring for patients' spiritual needs could also prompt healthcare workers to explore their own spiritual needs.[4]

Healing the body through mind and spirit is not a new concept; it is just something that is seldom acknowledged within the current scientific paradigm. The mind can have a powerful effect on the body and each person has the potential to heal their body.[5] Drawing on the latest research of the effect of positive emotions on health, it has been shown how feelings of wellbeing and love can greatly enhance recovery and healing.[6] Case histories of people who have helped heal themselves through their positive mindset illustrate how healthcare workers could incorporate simple techniques into practice (as well as their everyday lives) which promote a positive uplifting environment that would enhance patient care.[7] If the mind isn't healed, how can we expect the body to heal? Addressing the spiritual needs of patients would also greatly benefit those who have had an NDE.

*The Knowledge of Healthcare Workers*

It is obvious that people who undergo an NDE also undergo psychological changes. It is of paramount importance that all healthcare workers are educated about NDEs so that they can provide the necessary support to help with a speedy recovery and a greater understanding of their experience.

There are numerous cases in the literature where people who reported an NDE were misdiagnosed as having a psychiatric illness. A recent comparison study is suggestive that psychologists' knowledge of NDEs has remained the same for the past 20 years and that there is an overestimation of their knowledge of NDEs.[8] NDEs are often misdiagnosed as post-traumatic stress or a dissociative disorder, despite the literature warning against this, and they are categorized into conventional diagnostic illnesses that are not appropriate for NDEs.[9] In another study of hospital physicians the results showed that knowledge about NDEs was lacking in the majority of participants.[10]

The NDE had both an overwhelming and confusing effect on one lady whose case is reported by Dr Yvonne Kason. She found she was unable to discuss her experience with anyone as no one understood what she was trying to tell them. First she tried to talk with her husband, who didn't understand it and they ended up divorcing, then the pastor of her local church told her it was the work of the devil. She then went to her doctor, who'd never heard of NDEs and referred her to a psychiatrist, who'd also never heard of NDEs. It was suggested that she had unresolved emotional conflict that had caused delusions and that she should try long-term psychotherapy for the delusions and tranquilizers for her anxiety. She was increasingly confused because she felt such positive changes in her life and it was many years later when she came across a book on NDEs that she was finally able to understand her NDE.[11]

In a survey of nurses, despite 70 per cent of respondents reporting being familiar with NDEs, 89 per cent did not demonstrate good knowledge of NDEs when tested to assess their level of knowledge.[12] Similar findings have been reported by others.[13]

A study of the nature and meaning of NDEs for patients and criticalcare nurses highlighted that 'the NDE and related phenomena is a poorly understood event in the intensive-care unit'[14] and, having worked in one for the past 17 years, I agree. Despite NDEs being highly popularized in the media, healthcare workers still lack the knowledge to provide the level of care that these patients require.

As our technology is becoming so advanced many patients are now surviving critical illnesses that would have proved fatal 20 years ago. It would therefore seem logical to deduce that far more patients are likely to undergo an NDE. Unfortunately, the knowledge of healthcare workers remains quite superficial as there is simply not enough education about this phenomenon. It is encouraging to see that over the past two or three years more universities are beginning to broach the subject of NDEs. It is paramount that NDEs are incorporated into the education of all healthcare workers.

It would be helpful to include full educational modules on NDEs in the training of all healthcare workers and also offer post-registration courses on the subject. It would be advantageous to include in those modules NDErs talking about their NDEs. Becoming aware of NDEs through first-person description of the experience was found to be of great benefit to those trying to gain a greater understanding of the experience.[15] In my experience death, dying and death-related issues are what cause nurses and doctors, especially those who are inexperienced and junior, the most anxiety. Educational modules on death and dying in critical-care areas should be compulsory as they would help with the retention of staff in these specialized areas as well as being of great benefit to the patients and their families.

NDE modules incorporated into the training of medical students have been very successful and helped the students develop openness and respect for patients. The students engaged with the broader role of the physician and also interacted better with patients and colleagues with differing opinions.[16]

## Acknowledging and Responding to NDEs

If a person reports an NDE it has usually been done after a lot of thought and has taken a lot of courage to disclose such an overwhelming and often deeply personal experience. NDEs have such serious impact on the person that they have been likened to an existential crisis.[17] An NDE is a transcendent experience and there is nothing to compare it to. Many describe it as 'realer than real', so to have it dismissed as something trivial can be taken as an insult and shows total lack of understanding – often the person will withdraw and never try to communicate it again. People who have NDEs are usually reluctant to discuss their experience in public. In fact it may take some time to get to know the person before they will disclose the full extent of what they experienced, for a variety of reasons. Some patients will talk about a 'weird dream' or something similar to test the kind of response they will get before confiding their whole experience.[18] Most fear being disbelieved, ridiculed or considered crazy. Some don't fully understand the experience or integrate it into their life for many years. There is sometimes a great sense of guilt for wanting to continue further into the experience, knowing that they would be leaving loved ones, especially children, behind. For many, recall of the experience can evoke great emotion. For others it may be such a personal experience that they simply wish to keep it to themselves.

Listening to the patient is crucial to them coming to terms with their experience. It is vital that the experience is acknowledged and the person is given time to express it and that they are reassured that others have also experienced such a thing. Very often the person just requires validation of their experience, which allows them to move on.[19] Simple reassurance that they are not alone and that others have experienced similar events can be an enormous help. Caregivers should not discredit NDE/end-of-life experiences because they are at variance with their own worldview but should encourage the person to use it in a positive way and see it as a gift.[20] Although as nurses we are trained to 'correct' hallucinations, it is most important that NDEs are not treated in this way but listened to.[21]

If healthcare workers are not fully aware of the complexities of NDEs then responding appropriately becomes a very difficult task. These are usually the first people who come into contact with a person after their NDE and in some instances are subsequently involved in their long-term recovery. When I talk about healthcare workers I mean doctors, nurses, healthcare support workers, hospital chaplains, psychologists, psychiatrists: all people who have patient contact. However, this applies to all of us as sometimes family members are the first person in whom the person confides. NDEs are still regarded by some people as hallucinations and many try to explain them away as being due to drugs or lack of oxygen. This is not a criticism; when NDEs are taken at surface value these appear to be very rational, plausible explanations – in fact, these were my own initial reactions to NDEs. Research in the clinical area is now showing these factors to be inadequate explanations and such a response can be detrimental to the NDEr understanding and integrating their experience.

From a nurse's perspective, those who had cared for someone who reported an NDE felt that it instigated their own spiritual exploration. They became more sensitive to the needs of patients, more understanding and compassionate and felt more comfortable talking about death with patients and their families. They were also more aware of what they said during resuscitation.[22] This is certainly true for me.

It is essential that distressing NDEs are also recognized, as these appear to evoke the most emotion in people and some are left with some residual psychological trauma. Many people will not discuss a distressing NDE and some even have a sense of shame because theirs was distressing. Again, it is important that reassurance is given that they are not alone in experiencing this. I've found it beneficial for the patient to mention that there are documented cases where distressing experiences have turned into pleasant experiences as they have progressed.[23] There are many resources that the patient can be alerted to such as the IANDS website and the Horizon Research Foundation. It would be helpful to have a selection of resources in all healthcare settings as freely available as, for example, instructions for wound care.

Following a retreat to help further understand their experience, a group of NDErs suggested ways of improving support for future experiencers:[24]

- Understanding, well-informed healthcare workers
- Information on research, comparison with mystical traditions, historical perspectives, personal experiences and after effects
- Time to meditate, process the experience, pray or be in nature
- Spiritual counsellors, trained clergy, informed marriage and family counsellors, guides and mentors
- Workshops, retreats, conferences, support groups, classes, on-line support
- Self-help material
- Heightened public awareness of all that the NDE entails
- Venues to learn, speak, network and integrate the NDE into careers
- Retreat for childhood NDErs.

Many people are under the misconception that a person has to die to have an NDE – this is incorrect. NDEs, although more prevalent in cardiac arrest, can occur in varying contexts. Below is the example of Sherry, a 52-year-old lady from Lancashire who had an NDE while trapped in a car following a road traffic accident. When Sherry first contacted me it was clear that she did not understand her experience and the fact that it was dismissed by healthcare workers exacerbated her problem.

*I read the article in this morning's paper and want to share my experience that I have never fully understood. The reason I haven't understood it is that whenever I have tried to talk about it, it is dismissed because I was in fact not dying at the time, although I thought I was ... In fact I heard one of the emergency services team tell the ER doctors that he thought I was dying. I don't know how much information you want so all I can do is tell you my experience and hope it isn't too long.*

*Three [now eight] years ago I was involved in a car crash, I had a lift with two friends after we got lost. A car pulled up to ask the way to the place we were heading and gave us a lift. The car was tiny, the three of us got in the back. One friend entered the car first, followed by me, but as I put my head in the car I had a strong sensation of danger, I had no idea what that was but stepped back out and asked my other friend did she want to get in next (not a nice thing to do and I did confess later and apologized although she did seem very pleased!), somehow feeling that where she was sitting was dangerous for me. This also has been dismissed that lots of people don't like to sit in the middle. I couldn't make sense of how I was feeling but put my belt on . . . a move that saved my life. My other two friends did not put their belts on. We had only been in the car five minutes at the most and there was confusion as she was lost, my friend in the middle kept trying to get the driver to turn right and go back the way we came. I realized whilst everyone was busy looking right, to my horror, she was pulling out into a stream of on-coming traffic onto a busy carriageway!*

*What followed was in slow motion. I watched as a car came towards me and I just braced myself, hoping against hope it would either hit the front passenger or pass us by, but he hit me side on directly and because I was squashed up against the door as it was a tiny car I took the full impact. The car was spun round and sent back into the traffic. I knew straight away I was badly injured and before the car came to a standstill thought I was in the process of death. I struggled to breathe for what felt like an eternity. Everyone miraculously escaped serious injury and climbed out the driver's door. They were begging me to try and get out in case the car got hit again but I was trapped and too injured, and panicking not to be left. My experience has left me with post-trauma for which I am still receiving treatment but I am doing fantastic.*

*I was fighting for breath and shock from broken bones in my chest, pain, fear of dying and not seeing my daughter and husband, who didn't know I was even in a car because I had caught the train with my friend initially. My dear friend put her hand in the car and held my hand and I told her I was dying and to tell my husband and daughter I was sorry and I loved them. The emergency services were brilliant and one climbed in the car, one got through the back window and did the usual stuff – cut my clothes off, examined, keeping me talking. First I was saying, please don't let me die . . . my heart had taken a knock and was beating erratically. The fire brigade started cutting the roof off but they couldn't release me so started cutting the back of the car out, then the back of my seat . . . which was extremely painful as I had broken my pelvis. Being trapped, oxygen mask on, head brace on, hands around my face, people surrounding me, a guard put over my head whilst they smashed windows, etc. . . . just all became too much and I wanted to be gone. I looked at the ambulance man and he looked up above him and said to a fireman we need to get her out now!!! . . . I remember physically turning my head away to my left and closed my eyes. The ambulance man was talking to me and touching my face but it seemed so far away I didn't care. In my head I asked if there was someone there to help me and that I was ready to die. I had no fear or care any more about my daughter or husband; it became very personal and was just about me, nothing else seemed to matter, just a deep sense of 'going home'. I felt a deep sense of relief as I felt someone was coming for me.*

*What happened next still overwhelms me and I have never been able to really articulate it into words. I just felt as though I was being wrapped up in the most wonderful warmth that felt like a blanket of love, a sort of hug that was so tender and sort of full . . . I still can't put that into words, except it was so beautiful that I still cry thinking of it. Suddenly I was drawn back and being pulled out of the back of the car onto a body board and everything else was just chaos . . . cold, noise, pain, voices and a man's voice that said he was from the emergency room and would be with me when I arrived at hospital. I was in agony but it didn't seem to matter: all I could think about was that I was deeply loved by something that wasn't from this life.*

*I am still recovering physically and mentally from the accident but my experience never left me even in the dark days of recovery. When able, as soon as I could, I asked for a priest and was put on medication because I could not stop crying. I did suffer post-traumatic stress disorder and still have some symptoms now but my talk with the priest helped me. Once able to walk I asked for religious instruction that ended with my christening . . . baptism into the Catholic faith, a year later. I am not sure what my experience was, my priest jokingly said maybe it was the effects of the morphine!!*

*... I am not in the 'God squad' ... I just have a deep sense that something warm and wonderful awaits when we pass and for me, despite not actually being in the throes of death, as I thought ... I think something somewhere came and put its arms around me at my deepest hour of need. I have a very open mind on this: was it a guardian angel, was it a relative or do we have a very clever body that at times of trauma can comfort itself?*

*Weirdly I have too much static in my body, and keep getting shocks off the car door and in shops on the clothes rails, etc. I mention that because of what was written in your article, and it has just made me link it, as I never had this before, to this extent. I know my experience isn't in comparison with some of the people's in your article but it was something that had a profound effect on me and how I perceive myself now, in terms that dying is nothing to be feared. Although how you go still frightens me!! ... hope it's in my sleep and not being squashed by a car again! Good luck with your work.*

Five years after Sherry first contacted me, she has a better understanding of what she experienced. I asked how her care could have been improved at the time:

*Having had varying surgeries over the years I am getting fit again. I have also never forgotten my experience during my rescue eight years ago.*

*Looking back through fresh eyes now that I have no post-trauma, the memory is as strong now as then. That fearless carefree surge of something unexplainable, it was so beautiful it could make you cry. I didn't care any more about my husband and daughter, I wanted to go with this beautiful thing I can't articulate it with a word ... like a blanket of love surrounding me ... The contrast of the sudden shock, a horrible jolt of being pulled and being back in the cold, etc. Yes, I think it's something that can't be forgotten.*

*For me the NDE had a profound and positive effect in that I think most of us have a fear of dying, the unknown. It did make me feel like I couldn't talk about it with fear, I would be laughed at or thought of in a less favourable light. Of course I still fear death in so much as HOW I will die; I don't want to particularly feel the pain like in the accident, but to die itself, if it is anything like the experience I had, is really quite beautiful. I have always felt I don't want to die and leave my loved ones as I would miss them and as I am so nosey that would just be unbearable. The reality was that when that release came I just wanted to go with whatever was drawing me so much and all thoughts of previous life before just faded. There was a feeling of utter peace and at oneness. I can't articulate it, it was something I can't really describe in words as I don't know a word for it.*

*For me there was a feeling that I needed it explaining. They say there was a deep concern for me and I do remember at one stage the paramedic looking upwards to I presume the firemen and said, 'We have to get her out now,' in an urgent voice just at the time I wanted to give up and I did not wish to respond to instructions any more, willing myself out of it.*

*A priest was brought to speak with me as my family thought perhaps it was a religious experience. The priest said he felt it was a gift to treasure. I am not sure it was a religious experience necessarily, a sort of oneness, of peace and love; though the contrast to that was an unanswered question of what was it that came to my aid. There is a little apprehension in that.*

*You, Penny, were actually the one who made sense of how I felt and, following your thoughts that it did actually fulfil what would be deemed an NDE, to acknowledge it and not dismiss or laugh or disbelieve is fundamental in the patient making sense of something that makes no sense.*

*The medical staff should have been given some knowledge as part of their training, perhaps via your book. As part of the care of the patient and in the treatment plan if any leaflets as regards dressings, instructions maybe a leaflet in relationship to NDEs with perhaps a contact number or reference to your book could form part of any treatment plan, or left in hospital wards, reception, etc. I have never thought of myself as anything special, and so why would this happen to me and not anyone else? It would have helped to know that it was not unusual and to acknowledge its naturalness. It can feel quite profound to learn that perhaps we really do have a spirit and that it will leave when our body dies. Where it goes is another book for you, I think!!! I feel so honoured to have played a tiny speck part in this book, thank you, Penny, for giving me the opportunity to open my mind and find peace with my NDE.*

## Therapeutic Benefits

*Terminal Illness and Allaying the Fear of Death: How and When Do we Broach the Subject of Death?*

Recent years have seen great advances in our technology which have resulted in many ailments that were previously unrecoverable being treated successfully. New techniques are constantly being developed. If someone is very sick then we are lucky that such technology, along with medical and nursing skills, have been developed. I have always been very proud to work at a great hospital and intensive-care unit with such an amazing team. It is always rewarding to see a patient make a recovery after a critical illness – and many do. However, there are some patients who do not recover, despite every attempt to reverse their illness, often resulting in the last few days, weeks or sometimes months hovering in a semi-conscious state between life and death.

As a patient approaches the end of their life, making decisions with regards to how their treatment proceeds is a very difficult task for everyone involved. In intensive care, patients are admitted in emergency situations. Often patients are unconscious by the time of arrival in ITU so decisions about their treatment are made by the doctors treating them. We seldom consider end-of-life issues that may involve ourselves, mainly because we have no reason to think of such things during the day-to-day running of our lives. It is only when the unexpected happens – when people are faced with a situation they are often not prepared for. Even when people have a terminal diagnosis, some tend to avoid thinking about death.

Death is something that as a society we totally ignore or give little thought to. Even in areas where death may be expected, it remains a taboo topic for discussion. Unless the patient brings it up it is usually not appropriate to have a discussion about death. Knowing what to say to dying patients is one aspect of nursing care that causes great anxiety for many nurses. When is it the right time to bring up the subject of death? Does the patient even want to discuss death? When someone is newly diagnosed with a terminal illness how do we support that patient and help them come to terms with the diagnosis? As much as we may want to help, the patient may not be receptive to what we have to say or they may just want some privacy.

Despite my experience of working in ITU, I am still occasionally faced with events for which nothing can prepare me. ITU is a rapidly changing environment and often throws up new situations. Within each working day comes a new learning experience. Just two days after I had given a public lecture that had a huge attendance, I was faced with a situation that both upset me yet taught me so much. During the lecture I had mentioned that hearing accounts of NDEs can help people faced with terminal illness. This statement was put to the test that day.

As I arrived on the unit at 6.30am, I noticed that the lights were on in the high-dependency unit (HDU) – never a good sign: at that time of morning the patients in HDU are usually sleeping. I changed into my scrubs and checked the allocation board; I was looking after two patients in HDU. I opened the doors, to be greeted with equipment strewn everywhere, flustered nurses and two doctors attempting to put intravenous lines into a patient who was somewhere hidden underneath sterile towels which were soaked with blood. The nurse from the night shift handed over her two patients to me while the doctors successfully sited intravenous access.

I briefly introduced myself to the man I was looking after in the next bed but quickly turned my attention to the lady ('Sian'), who needed my attention more. I approached the bed, removed the sterile towels and introduced myself. The lady had sweat pouring off her face, her blood pressure was unrecordable and I could barely feel a pulse as I held her hand.

As I was attending to her and clearing away the equipment, the on-call consultant surgeon called to review the patient with his entourage of staff and explained to her that an operation might be necessary. I quickly went to the visitors' room to introduce myself to Sian's husband, son and two daughters and explained what was happening. Ten minutes later the surgical consultant for the morning turned up with *his* entourage. He stood at the bedside, shouting and demanding the notes of the patient, which were not available. At the same time the radiographer arrived to x-ray Sian.

The ITU consultant immediately reviewed Sian and on her instructions I administered drugs to support her blood pressure. As I hurriedly gathered the necessary equipment to transfer Sian to the operating theatre I tried to explain to this very frightened lady that after her operation she may be connected to a ventilator; there would be a tube in her mouth going down to her lungs and that she temporarily would not be able to speak. I completed the necessary paperwork and prepared Sian for the operating theatre in record time.

The surgeon returned and roughly poked me in the shoulder with his finger and asked if the people at the bedside were Sian's husband and children. He stepped behind the screens, held Sian's hand and in a voice that was gentle and authoritative (and loud!) said he'd viewed her CT scan and it would be futile to take her to theatre as she would not survive the operation. There was nothing more he could do.

There was utter devastation as she began crying loudly and hysterically, her family also. They were hugging each other and crying. The surgeon walked away and I was left feeling useless trying to console them all; I was totally caught off guard. The family ran out, hysterical, the son shouting angrily as loud as he could and I was left alone behind the screens with Sian. I held her hand but did not speak for two reasons: 1) I didn't know what to say and 2) even if I'd had anything useful to say I wouldn't have been able to get the words out because I was left with a lump in my throat and tears in my eyes. The whole of the HDU was in a stunned silence, there was not a word uttered by the other three patients who had all been in earshot of what was said. The ring of the phone pierced the silence and my colleague put her head around the screens with a message – I could see that she too had been crying.

Sian kept loudly screaming, 'I'm dying, I'm dying.' I asked if she was afraid of death and if she had any thoughts on what may happen. She hadn't thought much about death, she was just frightened. All the time at the back of my mind were the words I'd spoken in my lecture. Was it appropriate for me to broach the subject with Sian? In the past I'd spoken to patients about my research but that was after I'd had time to build up a rapport with them and I knew it would be appropriate to mention it. I'd only just met her, yet she'd had the most devastating news anyone could possibly have and she was literally staring death in the face – there was no escaping it.

It would have been far easier just to leave our conversation at that and not attempt to put into practice what I had said about NDEs helping to alleviate fear of death in those faced with terminal illness. I could have avoided talking about it further and busied myself with other tasks that needed doing. But she was devastated and I couldn't ignore it, I had to try to ease things for her. I decided to try to help as best I could and asked Sian exactly what frightened her most about dying. She didn't know, she'd never thought about it but she didn't want to die and was very afraid. I mentioned that I had spoken to many people who had actually died temporarily but had been resuscitated. I said that they had reported wonderful experiences and that if she wanted me to I would explain more about this in depth later if she so wished. I left it up to her but reiterated that I thought what I had to say would help both her and her family.

More doctors and specialist nurses arrived to review Sian and ensure her pain was well controlled. Her distraught family were fully updated by the medical team and came back to sit at her bedside. They all held hands and cried a little then tried to speak to each other in-between sobs.

To cut a very long story short, by 2pm Sian looked visibly better. At one point during the morning I thought she had only a few hours to live. The treatment that she'd received; albeit very briefly, had proved effective and had made a difference. She was sitting up in bed, wearing pyjamas, the sweat had stopped pouring from her face, her blood pressure had improved and she had colour in her cheeks. She was surrounded by family members and friends and she was saying that she was not ready to die; she wanted to take her grandson to Disneyworld, she wanted to do this and she wanted to do that. What would I do and what would go through my mind if I'd been told I was going to die imminently?

She then asked me if I'd come and talk with her about my research. She sent the remaining friends and family out but asked her husband, son and two daughters to stay. I knew it had comforted patients I'd looked after before, as well as my own grandfather while he was dying, but there is always a little bit of doubt when talking about death with patients. I pulled up a chair and explained that I had an interest in death because it is so common in ITU. I'd read about and researched something called near-death experiences and the majority of people who have these experiences no longer fear death and know that it is something wonderful. I explained the various different components and how all pain has been reported to disappear. I said that what I was explaining may not have any relevance to her at the moment but maybe as her death approached it would all make sense and help guide her through the process. I also reiterated that she'd have far more control over the time of her death than she realized. We sat and chatted for a while and I encouraged them all to ask questions then left her and her family to have some time alone.

I learned from the specialist nurse the next day that Sian had gone back to the ward and was sitting up in bed drinking a cup of tea with her family and was pain free. Being thrust into this situation gave Sian the time to say those things to her family that she may not have had the opportunity to say had the outcome been any different. As for the effectiveness of NDEs helping someone come to terms with their own death – all I can say is that Sian was a very different person from the time that my shift began to the time that my shift ended eight hours later. She appeared to be much calmer and she and her family were grateful for what I had explained. Had I not had the benefit of undertaking my research and my knowledge of NDEs I don't know how else I would have dealt with that situation.

In Sian's case, hearing about NDEs seemed to help her, or at least take her mind off what she was fearful of. When my maternal grandfather was dying I was coming to the end of my research. We had long conversations about death and he frequently asked me what patients were reporting. He was a very private person and very much kept his thoughts to himself but when confronted with his own mortality he wanted to know more about my work. He died at home with all of the family present and his death was quite quick and very peaceful.

These are not rare occurrences and cases like this occur daily. Hence if healthcare workers were more aware of the therapeutic benefits of understanding NDEs, many patients could be greatly helped during a time when they are most vulnerable and frightened.

## Sedation and Medication at the End of Life
Dying is a unique process and each patient's death is different. Some are very peaceful but some patients appear to be in great spiritual pain. They may become very agitated as they approach death; some may even be quite aggressive. Some may have unresolved guilt or fear punishment for things they have done in their life. It is unfortunate that maybe they have never had the opportunity to discuss their fears or concerns. Recognizing and addressing spiritual as well as physical needs can result in a reduction in painkillers and a peaceful transition into death.

When analysing the results of my research, one thing that I discovered was that the painkilling and sedative drugs we give patients appear to have an inhibitory effect on NDEs. This was also suggested by others.[25] Dr Yvonne Kason[26] referred to the case of Christina. During the birth of her son she was undergoing a spiritual experience (this is similar to an NDE but occurs in the absence of life-threatening circumstances) but the whole process stopped when morphine was administered. A similar but stronger experience occurred during the birth of her second child and this too stopped as soon as tranquilizers were administered.

My research and other cases I've studied has made me quite mindful of the possibility that the drugs we give at the end of life may actually deny patients valid aspects of the dying process. I want to emphasize that I am not advocating withholding such drugs at the end of life but it is important not to over-sedate a patient just because they are agitated as they approach death. It is a challenge for critical-care staff to distinguish between hallucinations and spiritual expressions. It has been recommended that medication be administered at times of spiritual expression only if the patient is a danger to themselves or if they request it.[27] If the patient is comfortable then there is no need to commence or increase sedation. This was the wish of a dying person, who wanted his pain relieved but didn't want to be rendered unconscious as he wanted to enjoy his last moments with his family and perform his spiritual practice.[28] This is highlighted by one of Rommer's cases: 'I fear the physical pain like everyone else. But since my NDE I pray that I am conscious when I die.'[29]

It would be beneficial for nurses who observe patients having death-bed experiences to share this information usefully with other nurses by documenting it in the patient's care plan and mentioning it on hand over. In fact this is a common part of hand over in many hospices.

In some cases patients do not require sedatives or opiates.[30] If physical pain does become an issue then doses can be adjusted to ensure that the individual is able to remain coherent and stay conscious. One hospice doctor was successful in adjusting the pain medication of one lady who wished to have conversations with her daughter and not miss out on valuable time with her. Although initially sleepy while her body adjusted, after a few days she was able to return to her usual state of consciousness, which resulted in her daughter commenting how nice it was to have her back.[31]

As my grandfather's condition deteriorated rapidly and his physical pain increased he was started on a painkilling infusion. We nursed him in his own home and in my discussion with the palliative-care team I requested that midazolam be omitted from the infusion (I had found this to contribute greatly to confusional experiences in my research), which was agreed unless he became unmanageable and it would then be reviewed. My mother had arrived from her home in France that evening and my grandfather was so pleased to see her. They had a brief chat, which was interrupted by the arrival of the evening nurses, who had never met him before. The painkilling infusion had only been running a few hours so, as they tried to move him, he screamed out in pain, understandably. Then it went silent, the nurses came out of his room and said that they'd given something to settle him and left. I checked his chart and he had been given midazolam. I was furious, I hadn't even thought to mention to them that I didn't want any given as he was fine and did not require it. After that my grandfather was unconscious and did not regain consciousness to continue his conversation with my mother. He never regained consciousness and died the next day, not having had the opportunity to say things that he may have wanted to say to his daughter.

With greater awareness of the dying process many individuals faced with terminal illness may decide to complete a death plan or complete an advanced decision to refuse treatment (ADRT) form with regards to their wishes as their condition deteriorates. It must also be borne in mind that the views of people can drastically change as their illness progresses.[32] If recovery from illness is likely then ITUs are the best places to help with recovery. However, if the overall picture indicates a slim chance of recovery then a death plan or ADRT would leave the individual in control rather than relying on the decisions of others.[33]

*Suicide and NDEs*

Therapeutic effects of NDEs have been recognized and used effectively by others.[34] As incongruous is it seems, NDEs have a very positive effect[35] and have been used therapeutically in the treatment of people who have had multiple suicide attempts.[36] It may seem that reports of wonderful places of peace, joy, love and being greeted by loved ones would encourage suicidal people to commit suicide, but in fact the opposite appears to be true. Professor Bruce Greyson found that patients who had had multiple suicide attempts but then experienced an NDE during the attempt were far less likely to attempt suicide again. Reasons for this could be a renewed appreciation of life and a sense of purpose in one's life.[37] In fact, those who had an NDE during a suicide attempt felt that suicide was not an option.[38] The NDE empowered them with a sense of purpose in life and prompted an overwhelming realization that they took their problems with them even when out of their body – there was simply no way to escape their problems, so to attempt suicide was futile.[39] Psychotherapist J. M. McDonagh[40] also found that suicidal thoughts and intent were reduced when introduced to NDE accounts; his patients were also encouraged to conduct their own research by looking up NDE websites.

The *Occidental Book of Death and Dying*, comprising NDE accounts, was developed by Engelbert Winkler.[41] This was cautiously used to treat the very difficult case of a young boy whose suicidal tendencies arose after the death of his father. The treatment was very successful for the young boy, as well as later difficult cases, and Winkler regards it as a 'highly useful healing tool'. He further proposed that NDE accounts be used as a 'high-tech' Book of Death and Dying – such books have been utilized by cultures throughout history but are currently absent in our society.

*Grief Therapy*

Getting over the loss of a loved one is not easy and can have a devastating impact. In fact, I have nursed some patients whose inability to cope with their grief has triggered lifestyle behaviours, such as alcoholism or self-neglect, which have resulted in them being admitted to ITU. Reading accounts of NDEs has also been useful for those who are grieving for loved ones and many grief counsellors suggest that clients familiarize themselves with the NDE literature. From a personal perspective, my knowledge of NDEs has certainly made a big difference to how I coped with the loss of loved ones after I began my research. It didn't take away the pain and sadness but it did help to ease those feelings. It has also helped friends when I have recommended NDE books to them.

Also, acknowledgement that after-death communications (ADCs) are common can greatly accelerate the grieving process. People who report ADCs are certain it is a genuine communication and consequently radically change their worldview and find new meaning in life and death. With a renewed perspective on life, emotional wounds are healed and peace of mind is attained.[42]

Psychologist Allan Botkin developed a technique called Induced After Death Communication (IADC) while treating patients suffering from post-traumatic stress disorder. During IADC therapy the patients report communicating with loved ones. Very often any unresolved issues are worked through during those communications, leaving the patient in a very positive frame of mind. In many instances IADC has signified a time when the patient was able to move on and there was no requirement for further treatment.[43] The therapy succeeded in stimulating self-healing in many cases.

There are many unreceptive attitudes, as this is such unusual therapy and one that seemingly has no scientific basis. However, the therapy has been shown to be greatly beneficial in many cases – whatever happens during the therapy has a healing quality and may benefit many people if made widely available to those open to receiving such therapy.

## Evolutionary Implications

*Positive Implications for our Interaction with Others*
The powerful life-changing potential of the NDE literature has long been recognized as those who have not had an NDE have gained comfort, hope and inspiration from reading the accounts of NDErs. The NDE has been likened to a 'benign virus' in that those who are open to NDEs and are exposed to testimonies of NDErs exhibit the same life changes as NDErs.[44] The overall message of the NDE is that we are all interconnected and we should treat others as we wish to be treated ourselves. Many NDErs find they have increased compassion, love, tolerance and understanding for others.

Following many years of teaching about NDEs in an undergraduate course, Professor Kenneth Ring noticed the powerful positive effect that the course had on the students. In his 'Omega Project', Ring found that his control group of people studying NDEs – but who had not experienced an NDE – reported the same changes as those who had had an NDE, though to a lesser degree.[45] The non-NDErs also became more self-accepting, more appreciative of life, more compassionate, more spiritual, had heightened concern for the environment and were less materialistic. Through means of an informal survey at the end of the course he found that 96 per cent were more convinced of the authenticity of NDEs, 61 per cent felt that they were more spiritually orientated and 68 per cent felt that they had a purpose in life. The survey was repeated twice in further courses, with almost the same results.

Ring comments: 'It appears as if some of the benefits of the NDE can be transmitted vicariously, simply by presenting relevant information on the subject to individuals who are or become interested in NDEs.'[46]

Professor Bruce Greyson[47] compared a group of NDErs with members of IANDS who had not had an NDE but had sufficient interest to join such a group. The four personal values he was particularly interested in were self-actualization, altruism, spirituality and being successful in life. Both non-NDErs and NDErs considered the important values to be self-actualization, altruism and spirituality with no statistical difference in the two groups. Both groups had less concern with success but NDErs statistically scored significantly lower.

Professor of Sociology Charles Flynn[48] incorporated videotaped interviews with NDErs into a course that he taught, called the 'Love Project'. His students were also instructed to behave in a loving manner to someone who they would not otherwise get to know. The results showed that there was an increased concern for others, increased personal growth and some value changes. There were also increases in self-understanding, increased self-worth and self-esteem and an increased sense of meaning and purpose in life.

On long-term follow-up of childhood NDErs, Dr Melvin Morse[49] found them to display physical, mental and spiritual stability and empathy for others; they were successful in school, ate healthy food and none of them had become addicted to drugs or alcohol.

In one prospective study of cardiac arrest survivors[50] it was discovered that NDErs developed altruistic tendencies. There were significantly greater increases in NDErs than non-NDErs in the ability to express love to others, listen to, tolerate and understand others, along with the desire to help others.

Nurses who had cared for patients who reported NDEs were also prompted to explore their own spirituality, which resulted in positive changes in their own personal and professional life. Their attitude to patients changed and they became more compassionate and sensitive to the needs of their patients and felt more comfortable discussing NDEs and death with their patients and their families.[51]

This contagion is not restricted to only those who are open to NDEs. Professor Neal Grossman reported the changes of a 'committed materialist' graduate student who attended his seminars on NDEs. Through listening to a professor discuss his own NDE, the student had no option but to review his previously held beliefs.

> *Listening to an NDEr narrate a deep experience, especially in a one-to-one setting, constitutes a profound experience for the listener and is more psychologically convincing than just reading a bunch of studies.*[52]

A similar comment was reported by Rominger:[53] 'I have never heard directly about the NDE other than reading books, and I felt, wow, this is real. I mean, it, it's not just a story . . . somebody did it for real.'

## Positive Implications for Individual Health and Wellbeing

One of the most powerful after effects of the NDE is a heightened sense of love and compassion for self, which ultimately is reflected onto others. In the DVD *I AM*[54] Dacher Keltner, professor of psychology at Berkeley, highlights how in Darwin's *Descent of Man* the word 'love' is mentioned 95 times and the phrase 'survival of the fittest' is mentioned only twice. Despite not having great strength and agility, or large fangs, etc., the human race has survived and greatly evolved and Darwin believed this to be due to our ability to co-operate and to have sympathy for others. Darwin considered sympathy to be the strongest instinct in nature – there are deep reasons why we have evolved to be good to others: it's wired into our DNA.

Unfortunately, this aspect was ignored and instead the focus was on the survival of the fittest aspect and so we were conditioned into a belief that we are all separate. With the belief that we are all separate, we adopt selfish behaviour and put our own needs before the needs of others. As Dean Radin comments,[55] if we lived with the understanding that we are all connected then our behaviour towards others would be very different. This is reinforced in the life review component of the NDE, where experiencers find themselves reliving the consequences of their actions on others from a third-person perspective – they actually experience the ways in which their actions harmed or benefited another person. This interconnectivity is literally experienced first hand and it is as if the experience resets the psyche of the NDEr and removes the misconceptions that have been conditioned into their belief system in their life prior to the NDE. Consequently, following their NDE they modify their future behaviour accordingly. So when we see ourselves as interconnected this is conducive not only to our survival as a species but also to our survival as a planet.

The interconnectivity that is reported by NDErs and is demonstrated by empathic death experiences was also apparent to Einstein, who called it 'spooky action at a distance'. In 1935 Einstein and his colleagues Rosen and Podolsky published the results of experiments they had conducted with electrons.[56] They found that when two electrons that had been in connection with each other were separated a huge distance apart, if the spin on one of the electrons stopped, the spin on the other electron also stopped at the exact same time. There is no known mechanism for this as there should be a time lag involved. This is now called quantum entanglement, but this would imply that we are connected at very deep levels. Again this reinforces what NDErs report and also what all of the great wisdom traditions of the world have always said – we are not separate but interconnected and part of a great whole.

Not only does this impact positively on our relationships with others but it also has a positive influence on our health. When compassion is experienced, levels of salivary immunoglobulin A (IgA) significantly increase – this is the body's first line of defence against pathogens in food.[57] It has also been noted that people with a strong sense of purpose, a sense of belonging and connection with others cope well with stress, are less prone to illness and live longer.[58] One of the most overwhelming insights that NDErs realize is that we are all interconnected.

*The sense of connectedness and responsibility, whether it be to people, pets or plants, seems to draw us out of ourselves and link us to a larger world. The predisposition to communicate with others, to bond, appears to be vital to our health.[59]*

Further changes experienced by NDErs include being motivated to undertake voluntary work and help others; again, there is evidence to show that this behaviour is correlated to high levels of overall health.[60] There is an abundance of peer-reviewed research articles which conclude how beneficial qualities of compassion, kindness and love are to our health. For an overview of such articles in relation to health, see the work of Dr David Hamilton.[61] So it would seem that having an NDE or familiarizing ourselves with them can lead to greater health and life expectancy.

NDEs are also very similar to 'peak' experiences, described by Abraham Maslow,[62] and mystical experiences. People who have undergone mystical experiences have been shown to be well adjusted and demonstrate psychological health.[63] Following a mystical or religious experience there is a corresponding shift in attitude, resulting in a sense of meaning and purpose in life.[64]

Many people engage in the practice of meditation or prayer following an NDE or mystical experience, which is conducive to promoting health and preventing disease.[65] Meditation plays a large part in rehabilitation of cardiac patients and is effective in lowering blood pressure. In our consumptive society the emphasis is on the need for more money and more material possessions, often putting individuals in highly stressful situations of high-pressure jobs with long working hours in order to maintain that lifestyle. It is apparent that the benefits of acknowledging spiritual aspects of life and engaging with spiritual practice can lead to both physical and psychological health as well as increasing the capacity for compassion and the reduction of materialism.

Another important way in which NDErs are affected is that they become more ecologically aware. With the rise of industrialization, humans are currently destroying nature for short-term gain. NDErs report an increased love for nature and the understanding that all people and things on the planet are interconnected: the same view as the Gaia Hypothesis. Environmentalist James Lovelock proposed that all organisms and their inorganic surroundings on the planet are closely integrated to form a single and self-regulating complex system, maintaining the conditions for life on earth.[66] Indeed, indigenous peoples have always understood this interconnectivity and continue to live with great respect for the land and the planet. If more people understood these insights it could result in a reassessment of the ways in which nature is being destroyed and could promote a balanced future with greater appreciation for nature. This leaves us with the encouraging prospect of a transformation of consciousness for the planet.

As more research is being undertaken into NDEs and consciousness, it is demonstrating that our understanding of consciousness is changing. Ironically, the technology developed by our science is actually helping us to arrive at this new understanding of what it means to be human. It is very apparent to me that our science is evolving to the next level, which will provide an even greater understanding of life as it will include spiritual aspects as well as physical aspects of life.

It is paramount that we keep an open mind about NDEs and do not just dismiss them. Whatever our personal perspectives on NDEs and end of life experiences, it is important to acknowledge that they have a very significant place in how we understand and treat those who are approaching death and those who undergo bereavement, as well as enhancing our health. It is therefore essential that as a society we take more notice of these experiences and that these issues are incorporated into the education system, especially that of healthcare workers. Then we can all reap the benefits of the NDE – without having to nearly die.

# 10

# Conclusion

*The NDE is not really about death but about life. It can, and has, inspired others who have not had any kind of transcendent experience to carry out the message and mandate of the light by living lives of love.*

Charles Flynn[1]

This is a very exciting time to be alive and to be doing research of any kind. It appears that the human race is on the verge of an evolutionary leap into the millennia ahead. This book is the result of the past 20 years of trying to make sense of death and in the process learning important lessons about life. I don't profess to know all of the answers and in fact my research has raised more questions than it has answered. It has opened my eyes to things I had never previously acknowledged, simply because they had never been brought to my attention; nor had I ever been educated about them. None of my school lessons or my nurse training mentioned the experiences of the dying I have been investigating.

Occasionally, I had read brief descriptions in newspapers about some anomalous experiences of what it was like to die: stories which were hyped up and shrouded in mystery. I had never given them much consideration as they seemed impossible and inexplicable. Since studying a vast number of subjective accounts of patients that I nursed who were dying or close to death, it is apparent that these accounts only remain mysterious when considered from the viewpoint of our current scientific paradigm that consciousness is a mere by-product of the brain.

Over the years I have worked in ITU, I have witnessed thousands of patients die. Each patient is usually under the care of different teams of doctors, such as the ITU anaesthetists, orthopaedic surgeons, general surgeons, medical physicians, renal physicians, etc. Decisions made about patient care are therefore usually a collaboration between teams. I once witnessed a situation in which a patient was clearly dying and the surgeon was called to review the patient. Within minutes he and his team had donned masks, sterile gowns and gloves, had exposed the patient's abdominal wound and were poking their fingers into her abdominal cavity to examine her for a possible cause for her deterioration. As healthcare professionals, sometimes we fail to see the whole picture. We don't see *the patient, the person, the human being, the mother* who had brought up a family who were desperately worried about her condition. Although there was a potential solution to the surgical problem, we failed to see the overall picture and understand that the patient was dying: she was unconscious, having large doses of potent drugs to maintain her blood pressure and maximum ventilation to assist her breathing. How much do we have to do before we can acknowledge our limitations? The avoidance of the subject of death was recognized over 32 years ago by Hampe, and it now persists to an even greater extent: 'Anyone who has ever been in hospital, or still more in an intensive-care unit, has found that there above all the subject of dying and death is avoided, benevolently and persistently, though this is the last place where one might expect this avoidance.'[2]

With advances in our technology, death is not as clearly defined as it once was and patients frequently die while connected to the latest life-saving equipment and in drug-induced comas, leaving no scope for the natural process of dying. Those individuals have no command over the way in which they die. Death has become an event that is viewed with embarrassment and hidden away in a side room with all control totally in the hands of the medical team. When patients die in hospital it is important not to forget the dying patient's relatives, as they often feel useless in the high-technology environment, and the different equipment and intravenous infusions can act as a barrier between patient and relatives. The loss of loved ones can have an enormous impact and the family should be supported by the knowledge that their loved one has been given the best possible chance to survive their illness.

It is 20 years since I first enquired about a course to help enhance my skills to care for dying patients in ITU. I am still waiting for such a course for critical-care nurses. In one sense improvements have been made, as

NDEs are now taught in some courses. However, generally, there is very little education about death and even in large teaching hospitals there is little or no provision made for the care of dying patients in critical-care areas. Death-related issues are noticeably absent on the programme for the introductory teaching period for new intensive-care nurses, yet it is these precise issues that cause great concern for many of them. I have therefore developed an educational course that specifically addresses these issues.

Our hospitals continue to get busier and continue to expand and people are living longer, yet we have not developed the understanding necessary to deal with patients dying amongst this technology. Many people of all ages spend the last few weeks or months of their lives hooked up to machines. During the last few days or hours before the life of the patient is extinguished, relatives are distanced, as the visiting of loved ones remains controlled by the routines of the nurses and doctors.

There are always going to be dying patients in ITU and situations where patients would sometimes have been better off if they had been admitted to a hospice. It is therefore of vital importance in all hospital settings that spiritual aspects of patient care are acknowledged and that we treat the whole person, not just the body.[3] Healthcare workers are in a unique position of being able to provide both physical and spiritual care; as death approaches, addressing the patient's spiritual needs is crucial. I regard nursing as one of the highest jobs, on a spiritual level, that can be done and I believe that being at the bedside of a dying patient is an absolute privilege.

Death should not be considered a defeat; it needs to be embraced. Indeed, the care of the dying should have the same value that our society places on the fight to save someone's life. We are a death-denying, materialistic society. Yet it is by contemplating death that we can actually stop and think about the way we are living our lives. The insights to be gained from those who have been clinically dead and report an NDE can induce great life changes that will ultimately serve to enhance current lifestyles and in some cases even reduce the likelihood of needing medical treatment. I hope that this book will benefit future patients and their families. In particular, I hope that reflection on personal mortality might encourage more people to re-evaluate their lives. The study of NDEs and, even more, the experience of NDEs may help give others a wider vision of what life may offer.

Contemplating one's own mortality can have a profound effect on one's life. Things that have never been considered suddenly become very relevant with the threat of death and often the emphasis can shift from the self to helping others. For example, having been diagnosed with a terminal illness at the age of 34, Juliet Boyd's life was thrown into turmoil. She was left with the daunting prospect of saying goodbye to her two-year-old daughter who would never know her. She compiled a list of things she wanted to say to her daughter along with memories of what she had done in her life so that her daughter would have a sense of who she was. Fortunately, Juliet later found that she had been misdiagnosed but the emotional angst that she went through left its mark. As a result she wanted to help others who were faced with a terminal illness. She set up a service[4] so that those faced with a terminal illness could leave a record of their lives to be passed on after their death.

As Chapter 8 has discussed, all cultures once had Books of the Dead, which helped prepare the dying for their own deaths but also guided those not dying on how to live. Our rapid acceleration in technological breakthroughs has not been accompanied by a spiritual growth, which leaves our current society at a loss about how to understand and cope with death. We have no 'Book of the Dead' in our current society yet it is apparent that this is something that is much needed.

The spiritual aspects of our life have not caught up with our intellectual developments. We are therefore left with highly advanced technology in healthcare but are not equipped to deal with its legacy – the alienation of death. Death denial is not restricted to hospitals; it is within each of us. None of us wants our loved ones to die, but unfortunately it is a fact of life. It is something we are never prepared for yet it would help if we were. Even after studying death for so long, it didn't take away the hurt and sense of loss when my relatives have died but I did feel better prepared in the months leading up to their deaths.

That's why I believe this research is so important; the people I have spoken to, who have nearly died or have been clinically dead and subsequently reported an NDE, do not believe death to be a bad thing. It is only sad for those left behind. Through personal experience I know that when our loved ones die we are left with a big gaping open wound that can take years to heal – and for many never heals. Yet NDErs come back with a message of hope which can help to activate the healing process, which is why they are so helpful in grief therapy. As NDEr Jules Lyons remarked:

# Conclusion

*There truly is no such thing as 'death'. What many see as 'the end' is really just a change, like a change of clothes, or a change of vehicle, or a change of residence. I do wish I could take away all fear of death from people, as, if anything, what we call 'death' is actually a release and an immensely beautiful journey.*

*It's heartbreaking to hear people grieving for loved ones they feel have 'gone forever'. I wish I could help people know that the loved ones we have 'lost' are very much alive and, in fact, are much closer to us than we realize!*

As more people are successfully resuscitated and recover from severely life-threatening illnesses it is likely that there will be a corresponding increase in people who report NDEs. It is essential that we acknowledge these experiences and respond in a supportive manner, as opposed to dismissing them with the unproven assumption that they are hallucinations or the mere product of a dysfunctional brain. It is hoped that those who are trying to come to terms with and understand their NDE will be encouraged to seek people to discuss it with. Most importantly, I hope NDEs will be acknowledged by everyone, especially healthcare workers, and, despite their own ideas about what NDEs are, that they are sympathetic to people reporting an NDE and will be able to guide these patients to the resources which offer helpful, practical information.

The two deepest NDErs in my prospective study now have absolutely no fear of death and remain adamant that death is nothing to fear. This research, along with other prospective NDE research,[5] demonstrates that such people were reporting clear, lucid, conscious experiences during a time when their brains had ceased to function or were not functioning optimally. These are not anecdotal cases that can be explained away. These are thoroughly documented cases, with the backup of medical and nursing notes, along with the testimonies of the patients and members of staff present during the events. Further to that, the prospective research was highly consistent with anecdotal cases that have been previously reported in the literature.

To recap briefly, my research showed that NDEs can occur in all contexts but are more prevalent in conditions of cardiac arrest. This would suggest that the closer one comes to death the more likely one is to report an NDE. One patient reported an OBE where he accurately reported the actions of the doctor, nurse and physiotherapist during a time when he was deeply unconscious. In contrast, when the control group were asked to re-enact their resuscitation the majority didn't have a clue and the few who made guesses were inaccurate and demonstrated misconceptions in the procedure carried out and the equipment used. The NDE is an under-reported phenomenon: out of the 15 NDEs only two of the patients volunteered the information. Both of these NDEs were very deep and had sufficient impact on the patients to motivate them to tell others. The remaining 13 patients would not have discussed their NDE had I not asked specifically if they recalled anything during the time that they were unconscious. There were also three patients who reported an NDE but died very soon after. It may therefore be the case that patients undergo an NDE during the acute phase of their illness but do not recover sufficiently to report it before they die. The materialist theories were not supported by this research and, if anything, drugs appear to inhibit the NDE as opposed to create it. The aspects of meeting deceased relatives who they did not know to be dead at the time of their experience (patient 19), gaining information in ways other than through the senses (patient 11, patient 295) and the inexplicable spontaneous healing of a congenital abnormality (patient 10) cannot be explained by any of the physiological, psychological or cultural factors.

It is easy to see that when NDEs are taken at surface value so many people initially dismiss these experiences as hallucinations. However, when you consider the complexities of these experiences and engage with them and the people who report them, they become much more difficult to explain away. After the NDE, not only are there enormous psychological and sociological changes, but in some cases physiological changes in electrical field and spontaneous healings. After over 30 years of research into NDEs there is still no theory within the current scientific paradigm that adequately explains all aspects of the phenomenon. The fact that prospective hospital research is now showing that the proposed theories that NDEs are attributable to anoxia, hypercarbia or the drugs administered are not supported gives us no option other than to explore consciousness from a different angle.

It is unfortunate that the predominant mode of thought equates the mind with the brain. Although certain parts of the brain may be involved with experiencing the NDE it is regrettable that these correlations have been confused with causations.[6] From this perspective NDEs will never be adequately explained. However, if we consider the possibility that consciousness is primary, not the body, and that the brain mediates rather than creates consciousness, then there is a much better way to understand consciousness. Although NDEs and other anomalous experiences have been referred to as paranormal or supernatural, from this new perspective there would be nothing supernatural about these experiences and in fact they would be quite normal.

Prospective studies, coupled with the multitude of previous NDE studies, indicate that the premise that consciousness is a by-product of the brain is an outdated concept. Unfortunately, the belief that consciousness is created by the brain is so thoroughly ingrained within our current belief system that anything that suggests otherwise is immediately discounted or dismissed because it poses such a threat. This is summarized nicely by Chris Carter: 'Science cannot be an objective process of discovery if it is wedded to a metaphysical belief that is accepted without question and that leads to the exclusion of certain lines of evidence on the grounds that these lines of evidence contradict the metaphysical belief.'[7] However, I am not here to argue this point – instead I would like to concentrate on how we can benefit from a greater understanding of NDEs.

Chapter 9 mentioned how we can benefit from acknowledging and engaging with NDEs. They have been shown to be effective in the prevention of suicide and in grief therapy. Following an NDE, many people become more concerned with ecological issues, and conservation of the planet becomes very important to them. Many NDErs display altruistic behaviour as a result of their experience. Some of the most commonly reported after effects, such as feelings of compassion and love for others, are actually conducive to good health. The fact that some people report healing abilities and spontaneous healings which can't be easily dismissed have the potential of working for us all if only we understood the mechanism.

As long as NDEs are explained away or dismissed and discounted as aberrations of a disorganized brain then we will never have the opportunity to incorporate these abilities to our benefit. If these healing abilities were investigated scientifically and better understood it is possible that non-invasive healing techniques could be developed which would serve to complement conventional medicine and accelerate recovery from illness. By dismissing and ignoring these healing abilities we are denying the evolution of our healthcare and denying future generations the chance to enhance their health by acknowledging all aspects of health, not just the physical. Using the message of the NDE to our own advantage could potentially empower us so much that we would remain in good health for longer and the need to go to hospital would be greatly reduced. These are new concepts and many may consider them idealistic or unrealistic but, if we don't take notice and investigate them, we will never know.

Our science is amazing and has been very important in our development and in getting us to our current point in evolution. The scientific process is precise and rigorous; it advances through measuring things and replicating experiments. Without science we wouldn't be where we are today, none of the technology would exist and there would not have been the advances in healthcare that have increased our life expectancy. Unfortunately, science is concerned with the physical and anything that can't be measured is not considered to be real. Science advanced with a great disconnection of the mind from the body. However, there is one thing that can't be measured, which every human being would agree is real, and that is love.

Now this is the exciting thing for me. When I reflect on how we came to this worldview it is evident that throughout history science has changed and always advances to the next level once certain discoveries have been made.

Religion was once the dominant worldview, which was then superseded by the Scientific Revolution. Proponents of science such as Isaac Newton and Galileo advanced the belief that the universe was a giant clock and humans were reduced to being machines. All spiritual aspects of life were left to the domain of the Church, while science investigated the physical. It would appear that some of our advances in technology have been to the detriment of the spiritual nature inherent within us all. Spiritual aspects of life are not acknowledged and this neglect has resulted in the inability to understand crucial experiences at the root of the human psyche.

Many aspects of life considered to be scientific facts were later discovered to be incorrect. It was considered a 'scientific fact' that the earth was flat until c1500 AD; it was considered a 'scientific fact' that the earth was the centre of the universe until the fourth century. It is considered that consciousness is created by the brain, and it is only in the last few decades that this has been questioned. Now, many proponents in the field of NDEs and consciousness research, myself included, believe consciousness to be mediated through the brain but not created by it. However, this is a bold statement that opposes the current worldview, which is fiercely defended by those who believe consciousness to be created by the brain.

Another point I would like to leave you with is that science says that we are all made up of energy. Our science also says that energy can be neither created nor destroyed – so when our physical bodies die, what happens to that energy?

The simple fact is that science changes as it makes new discoveries through the scientific process, and things that we now take for granted were initially considered preposterous. Take, for example, the electric light bulb. Here are some quotes from when its invention was first announced:

- 'Good enough for our transatlantic friends ... but unworthy of the attention of practical or scientific men.' The British Parliamentary Committee, 1878.
- 'Such startling announcements as these should be deprecated as being unworthy of science and mischievous to its true progress.' William Siemens, 1880.[8]

With regards to healthcare the following statements now seem absolutely unbelievable:

- 'The abolishment of pain in surgery is a chimera. It is absurd to go on seeking it ... knife and pain are two words in surgery that must forever be associated in the consciousness of the patient.' Dr Alfred Velpeau, French surgeon, 1839.
- 'Louis Pasteur's theory of germs is ridiculous fiction.' Pierre Pachet, British surgeon and Professor of Physiology at Toulouse, 1872.
- 'The abdomen, the chest, and the brain will forever be shut from the intrusion of the wise and humane surgeon.' John Eric Ericksen, British surgeon, appointed surgeon extraordinary to Queen Victoria, 1873.[9]

NDEs have previously been considered unworthy of science but, now that these experiences are being seriously acknowledged and are a valid area for scientific study, it seems that we are on the threshold of expanding our current knowledge about the meaning of life and death. There is no denying that they occur, we simply can't explain them yet. This is no reason to disregard them. There is so much evidence out there to support the importance of embracing the spiritual in our lives and in healthcare, it's time that we paid attention and took advantage of this evidence to enhance our current healthcare systems.

NDEs certainly occur and have very powerful life-changing effects – not only on those who experience an NDE but those who become familiar with NDEs. Again, Jules Lyons:

*Having an NDE awakened and changed me in many ways. It also brought me full understanding that nobody is here on earth 'by accident', that we each have a purpose, something we came here to do in this lifetime, before we return 'home'.*

*When I look at the world, it seems that more and more, humans are living out their lives as if their sole purpose is to 'get', rather than concentrating on living their **soul** purpose . . . which is to **give**.*

It is ironic that the science that has led to the development of the technology that is resulting in more people surviving life-threatening illness – therefore increasing the number of people reporting NDEs and ELEs – still does not acknowledge these as valid experiences because there is no room to accommodate or understand spiritual aspects of life in the current scientific paradigm. However, that very science was of no use to the parents, grandparents and siblings of the two-year-old boy who tragically died on Christmas Day, it was of no use to the husband and sons of the woman who contracted a deadly virus while on holiday and died two days later, it was of no use to the man whose wife and life-partner of 65 years died after many weeks of illness, to mention just a tiny minority of tragic cases I have dealt with and which have stuck in my mind during the course of my career.

Science works so well because it can measure and weigh things and experiments can be replicated. This is not possible for spiritual aspects of life. Pathologist's can't perform a post mortem and discover the thoughts, feelings and memories of the person at a certain location within the body. We all have thoughts, feeling and memories, but just because we can't measure them doesn't mean they are not important to our everyday lives. There is no doubt in my mind that I am five foot and half an inch tall (that half inch is very important!). Science confirms this is true because it can measure it. There is no doubt in my mind that I love my husband very much but science has no way of measuring or confirming that. Yet no one can deny that love exists.

Previous investigations into NDEs have focused on establishing a materialist cause for the experience, which has served to detract from the very important spiritual insights that may be gained. It is time to stop concentrating solely on pathologizing these experiences and reflect on what they can actually teach us about living.

Unfortunately spirituality is often confused as being the same as religion – it is not. Someone can be spiritual without having a religion. Spiritual needs are inherent in us all. Whether we declare ourselves atheists or scientists with no belief in the spiritual we all have varying spiritual needs that give meaning to our lives no matter how much we try to deny them. In some cases it is only as death approaches that these spiritual needs become apparent. It is unfortunate that I have witnessed many patients undergo spiritual distress as they get closer to death: many fear what is happening to them and many fear leaving their loved ones or losing their material possessions. In some cases it is fear of the unknown or loss of control. Contemplating our spiritual needs while still alive may ensure that as our own death approaches we are content that we have done and said the things we wanted to and that nothing fearful awaits us.

Spiritual aspects of life help develop compassion for others and indeed this happens in a very profound way to most NDErs because they undergo a complete spiritual transformation. To have a meaningful life it is essential that both physical and spiritual aspects of life are balanced. In short, science and spirituality go hand in hand. One seeks validation whereas the other seeks understanding, both being crucial to human experience. Yet our science has ignored the spiritual, resulting in the majority of people living in a highly unbalanced world. Research into altruism, love, compassion and gratitude (all qualities of the NDE) shows that these are all conducive to good health and our continuing evolution.

An NDE is an accelerated spiritual transformation – these people have literally encountered death in a totally unexpected and sudden way. It has taken something to shake the foundations of their being and to experience life in ways other than what they have been conditioned to believe. We too can learn from their spiritual insights through our own spiritual development. The spiritual transformation resulting from the NDE instils qualities that are highly conducive to the evolution of our species and the planet as a whole. We are continuously evolving. When things are considered from a global perspective, spiritual development will lead to a reconsideration of how we live alongside our fellow humans, animals and plants in the world and result in a balance which is necessary for our survival as a planet.

We have been conditioned to believe that death is a terrible, sad and fearful thing. However, the majority of NDErs who have experienced a temporary death report a wonderful, peaceful experience. Being mindful of the way in which we live our lives can result in the peace and harmony that we all crave. We spend so much time reminiscing about the past or looking forward to future events that we forget about living in the moment. It is time to embrace the spiritual, along with science, and regain the equilibrium so that we can lead fulfilled lives and, most importantly, live in the moment because yesterday is history and tomorrow may never come.

We can also be mindful of the way in which we live our lives by listening to NDErs. Many talk about their NDE with great reluctance due to concerns that they will be disbelieved or fears that they will be thought mentally unstable. Yet the insights that they have gained have much to teach us. Don't ignore death, think about it. Think about how you would feel if you were diagnosed with a terminal illness, what if this was the last day or week of your life – would you be doing something different right now? Be mindful of the way you live your life and don't take things for granted. Living in the present is what mindfulness ultimately leads to.

From the number of people who have contacted me over the years it is obvious that these experiences that surround death and dying are common. In fact, I would guess that most readers have experienced or know someone who has experienced some of these phenomena – they just don't talk about it. One thing that was particularly apparent during the course of writing this book was how grateful the people whose experiences have featured in this book have all been that their experience has been acknowledged and not discredited. To reach the full extent of the NDEs featured, in some cases, took months (up to ten years in a few cases) and several meetings, emails or phone conversations for the people to disclose all aspects, because they were so cautious. They are certainly not attention seekers; as you can see, many NDErs have chosen to remain anonymous. In fact, whenever journalists contact me asking for NDErs to appear on TV or radio there is usually a resounding 'no' in response from most of the NDErs. These people have undergone a life-changing experience which seems so implausible that some are literally terrified of talking about it with anyone else. It's time to acknowledge that NDEs are a very valid phenomenon and to treat people who have an NDE with the respect that they deserve.

Many NDErs are profoundly illuminated during their NDE and become aware of the implications of their thoughts and actions, thus radically changing their behaviour following the experience. It fills me with hope to think that if such practices were adopted by an increasing number of the population the world would become a better place. Previous research has shown that becoming familiar with NDEs can have life-enhancing qualities and people who have not had an NDE also reported the same positive changes as NDErs, though to a lesser extent. Imagine if everyone had an NDE and was as profoundly affected as those I have mentioned throughout this book. Imagine if everyone changed their perspective on life and saw each other as interconnected and valuable people, all part of the same underlying consciousness. What if everyone put the needs of others before their own needs? How radically transformed the whole world would be.

Christine Stewart (whose NDE is described in Chapter 3):

*My belief is that if everyone had an NDE there would never be another war, no one would starve or be the victim of violence and greed would become a thing of the past.*

Jules Lyons:

*I often think that if every single person on earth had an NDE tonight, and ventured to the world beyond, then tomorrow morning, we would all wake up to the dawn of a very different world here on earth.*

During the NDE there is an overwhelming understanding that everything is interconnected. Coupled with the message from the life review, this points to the notion that what we do to others we ultimately do to ourselves. This resonates with the 'golden rule' which is at the heart of each religion and spiritual tradition: 'Do unto others as you would have done unto you.' This is not some airy-fairy new-age slogan – it is a deep spiritual truth which if we all heeded and understood would result in respect, love and peace. NDErs show us that living consciously not only prepares us for our own death, it also has the dual effect of respecting each other and giving meaning to our lives. Whether we take on board their insights, of course, is entirely our individual choice. What will you choose?

# Epilogue

*The most important thing in life is to learn how to give out love, and to let it come in.*

Morrie Schwartz[1]

Oh no ... I heard my colleague call for help, then the unmistakable sound of the cardiac arrest buzzer pierced my ears. I stopped what I was doing and looked around, I was the only one at my end of ITU in a position to go and assist. I asked my colleague to keep an eye on my patient and slowly walked to the bed area where the screens had been frantically pulled around. There were several members of staff already attending to the emaciated patient who was at the end of her life. One had deflated the air mattress of the bed, the newly qualified nurse had begun CPR, one was attending to the airway, one got the defibrillator and one administered the drugs – a perfectly orchestrated sequence of events with each team member carrying out their specific role with great skill and efficiency. The scenario continued for a further half an hour, now a very fast irregular heartbeat registered on the cardiac monitor but no cardiac output; it was highly unlikely that the lady would survive.

I tried to locate her body underneath the defibrillator leads and empty boxes of resuscitation drugs; I couldn't even see her hand, let alone hold it, so I spoke to her in my mind reassuringly, hoping it helped in some small way. The young nurse and doctor took turns to do chest compressions (after a few minutes it gets very tiring). I stayed in the background; there were so many people present that I didn't have to participate in pounding on the chest of the frail 86-year-old lady. I didn't have to feel the crunch of broken ribs under my hands as I pushed down on her chest. I didn't have to see the vomit rolling from the sides of her mouth, feel the cold, clammy, paper-thin skin or see the vacant look in her eyes that just stared into space as her body moved up and down on the bed underneath the hands of the medical team. The nurse briefly disconnected the tube to the ventilator to suction the secretions coming up from her lungs and the team were sprayed with a mixture of blood and mucous, which then slid down her face into her already vomit-soaked hair. I quietly slipped outside the curtains and walked away unnoticed, thankful that I wasn't needed . . .

'Ok, we've been 40 minutes now. I think it's time to stop, do you all agree?' On hearing the words of the doctor, everyone stopped what they were doing. The erratic wide complex rhythm of the heart that was now registering on the cardiac monitor slowed down as soon as the CPR was discontinued. No cardiac output registered. The heart rhythm changed to a flat line: asystole. The nurse turned the cardiac monitor off and the doctor certified the body and turned off the ventilator. The team removed their plastic aprons and gloves, washed their hands and left the bedside, leaving the nurse to clean up the carnage before the family were told the sad news and brought in to see their dearly loved mum, grandmother and sister for the last time.

This is based on a resuscitation that I recently witnessed. Two days previously the lady's breathing had deteriorated on the ward so she had been transferred to the HDU for further management. I was the admitting nurse and the plan was to treat the lady with non-invasive oxygen therapy. She was very frail and frightened on arrival and was gasping for breath through her oxygen mask so could not speak. About an hour after treatment had commenced her breathing began to improve and she was able to speak in short sentences. After another two hours her oxygen requirements had reduced and she was able to talk. She had expressed a wish to die; she lived alone and her husband had died the year before and she just wanted to be with him. Although she loved her family and was grateful for all that they were doing for her, she was becoming more debilitated and knew she was ready to die – she didn't want to be in hospital. I tried to reassure her that with a few more hours of oxygen therapy she would feel a lot better and might even be able to go back to the ward the following day. Unfortunately her condition deteriorated during the night and she became unconscious and required intubation and ventilation.

Over the years my views have changed a lot and things that I once considered to be heroic now seem barbaric. Sometimes there is a fine line between being admitted to a hospice or ITU. When I was a student nurse there were few patients who were considered appropriate admission for ITU due to their poor prognosis. Over 21 years later there are very few patients who are *not* referred to ITU. What I have been trying to do with my research is to ensure that future patients don't have to undergo indignities at the end of their life when they are clearly not going to survive their illness, especially if it is against their wishes. However, that is a huge task as it would involve a change of mass consciousness, not just my own.

It is reassuring to know that in my study over 80 per cent of the patients who were successfully resuscitated had no recollection of their resuscitation. Of those who did have memories of their resuscitation the majority recalled an NDE that was very peaceful and comforting. None of the patients recalled any pain during the time of their resuscitation, but a few reported a sore chest after regaining consciousness. Of the minority of patients who reported a distressing NDE during their resuscitation, I hope that the information in this book and other resources will help healthcare workers to recognize these as well as the pleasant experiences and their associated complexities so that these patients are better supported psychologically and spiritually throughout their recovery.

Had it not been for that encounter with the dying patient described at the beginning of this book, I would probably be living my life in a totally unconscious way and be happy to go along with the mass consciousness. I'm sure many of you have never considered these issues – they seem irrelevant when you're young, fit and healthy. But what if one day, like many patients I have nursed, you leave your house in the morning to go to work but never get there? What if the bus you are travelling on or the car you are driving is involved in an accident or you are run over as you cross the road? Would you be satisfied that your life had been well lived? Would there still be things that you would have liked to have done? Are there things that you still want to say or do? Don't leave these things left undone until the time of your death – the most important thing the patients have taught me is *to live my life now*. So many times I have witnessed relatives tell their loved ones that when they get better they will all go away on holiday; very often these promises are unfulfilled as the patient does not recover. We are so busy striving to get the things we don't have that we fail to see the very things we do have. Of all of the thousands of patients I have nursed to their death I have never heard one of them say on their deathbed that they wished they had worked longer hours.

My life has changed drastically since the encounter with the patient I mentioned in the introduction – it forced me to 'go within'. Consequently I became obsessed with finding out more about death and once I read about NDEs there was no turning back as I was compelled to learn more. My original scepticism – which I once believed to be rational – I now view as irrational, because at the time I was judging NDEs from a pre-conceived perspective and did not have an open mind to other possibilities and no in-depth knowledge of them. It is only since I was forced to look at the wider picture and think outside the box by fully engaging with the range of complexities associated with NDEs that I realized my previous explanations were wrong and misconceived – I had fallen into the trap of being dragged along by mass consciousness.

Once I'd worked through the awful depression that I went through after I looked after the dying patient I described in the introduction, I found something positive I could do for others. As a result my whole world seemed different; my values were a total contrast to what they had been. Whereas I'd always been quite ambitious, with the intention of becoming a nursing sister, all of a sudden those things didn't matter in the least to me. I undertook my PhD not for a qualification but as a means to learn more about death, dying and NDEs. When I first discussed undertaking this research with Professor Paul Badham I twice turned down the offer of a PhD. In fact, after I had achieved my PhD I continued to work as a Band 5 staff nurse (the lowest pay scale for qualified nurses) because to me it was more important to be with the patients – status and earning vast sums of money have absolutely no allure for me any more. Engaging with and studying NDEs has given my life meaning and taught me much about living; it has enriched my life, which is something I will always be grateful for. If everyone who reads this book is as 'infected' by this fascinating phenomenon as I have been and is as happy as I feel as a result of my research then the world could be a better place. It gives me hope to think that the whole world could be one of peace, love and respect for others.

It would be nice to think that as death approaches we will all experience feelings of peace, joy and unconditional love. However, these are only experienced in the time leading up to death – we won't know what happens *after* we die until we experience it fully at our own death. The most we can hope for at our death is a life well lived. In my lectures I often get asked if NDErs have really been to heaven. One thing I've come to realize over the past few years is that heaven is not a location – it is a state of mind and is within us all. We just have to go within and find it. I really hope this book will inspire every reader to embark on their own investigation into this mysterious thing we call death and in turn be as fulfilled, enriched and happy as I am, and then we can all experience heaven while here on earth.

# Notes

## Introduction

1 Morrie Schwartz in Albom, M. 2003, pp. 81, 83.
2 Sartori, P. 2008.

## Chapter 1

1 Dossey, L. 2011, p. 62.
2 Nahm, M. 2009a.
3 Zaleski, C. 1987.
4 Evans-Wenz, W. Y. 1960.
5 Drolma, D. 1995; Cuevas, B. J. 2003, 2008.
6 Sabom, M. 1982, 1998.
7 Morse et al 1989, Morse, M. 1990.
8 Holden, J. 1988, 1989.
9 Lawrence, M. 1995, 1998.
10 Rawlings, M. 1979, 1993.
11 Van Lommel et al 2001.
12 Schwaninger et al 2002.
13 Greyson, B. 2003.
14 Parnia et al 2001.
15 Moorjani, A. 2012.
16 Alexander, E. 2013.
17 Ring, K. and Cooper, S. 1999.
18 Kellehear, A. 1993.
19 Ring, K. 1980, p. 67.
20 Hampe, J. 1979, pp. 65–91; Greyson, B. 1993, pp. 390–9; Lundahl, C. R. 1993, pp. 63–76; Amatuzio, J. 2004, p. 186; Atwater, P. M. H. 1999, p. 64.
21 Atwater, P. M. H. 1999, p. 64.

22  Bush, N. E. 1994; Ellwood, G. F. 2001; Grey, M. 1987; Greyson, B. and Bush, N. 1992; Rawlings, M. 1979, 1993; Rommer, B. 2000; Storm, H. 2000; Rominger, R. A. 2009.

23  Sartori, P. 2008, p. 365.

24  Zaleski, C. 1987.

25  Jakobsen, M. D. 1999.

26  Rawlings, M. 1979, 1993.

27  Grey, M. 1987, p. 72.

28  Greyson, B. and Bush, N. 1992.

29  Rommer, B. 2000, pp. 87–96.

30  Parnia, S., comment made at Consciousness Research Group Meeting, Fetzer Institute, Kalamazoo, Michigan, 2007.

31  Ring, K. 1994.

32  Greyson, B. and Bush, N. 1992, p. 100; Ring, K. 1984, p. 8; Storm, H. 2000, pp. 29–30; Bonenfant, R. J. 2004.

33  Bonenfant, R. J. 2004.

34  http://www.drrajivparti.us/my-near-death-experience.

35  Zaleski, C. 1987, pp. 45–52.

36  Rommer, B. 2000, pp. 97–193.

37  Grey, M. 1987, p. 110.

38  Bush, N. 2012.

39  Bache, C. 2000, pp. 95–124.

40  Rosen, D. H. 1975, pp. 289–94; Ring, K. 1980, pp. 118–24, 199; Fenwick, P. and Fenwick, E. 1996, pp. 280–3.

41  Garfield, C. cited in Lundahl, C. R. 1982.

42  Lindley, J., Bryan, S. and Conley, B. 1981.

43  Grey, M. 1987, p. 72.

44  Atwater, P. M. H. 1992.

45  Rommer, B. 2000, pp. 24–5.

## Chapter 2

1  Interview broadcast on ABC News, 23 March 2011, see http://abcnews.go.com/WNT/Video/elizabeth-taylor-death-experience-13201786.

2  Atwater, P. M. H. 1988; Dougherty, C. M. 1990; Greyson, B. 1992, 1992–93, 1996, 1997; Greyson, B. and Bush, N. 1992; Groth-Marnat, G. and Summers, R. 1998; Kellehear, A. 1990; Musgrave, C. 1997; White, P. R. 1997.

3   Grosso, M. 1981.
4   Bush, N. 1991; Christian, S. R. 2006; Stout et al 2006, p. 56.
5   Stout et al 2006.
6   Stout et al 2006.
7   Wren-Lewis, J. 2004.
8   Christian, S. R. 2006.
9   Kircher, P. 1995; Atwater, P. M. H. 1999.
10  Van Lommel, P. 2010; Morris, L. and Knafl, K. 2003.
11  Fracasso, C., Friedman, H. and Young, M. 2010, p. 275.
12  Atwater, P. M. H. 1999, p. 41.
13  Kircher, P. 1995, pp. 16, 21.
14  Storm, H. 2000.
15  Van Lommel, P. 2010.
16  Matthews, C. 2009.
17  Atwater, P. M. H. 1994; Morse, M. and Perry, P. 1993; Ring, K. 1992; Ring, K. and Valarino, E. 1998.
18  Nouri, F. M. and Holden, J. 2008.
19  Ken Ebert's website has full details of his book. The first three chapters are available to read on his website, www.kenebert.com.
20  Kason, Y. 2000, p. 112.
21  Sutherland, C. 1992, 1995a.
22  Morse, M. and Perry, P. 1993, pp. 142–144. See also the case of Janet, pp. 138–9.
23  Dossey, L. 2011.

## Chapter 3

1   Bush, N. E. 1983; Sutherland, C. 1995a, p. 11.
2   Bush, N. E. 1983; Serdahely, W. 1991.
3   Morse et al 1985, 1986; Morse, M. and Perry, P. 1990.
4   Morse, M. and Perry, P. 1990; Sutherland, C. 1995a, pp. 11, 186.
5   Atwater, P. M. H. 1999, p. 42.
6   Atwater, P. M. H. 1999. p. 43.
7   Morse, M. and Perry, P. 1990.
8   Lerma, J. 2009, pp. 189–220.
9   Bush, N. E. 1993; Sutherland, C. 1995a.
10  Sutherland, C. 1995a, p. 11.
11  Atwater, P. M. H. 1999, p. 63.

12  Morse et al 1985, 1986.
13  Atwater, P. M. H. 1999, p. 64; Sutherland, C. 1995a, pp. 27–30.
14  Serdahely, W. 1990.
15  Sutherland, C. 1995a, p. 188.
16  Stout et al 2006.
17  Sutherland, C. 1995a, p. 13.
18  Herzog, D. and Herrin, J. 1985.
19  Atwater, P. M. H. 1999.
20  Sutherland, C. 1995a, p. 20.
21  Atwater, P. M. H. 1999, p. 81.
22  Atwater, P. M. H. 1999, p. 65.
23  Sutherland, C. 1995a.
24  Atwater, P. M. H. 1999, p. 109.
25  Atwater, P. M. H. 1999, p. 93.
26  Morse, M. and Perry, P. 2000, pp. 2, 12.
27  Atwater, P. M. H. 1999, p. 108.
28  Sutherland, C. 1995a, p. 38.
29  Atwater, P. M. H. 1999, p. 116.
30  Hoffman, E. 1992, pp. 47, 69, 99, 133.
31  Atwater, P. M. H. 1999, pp. 68–128.
32  Atwater, P. M. H. 1999, p. 113.
33  Atwater, P. M. H. 1999, p. 118.

# Chapter 4

1  Gallup, G. and Proctor, W. 1984, p. 12.
2  Perera et al 2005.
3  Knoblauch et al 2001.
4  Thrum, T. 1907; Pommaret, F. 1989; Kellehear, A. 2001.
5  Drolma, D. 1995; Kellehear, A. 2001.
6  Murphy, T. 2001.
7  Zaleski, C. 1987.
8  Osis, K. and Haraldsson, E. 1977.
9  Pasricha, S. and Stevenson, I. 1986.
10  Pasricha, S. 2008.
11  Murphy, T. 2001.
12  Murphy, T. 2001, p. 173.

# Notes

13 Pommaret, F. 1989; Epstein, L. 1982; Carr, C. 1993; Sogyal, R. 1995; Drolma, D. 1995; Bailey, L. 2001; David-Neel, A. 1997; Cuevas, B. J. 2008.

14 Morse, M. and Perry, P. 1993, p. 127; Tachibana, T. 1994.

15 Iwasaka, M. and Toelken, B. 1994, p. xv; Yanagita, K. 1975, pp. 68–9.

16 Corazza, O. 2008.

17 Hadfield, P. 1991.

18 Becker, C. 1981.

19 Becker, C. 1984.

20 Vaughan, L. 1920, pp. 42–6.

21 Gomez-Jeria, J. S. 2006.

22 Zhi-ying, F. and Jian-xun, L. 1992.

23 Warner, L. 1937; Berndt, R. and Berndt, C. 1989 cited in Kellehear, A. 2008.

24 King, M. 1985; Kellehear, A. 2008.

25 Green, J. T. 1984.

26 Counts, D. 1983.

27 In Morse, M. and Perry, P. 1993, pp. 120–4.

28 McClenon, J. 2006.

29 Bockie, S. 1993 in McClenon 2006, pp. 25–8.

30 Keable, R. 1921 in McClenon 2006, pp. 30–2.

31 Hallowell, A. I. 1967/1940; Barrett, S. M. 1970/1906; Schoolcraft, H. R. 1975/1825; Barbour, P. L. 1983; Kalweit, H. 1988 cited in Wade 2003.

32 Talayesva, D. 1942 cited in Green, J. T. 2008.

33 Neihardt, J. G. 1932/1995.

34 Wade, J. 2003.

35 Thrum, T. 1907 cited in Kellehear, A. 2001.

36 Gomez-Jeria, J. S. 1993.

37 Kreps, J. I. 2009.

38 Nahm, M. and Nicolay, J. 2010; Fracasso et al 2010a.

39 Nahm, M. and Nicolay, J. 2010, p. 258.

40 Nahm, M. and Nicolay, J. 2010, p. 257.

41 Blackmore, S. 1993a.

42 Kellehear, A. 1993.

43 Jung, C. G. 1996/1959.

# Chapter 5

1   Gurney, E., Myers, F. W. H. and Podmore, F. 1886.

2   Osis, K. and Haraldsson, E. 1977.

3   Cooke, A. 1968; Hoffman, E. 1992; Lerma, J. 2009.

4   Morse, M. and Perry, P. 1994; Brayne, S. 2010; Fenwick, P. and Fenwick, E. 2008.

5   Brayne et al 2006; Brayne et al 2008; Fenwick et al 2009.

6   Brayne et al 2006, pp. 4, 5.

7   Callanan, M. and Kelley, P. 1992, pp. 11–27; Sanders, M. A. 2007, pp. 24–35.

8   Fenwick et al 2009, p. 6.

9   Brayne et al 2006, p. 7.

10  Brayne et al 2006; Brayne et al 2008; Fenwick et al 2009.

11  Brayne et al 2008.

12  Brayne, S. and Fenwick, P. 2008.

13  Alvarado, C. 2006a, 2006b.

14  Osis, K. and Haraldsson, E. 1977; Nahm, M. 2009b; Nahm, M. and Greyson, B. 2009; Moody, R. A. and Perry, P. 2010.

15  Swaddling, M. 2006.

16  Kircher, P. 1995, p. 140; Fenwick, P. and Fenwick, E. 1996a; Howarth, G. and Kellehear, A. 2001; Kason, Y. 2000; Moody, R. A. 1999; Moody, R. A. and Perry, P. 2010; Van Lommel, P. 2010.

17  Kason, Y. 2000, p. 86.

18  Osis, K. and Haraldsson, E. 1977; Kircher, P. 1995, p. 71; Nahm, M. and Greyson, B. 2009; Nahm, M. 2009b; Moody, R. A. and Perry, P. 2010, pp. 15, 29.

19  Nahm, M. 2009b.

20  Kircher, P. 1995, p. 139.

21  Lerma, J. 2009, p. 101.

22  Lerma, J. 2009, p. 163.

23  Kircher, P. M. 1995, p. 140.

24  Guggenheim, B. and Guggenheim, J. 1996; Devers, E. 1997; LaGrand, L. E. 1997; Houck, J. A. 2005.

25  Rees, W. D. 1971.

26  Moody, R. 1992, 1993.

27  Botkin, A. L. 2000; Botkin, A. L. and Hogan, R. C. 2005.

28  Rees, W. D. 1971.

29  Kircher, P. 1995; Betty, L. S. 2006.
30  Fenwick et al 2009; Van Lommel, P. 2010.
31  Aries, P. 1981.

# Chapter 6

1  Planck, M. 1948.
2  Henderson, Y. and Haggard, H. W. 1927; McFarland, R. A. 1932; Whinnery, J. 1990, 1997.
3  Christensen at al 1990; Marshall et al 2001.
4  Van Lommel, P. 2004b.
5  Whinnery, J. 1997.
6  Fenwick, E. and Fenwick, P. 1996a, p. 309.
7  Blackmore, S. 1993, pp. 67–93; Woerlee, G. 2003, 2004, pp. 207–15.
8  Woerlee, G. 2004, pp. 207–15.
9  Kellehear, A. 1993.
10  Meduna, C. 1950.
11  Grof, S. and Halifax, J. 1977; Masters, R. and Houston, J. 2000/1966; Saunders et al 2000; Jansen, K. 2001.
12  Masters, R. and Houston, J. 2000/1966, p. 127.
13  Corazza, O. 2008.
14  Greyson, B. 1983a.
15  Strassman, R. 2001.
16  Strassman, R. 2001, pp. 224–5.
17  Eadie, B. 1992.
18  Brinkley, D. and Perry, P. 1994.
19  Sotelo et al 1995.
20  Kellehear, A. 1996.
21  Jansen, K. 1997a; Fenwick, P. and Fenwick, E. 1996a, pp. 315–17.
22  Oyama et al 1980.
23  Oyama et al 1980; Halifax, J. in Varela, F. J. 1997, p. 201.
24  Fenwick, P. and Fenwick, E. 1996a, pp. 315–17.
25  D'Aquili, E. and Newberg, A. 1999; Marsh, M. 2010, pp. 170–86.
26  Chalmers, D. 1995.
27  Badham, P. and Badham, L. 1984.
28  Mitchell, E. D. 1974; Morris et al 1978; Osis, K. 1972; Rogo, S. 1978.
29  Tart, C. 1968, 1998; Mitchell, E. D. 1974.
30  Osis, K. 1972.

31 Lukianowicz, N. 1958.

32 Gabbard, G. O. and Twemlow, S. W. 1984.

33 Lhermitte, J. 1939, 1951; Damas Mora et al 1980.

34 Dewhurst, K. and Beard, A. W. 1970; Gloor et al 1982; Devinsky et al 1989; Saver, J. L. and Rabin, J. 1997.

35 Devinsky et al 1989.

36 Ruttan, L. and Persinger, M. A. 1990; Healy, F. and Persinger, M. A. 1996; Persinger, M. A. 2003.

37 Adams, J. and Rutkin, B. 1970.

38 Rodin, E. 1989.

39 Fenwick, P. 1997.

40 Persinger, M. A. and Healey, F. 2002.

41 Granqvist et al 2004; for a more expanded critique of this research, see Beauregard, M. and O'Leary, D. 2007.

42 Penfield, W. 1955, 1975; Penfield, W. and Perrot, P. 1963; Gloor et al 1982; Blanke et al 2002, 2004.

43 Penfield, W. 1955, 1975; Penfield, W. and Perrot, P. 1963; Gloor et al 1982.

44 Blanke et al 2002, 2004.

45 Holden, J., Long, J. and McClurg, J. 2006.

46 Blanke et al 2002.

47 Clark, K. 1984; Sabom, M. 1982, 1998; Cook, E., Greyson, B. and Stevenson, I. 1998; Kelly, E., Greyson, B. and Stevenson, I. 1999–2000; van Lommel et al 2001; Sartori, P., Badham, P. and Fenwick, P. 2006; Sartori, P. 2008.

48 Holden, J. 1998, 1989; Holden, J. and Joesten, L. 1990; Lawrence, M. 1995, 1998.

49 Parnia et al 2001.

50 Sartori, P., Badham, P. and Fenwick, P. 2006, Sartori, P. 2008.

51 The AWARE (AWAreness during REsuscitation) study is the first launched by the Human Consciousness Project, a multidisciplinary collaboration of international scientists and physicians who have joined forces to study the relationship between mind and brain during clinical death.

52 Mavromatis, A. 1987.

53 Muldoon, S. 1965; Green, C. 1967, 1968; Muldoon, S. and Carrington, H. 1974; Monroe, R. 1974.

54 Gabbard, G. O. and Twemlow, S. W. 1984.

55 Tart, C. 1968; Twemlow, S. W. 1977.
56 Nelson et al 2006; Nelson et al 2007.
57 Long, J. and Holden, J. 2007.
58 Nelson et al 2006.
59 Butler, R. N. 1963.
60 Olson, M. and Dulaney, P. 1993.
61 Heim, A. 1892.
62 Stevenson, I. and Cook, E. 1995.
63 Spiegel, D. and Cardena, E. 1991.
64 Putnam, F. W. 1991.
65 Spencer, M. 1996, p. 152.
66 Greyson, B. 2000.
67 Gabbard, G. O. and Twemlow, S. W. 1984, pp. 46–7.
68 Noyes, R. and Slymen, D. 1979, p. 319.
69 Gabbard, G. O. and Twemlow, S. W. 1984, pp. 56–8.
70 Noyes, R. and Kletti, R. 1977.
71 Woodrow, P. 2000; Milner, Q. J. and Gunning, K. E. 2000; Shelly, M. P. 1993; Mundigler et al 2002; McInroy, A. and Edwards, S. 2002; Christensen, A. J. 2002.
72 Roberts, B. and Chaboyer, W. 2004; Sartori, P. 2008, pp. 465–501.
73 Augustine, K. 2007a, 2007b, 2007c.
74 Augustine, K. 2007, p. 91.
75 Greyson, B. 2007, p. 130.
76 Athapilly, G. K., Greyson, B. and Stevenson, I. 2006; Long, J. and Long, J. 2003.

# Chapter 7

1 Sartori, P. 2008.
2 Holden, J. 1988, 1989; Holden, J. and Joesten, L. 1990.
3 Lawrence, M. 1995, 1998.
4 Sartori, P., Badham, P. and Fenwick, P. 2006.
5 Gurney, E., Myers, F. W. H. and Podmore, F. 1886; Morse, M. and Perry, P. 1994; Moody, R. and Perry, P. 2010.
6 Lukianowicz, N. 1958.
7 Sabom, M. 1982.
8 Blackmore, S. 1993, pp. 119–20.
9 Ring, K. 1984, p. 42.

10  Osis, K. and Haraldsson, E. 1977; Ring, K. 1980, pp. 211–12; Sabom, M. 1982; Grey, M. 1987, pp. 90, 175; Greyson, B. 1982, 2000b; Atwater, P. M. H. 1994; Rommer, R. A. 2000, p. 22; Greyson, B., Holden, J. and Mounsey, J. P. 2006, p. 95.
11  Sartori, P. 2008.
12  Greyson, B. 2007.
13  Oyama et al 1980.
14  Ehrenwald, J. 1974, 1978; Noyes, R. and Kletti, R. 1976; Noyes et al 1977; Owens, J., Cook, E. and Stevenson, I. 1990.
15  Van Lommel et al 2001; Schwaninger et al 2002.
16  Van Lommel et al 2001; Parnia et al 2001; Greyson, B. 2003; Schwaninger et al 2002.
17  This section is only a very brief summary of the main aspects of the work that I carried out and it does not adequately convey the full extent of what the research entailed. For more information see the study, which has been published in its entirety.

# Chapter 8

1   Grof, S. 1994.
2   Wallis Budge, E. A. 2008.
3   Evans Wenz, W. Y. 1960.
4   Christensen, A. J. 2003.
5   Aries, P. 1981, 1994.
6   Sogyal, R. 1995, p. 7.
7   Ballard, P. 1996, pp. 7–28.
8   Kessler, D. 1997, pp. 152–62.
9   Longaker, C. 1997, pp. 45–59; Van Lommel, P. 2010, p. 354.
10  Grof, S. 1994, p. 7.

# Chapter 9

1   Kellman, R. 2004, p. 50.
2   Funning, B. 2010.
3   Sartori, P. 2010a, 2010b.
4   Morris, L. and Knafl, K. 2003.
5   Lipton, B. 2005; Hamilton, D. 2008.
6   Lipton, B. 2005; Hamilton, D. 2008.

Notes

7   Hamilton, D. 2008.
8   Fracasso, C., Friedman, H. and Young, M. S. 2010, p. 279.
9   Fracasso, C., Friedman, H. and Young, M. S. 2010, p. 275.
10  Moore, L. H. 1994.
11  Kason, Y. 2000, pp. 73–4.
12  Orne, R. M. 1986.
13  Bucher et al 1997; Hayes, E. R. and Orne, R. M. 1990.
14  Morris, L. and Knafl, K. 2003.
15  Ring, K. 1995; Rominger, R. A. 2009.
16  Sheeler, R. D. 2005.
17  Van Lommel, P. 2010, p. 45.
18  Morris, L. and Knafl, K. 2003, p. 164; Sartori, P. 2008, pp. 294–6.
19  Morris, L. and Knafl, K. 2003, p. 154.
20  LaGrand, L. E. 2005.
21  Morris, L. and Knafl, K. 2003, p. 165.
22  Morris, L. and Knafl, K. 2003.
23  Storm, H. 2000; Bonenfant, R. J. 2004.
24  Stout et al 2006.
25  Osis, K. and Haraldsson, E. 1977; Grey, M. 1987, pp. 90, 175; Greyson, B. 1982, 2000b; Atwater, P. M. H. 1994; Morse, M. and Perry, P. 1993, p. 19; Ring, K. 1980, pp. 211–12, 1995; Rommer, B. 2000, p. 22; Greyson, B., Holden, J. and Mounsey, J. P. 2006, p. 95.
26  Kason, Y. 2000 pp. 60–1.
27  Arslanian-Engoren, C. and Scott, L. D. 2003.
28  Longaker, C. 1997, p. 19.
29  Rommer, B. 2000 p. 172.
30  Lerma, J. 2009, p. 216.
31  Kircher, P. 1995, p. 130.
32  Finlay, I. 1996, p. 78.
33  Kircher, P. 1995, p. 134.
34  Schenk, P. 2006; Winkler, E. 1996, 2003.
35  Greyson, B. 1981, 1984, 1992–93.
36  McDonagh, J. M. 1979, 2004.
37  Kelly et al 2007.
38  Kircher, P. 1995, p. 127.
39  Greyson, B. 1984; Kason, Y. 2000, pp. 74–6.
40  McDonagh, J. M. 1979, 2004.
41  Winkler, E. 1996.

42  LaGrand, L. E. 2005.
43  Botkin, A. L. 2000; Botkin, A. L. with Hogan, R. C. 2005.
44  Ring, K. and Valarino, E. 1998, pp. 200–15.
45  Ring, K. 1992; Ring, K. and Valarino, E. 1998, p. 202.
46  Ring, K. and Valarino, E. 1998, p. 208.
47  Greyson, B. 1983b.
48  Flynn, C. 1986, pp. 120–49.
49  Morse, M. and Perry, P. 2000, pp. 2, 12.
50  Schwaninger et al 2002.
51  Morris, L. and Knafl, K. 2003.
52  Grossman, N. 2010, p. 225.
53  Rominger, R. A. 2009, p. 21.
54  *I AM* 2011, Flying Eye Productions, directed by Tom Shadyac.
55  *I AM* 2011, Flying Eye Productions, directed by Tom Shadyac.
56  Einstein, A., Podolsky, B. and Rosen, N. 1935, pp. 777–80.
57  McClelland, D. C. and Kirshnit, C. 1988; Rein, G., McCraty, R. M. and Atkinson, M. 1995.
58  Pelletier, K. R. 1994.
59  Ornstein, R. and Sobel, D. 1987.
60  Luks, A. 1991.
61  Hamilton, D. 2010.
62  Maslow, A. 1964.
63  Maslow, A. 1954; Hood, R. 1976, 1979; Hay, D. 1982.
64  Hardy, A. 1979.
65  Nataraja, S. 2008.
66  Lovelock, J. 1995.

## Chapter 10

1  Flynn, C. 1986, p. 7.
2  Hampe, J. 1979, p. 24.
3  Sartori, P. 2010a, 2010b, 2010c.
4  www.infinipartners.com.
5  Sabom, M. 1998; Parnia et al 2001; van Lommel et al 2001; Schwaninger et al 2002; Greyson, B. 2003.
6  Marsh, M. 2010; Nelson et al 2006, 2007.
7  Carter, C. 2010 p. 237.
8  http://en.wikiquote.org/wiki/Incorrect_predictions#Light_bulb.

9   http://en.wikiquote.org/wiki/Incorrect_predictions#Light_bulb.

# Epilogue

1   Morrie Schwartz in Albom, M. 2003, p. 52.

# References

Adams, J. and Rutkin, B. (1970). 'Visual Responses to Subcortical Stimulation in the Visual and Limbic System'. *Confinia Neurologica*, vol. 32, pp. 158–64.

Albom, M. (2003). *Tuesdays with Morrie*. London: Time Warner Paperbacks. First published 1997.

Alexander, E. (2013). *Proof of Heaven: A Neurosurgeon's Journey into the Afterlife*. London: Piatkus.

Alvarado, C. S. (2006a). 'Neglected Near-Death Phenomena'. *Journal of Near-Death Studies*, vol. 24, no. 3, spring, pp. 131–51.

Alvarado, C. S. (2006b). 'Letters'. *Journal of Near-Death Studies*, vol. 25, no. 2, winter, pp. 129–31.

Amatuzio, J. (2004). *Forever Ours: Real Stories of Immortality and Living from a Forensic Pathologist*. Novato, CA: New World Library.

Aries, P. (1981). *At the Hour of Death*. Middlesex, England: Penguin Books.

Aries, P. (1994). *Western Attitudes to Death from the Middle Ages to Present*. Southampton: Itchen Printers Ltd. First published 1974 by Johns Hopkins University Press.

Arslanian-Engoren, C. and Scott, L. D. (2003). 'The Lived Experience of Survivors of Prolonged Mechanical Ventilation: A Phenomenological Study'. *Heart and Lung*, vol. 32, pp. 328–34.

Athapilly, G. K., Greyson, B. and Stevenson, I. (2006). 'Do Prevailing Society Models Influence Reports of Near-Death Experiences: A Comparison of Accounts Reported Before and After 1975'. *Journal of Nervous and Mental Disease*, vol. 194, no. 3, pp. 218–33.

Atwater, P. M. H. (1988). *Coming Back to Life: The After Effects of the Near-Death Experience*. New York: Dodd, Mead.

Atwater, P. M. H. (1992). 'Is There a Hell? Surprising Observations About the Near-Death Experience'. *Journal of Near-Death Studies*, vol. 10, no. 3, pp. 149–60.

207

# References

Atwater, P. M. H. (1994) *Beyond the Light: Near-Death Experiences – The Full Story*. London: Thorsons.

Atwater, P. M. H. (1999). *Children of the New Millennium: Children's Near-Death Experiences and the Evolution of Humankind*. New York: Three Rivers Press.

Augustine, K. (2007a). 'Does Paranormal Perception Occur in Near-Death Experiences?' *Journal of Near-Death Studies*, vol. 25, no. 4, summer, pp. 203–36.

Augustine, K. (2007b). 'Near-Death Experiences with Hallucinatory Features'. *Journal of Near-Death Studies*, vol. 26, no. 1, fall, pp. 3–32.

Augustine, K. (2007c). 'Psychophysiological and Cultural Correlates Undermining a Survivalist Interpretation of Near-Death Experiences'. *Journal of Near-Death Studies*, vol. 26, no. 2, winter, pp. 89–126.

Bache, C. (2000) *Dark Night, Early Dawn*. Albany, NY: State University of New York Press.

Badham, P. and Badham, L. (1984). *Immortality or Extinction?* London: SPCK. Second edition. First published 1982.

Bailey, L. (2001). 'A "Little Death": The Near-Death Experience and Tibetan Delogs'. *Journal of Near-Death Studies*, vol. 19, no. 3, spring, pp. 139–59.

Ballard, P. (1996). 'Intimations of Mortality: Some Sociological Considerations'. In *Facing Death*, Badham, P. and Ballard, P. (eds), Cardiff: University of Wales Press.

Barbour, P. L. (ed.) (1983). *The Complete Works of Captain John Smith (1580–1631) in Three Volumes. Vol. II: The Generall Historie of Virginia, the Somer Isles, and New England with the Names of the Adventurers and their Adventures*. Chapel Hill, NC: University of North Carolina Press. Original work published 1623.

Barrett, S. M. (ed.) (1970). *Geronimo: His own Story*. New York: Dutton. Original published in New York by Duffield in 1906.

Barrett, W. F. (1926). *Death Bed Visions*. London: Methuen.

Beauregard, M. and O'Leary, D. (2007). *The Spiritual Brain: A Neuroscientist's Case for the Existence of the Soul*. New York: Harper Collins Publishers.

Becker, C. (1981). 'The Centrality of Near-Death Experiences in Chinese Pure Land Buddhism'. *Anabiosis – The Journal for Near-Death Studies*. vol. 1, pp. 154–71.

Becker, C. (1984). 'The Pure Land Revisited: Sino-Japanese Meditations and Near-Death Experiences of the Next World'. *Journal of Near-Death Studies*, vol. 4, no. 1, pp. 51–68.

# References

Berndt, R. and Berndt, C. (1989). *The Speaking Land: Myth and Story in Aboriginal Australia.* Harmondsworth: Penguin.

Betty, L. S. (2006) 'Are They Hallucinations or Are They Real? The Spirituality of Deathbed and Near-Death Visions'. *Omega*, vol. 53, pp. 37–49.

Blackmore, S. J. (1993). *Dying to Live.* London: Grafton.

Blanke, O., Ortigue, S., Landis, T. and Seeck, M. (2002). 'Stimulating Illusory Own-Body Perceptions'. *Nature*, vol. 419, September, p. 269.

Blanke, O., Landis, T., Spinelli, L. and Seeck, M. (2004). 'Out-of-Body Experience and Autoscopy of Neurological Origin'. *Brain*, vol. 127, pp. 243–58.

Bockie, S. (1993). *Death and the Invisible Powers: The World of Kongo Belief.* Bloomington, IN: Indiana University Press.

Bonenfant, R. J. (2004). 'A Comparative Study of Near-Death Experience and Non-Near-Death Experience Outcomes in 56 Survivors of Clinical Death'. *Journal of Near-Death Studies*, vol. 22, no. 3, spring, pp. 155–78.

Botkin, A. L. (2000). 'The Induction of After-Death Communications Utilizing Eye-Movement Desensitization and Reprocessing: A New Discovery'. *Journal of Near-Death Studies*, vol. 18, no. 3, spring. pp. 181–209.

Botkin, A. L. with Hogan, R. C. (2005). *Induced After Death Communication: A New Therapy for Healing Grief and Trauma.* Charlottesville, VA: Hampton Roads Publishing Company Inc.

Brayne, S. (2010). *The D Word.* London and New York: Continuum Publishing Corporation.

Brayne, S. and Fenwick, P. (2008). 'The Case for Training to Deal with End of Life Experiences'. *European Journal of Palliative Care, vol.* 15, no. 3, pp. 118–20.

Brayne, S. et al (2006) 'Deathbed Phenomena and Their Effect on a Palliative Care Team: A Pilot Study'. *American Journal of Hospice and Palliative Medicine*, vol. 23, no. 1, pp. 17–24.

Brayne, S. et al (2008) 'End-of-Life Experiences and the Dying Process in a Gloucestershire Nursing Home as Reported by Nurses and Care Assistants'. *American Journal of Palliative Care*, vol. 25, no. 3, pp. 195–206.

Brinkley, D. and Perry, P. (1994). *Saved by the Light.* London: Piatkus.

Bucher, L., Wimbush, F. B., Hardie, T. and Hayes, E. R. (1997). 'Near-Death Experiences: Critical Care Nurses Attitudes and Interventions'. *Dimensions of Critical Care Nursing*, vol. 16, no. 4, pp. 194–201.

Bush, N. E. (1983). 'The Near Death Experience in Children: Shades of the Prison-House Reopening'. *Anabiosis: The Journal of Near-Death Studies*, vol. 3, pp. 177–93.

# References

Bush, N. E. (1991). 'Is Ten Years a Life Review?' *Journal of Near-Death Studies*, vol. 10, no. 1, fall, pp. 5–9.

Bush, N. E. (1994). 'The Paradox of Jonah: Response to "Solving the Riddle of Frightening Near-Death Experiences"'. *Journal of Near-Death Studies*, vol. 13, no. 1, fall, pp. 47–54.

Bush, N. E. (2012). *Dancing Past the Dark: Distressing Near-Death Experiences.* Durham, NC: International Association of Near-Death Studies.

Butler, R. N. (1963). 'The Life Review: An Interpretation of Reminiscence in the Aged'. *Psychiatry*, vol. 26, pp. 65–76.

Callanan, M. and Kelley, P. (1992). *Final Gifts: Understanding and Helping the Dying.* London: Hodder & Stoughton.

Calvey, T. N. and Williams, N. E. (1998). *Principles and Practice of Pharmacology for Anaesthetists.* London: Blackwell Science. Third edition. First published 1982.

Carr, C. (1993). 'Death and Near-Death: A Comparison of Tibetan and Euro-American Experiences'. *Journal of Transpersonal Psychology*, vol. 25, pp. 59–110.

Carter, C. (2010). *Science and the Near-Death Experience: How Consciousness Survives Death.* Vermont, Canada: Inner Traditions.

Chalmers, D. (1995). 'Facing Up to the Problem of Consciousness'. *Journal of Consciousness Studies*, vol. 2, no. 3, pp. 200–19.

Christensen, A. J. (2003). *Popol Vuh: The Sacred Book of the Maya.* Hants, NY: O Books.

Christensen, M. (2002). 'The Physiological Effects of Noise: Considerations for Intensive Care'. *Nursing in Critical Care*, vol. 7, no. 6, pp. 300–5.

Christensen, S. F., Stadeager, C. and Siemkowicz, E. (1990). 'Estimation of Cerebral Blood Flow During Cardiopulmonary Resuscitation in Humans'. *Resuscitation*, vol. 19, pp. 115–23.

Christian, S. R. (2006). 'Marital Satisfaction and Stability Following a Near-Death Experience of One of the Marital Partners'. *Dissertation Abstracts International Section A: Humanities and Social Sciences*, vol. 66, (11-A), 3925.

Cooke, A. (1968). *Out of the Mouth of Babes: Extra-Sensory Perception in Children.* Cambridge and London: James Clarke & Co. Ltd.

Corazza, O. (2008). *Near-Death Experiences: Exploring the Mind–Body Connection.* London and New York: Routledge.

# References

Counts, D. (1983). 'Near-Death and Out-of-Body Experiences in a Melanesian Society'. *Anabiosis – Journal of Near-Death Studies*, vol. 3, pp. 115–35.

Cuevas, B. J. (2003). *The Hidden History of the Tibetan Book of the Dead*. Oxford: Oxford University Press.

Cuevas, B. J. (2008). *Travels in the Netherworld*. Oxford: Oxford University Press.

Damas Mora, J., Jenner, F. and Eacott, S. (1980). 'On Heatoscopy or the Phenomenon of the Double: Case Presentation and Review of the Literature'. *British Journal of Medical Psychology*, vol. 53, pp. 75–83.

d'Aquili, E. and Newberg, A. (1999). *The Mystical Mind*. Minneapolis: Fortress Press.

David-Neel, A. (1997). *Magic and Mystery in Tibet*. London: Thorsons. Originally published in Britain by Souvenir Press Ltd in 1967.

Devers, E. (1997). *Goodbye Again: Experiences with Departed Loved Ones*. Kansas City, MO: Andrews and McMeel.

Devinsky, O., Feldmann, E., Burrowes, K. and Bromfield, E. (1989). 'Autoscopic Phenomena with Seizures'. *Archives of Neurology*, vol. 46, October, pp. 1080–8.

Dewhurst, K. and Beard, A. W. (1970). 'Sudden Religious Conversions in Temporal Lobe Epilepsy'. *British Journal of Psychiatry*, vol. 117, pp. 497–507.

Dossey, L. (2011). 'Dying to Heal: A Neglected Aspect of NDEs'. *Explore*, vol. 7, no. 2, March/April, pp. 59–62.

Dougherty, C. M. (1990). 'The Near-Death Experience as a Major Life Transition'. *Holistic Nursing Practice*, vol. 4, no. 3, pp. 84–90.

Drolma, Delog Dawa (1995). *Delog: Journey to Realms Beyond Death*. Junction City, CA: Padma Publishing.

Eadie, B. (1992). *Embraced by the Light*. New York, Toronto, London, Sydney and Auckland: Gold Leaf Press.

Edgar, E. (1996). 'Death in Our Understanding of Life'. In *Facing Death*, Badham, P. and Ballard, P. (eds), Cardiff: University of Wales Press.

Ehrenwald, J. (1974). 'Out-of-the-Body Experiences and the Denial of Death'. *Journal of Nervous and Mental Disease*, vol. 159, no. 4, pp. 227–33.

Ehrenwald, J. (1978). *The ESP Experience: A Psychiatric Validation*. New York: Basic Books.

Einstein, A., Podolsky, B. and Rosen, N. (1935). 'Can Quantum-Mechanical Description of Physical Reality Be Considered Complete?', *Physical Review*, vol. 47, pp. 777–80.

# References

Ellwood, G. F. (2001). *The Uttermost Deep: The Challenge of Near-Death Experiences.* New York: Lantern Books.

Epstein, L. (1982). 'On the History and Psychology of the "Das-Log"'. *Tibet Journal*, vol. 7, pp. 20–85.

Evans-Wentz, W. Y. (1960). *The Tibetan Book of the Dead.* London: Oxford University Press. First published in 1927.

Fenwick, E. and Fenwick, P. (1996a). *The Truth in the Light.* London: Headline.

Fenwick, P. (1997). 'Is the Near-Death Experience Only N-Methyl-D-Aspartate Blocking? *Journal of Near-Death Studies*, vol. 16, no. 1, fall, pp. 43–53.

Fenwick, P. and Fenwick, E. (2008). *The Art of Dying.* London and New York: Continuum International Publishing Group.

Fenwick, P. et al (2009). 'Comfort for the Dying: Five Year Retrospective and One Year Prospective Studies of End of Life Experiences'. *Archives of Gerontology and Geriatrics*, vol. 51, no. 2, pp. 173–80.

Finlay, I. (1996). 'Ethical Decision Making in Palliative Care'. In *Facing Death*, Badham, P. and Ballard, P. (eds), Cardiff: University of Wales Press.

Flynn, C. P. (1986). *After the Beyond: Human Transformation and the Near-Death Experience.* Englewood Cliffs, NJ: Prentice-Hall.

Fracasso, C., Aleyasin, S. A., Friedman, H. and Young, M. S. (2010a). 'Near-Death Experiences Among a Sample of Iranian Muslims'. *Journal of Near-Death Studies*, vol. 29, no. 1, fall, pp. 265–72.

Fracasso, C., Friedman, H. and Young, M. S. (2010b). 'Psychologists' Knowledge of and Attitudes about Near-Death Experiences: Changes over Time and Relationship to Transpersonal Self-Concept'. *Journal of Near-Death Studies*, vol. 29, no. 1, fall, pp. 273–81.

Funning, B. (2010). 'Spirituality'. *RCN Bulletin*, 19 May, p. 5.

Gabbard, G. O. and Twemlow, S. W. (1984). *With the Eyes of the Mind: An Empirical Analysis of Out-of-Body States.* New York: Praeger.

Gallup, G. and Proctor, W. (1984). *Adventures in Immortality.* London: Corgi Books.

Gliksman, M. D. and Kellehear, A. (1990). 'Near-Death Experiences and the Measurement of Blood Gases'. *Journal of Near-Death Studies*, vol. 9, no. 1, fall, pp. 41–4.

Gloor, P., Olivier, A., Quesney, L. F., Andermann, F. and Horowitz, S. (1982). 'The Role of the Limbic System in Experiential Phenomena of Temporal Lobe Epilepsy'. *Annals of Neurology*, vol. 12, no. 2, August, pp. 129–44.

# References

Gomez-Jeria, J. S. (2006). 'The Near-Death Experience in Pu Songling's *Strange Tales from the Liaozhai Studio*'. *Journal of Near-Death Studies*, vol. 25, no. 2, winter, pp. 113–20.

Granqvist, P., Fredrikson, M., Larhammar, D., Larsson, M. and Valind, S. (2004). 'Sensed Presence and Mystical Experiences are Predicted by Suggestibility, Not by the Application of Transcranial Weak Complex Magnetic Fields'. *Neuroscience Letters*, doi: 10.1016/j.neulet.2004.10.057.

Green, C. (1967). 'Ecsomatic Experiences and Related Phenomena'. *Journal of the Society for Psychical Research*, vol. 44, pp. 111–30.

Green, C. (1968). *Out-of-Body Experiences*. London: Hamish Hamilton.

Green, J. T. (1984). 'Near-Death Experiences in a Chamorro Culture'. *Vital Signs*, vol. 4, nos 1–2, pp. 6–7.

Green, J. T. (2008). 'The Death Journey of a Hopi Indian: A Case Study'. *Journal of Near-Death Studies*, vol. 26, no. 4, summer, pp. 283–93.

Grey, M. (1985). *Return From Death*. London: Arkana.

Grey, M. (1987). *Return From Death: An Explanation of the Near-Death Experience*. London and New York: Arkana.

Greyson, B. (1981). 'Near-Death Experiences and Attempted Suicide'. *Suicide and Life-Threatening Behaviour*, vol. 2, pp. 10–16.

Greyson, B. (1983a). 'The Near-Death Experience Scale: Construction, Reliability and Validity'. *Journal of Nervous and Mental Disease*, vol. 171, pp. 369–75.

Greyson, B. (1983b). 'Near-Death Experiences and Personal Values'. *American Journal of Psychiatry*, vol. 140, no. 5, pp. 618–20.

Greyson, B. (1992). 'Reduced Death Threat in Near-Death Experiencers'. *Death Studies*, vol. 16, pp. 535–46.

Greyson, B. (1992–93). 'Near-Death Experiences and Antisuicidal Attitudes'. *Omega, Journal of Death and Dying*, vol. 26, pp. 81–9.

Greyson, B. (1993) 'Varieties of Near-Death Experiences'. *Psychiatry*, vol. 56, November, pp. 390–9.

Greyson, B. (1996). 'The Near-Death Experience as a Transpersonal Crisis'. In *Textbook of Transpersonal Psychiatry and Psychology*, Scotton B. W., Chinen, A. B. and Battista, J. R. (eds), New York: Basic Books.

Greyson, B. (1997). 'The Near-Death Experience as a Focus of Clinical Attention'. *Journal of Nervous and Mental Disease*, vol. 185, May, pp. 327–34.

Greyson, B. (2000). 'Dissociation in People Who Have Near-Death Experiences: Out of Their Bodies or Out of Their Minds?' *Lancet*, 355, pp. 460–3.

Greyson, B. (2003). 'Incidence and Correlates of Near-Death Experiences in a Cardiac Care Unit'. *General Hospital Psychiatry*, vol. 25, pp. 269–76.

Greyson, B. (2007). 'Commentary of Psychophysiological and Cultural Correlates Undermining a Survivalist Interpretation of Near-Death Experiences'. *Journal of Near-Death Studies*, vol. 26, no. 2, winter, pp. 127–45.

Greyson, B. and Bush N. E. (1992). 'Distressing Near-Death Experiences'. *Psychiatry: Interpersonal and Biological Processes*, vol. 55, no. 1, pp. 95–10.

Greyson, B., Holden, J. M. and Mounsey J. P. (2006). 'Failure to Elicit Near-Death Experiences in Induced Cardiac Arrest'. *Journal of Near-Death Studies*, vol. 25, no. 2, winter, pp. 85–98.

Grof, S. (1994). *Books of the Dead: Manuals for Living and Dying*. London: Thames and Hudson.

Grof, S. and Halifax, J. (1977). *The Human Encounter with Death*. New York: E. P. Dutton.

Grossman, N. (2010). 'Book Review'. *Journal of Near-Death Studies*, vol. 28, no. 4, summer, pp. 211–32.

Grosso, M. (1981). 'Toward an Explanation of Near-Death Phenomena'. *Anabiosis: The Journal of Near-Death Studies*, vol. 1, pp. 3–25.

Groth-Marnat, G. and Summers, R. (1998). 'Altered Beliefs, Attitudes and Behaviours Following Near-Death Experiences'. *Journal of Humanistic Psychology*, vol. 38, no. 3, pp. 110–25.

Guggenheim, B. and Guggenheim, J. (1996). *Hello from Heaven! A New Field of Research Confirms that Life and Love are Eternal*. New York: Bantam.

Gurney, E., Myers, F. W. H. and Podmore, F. (1886). *Phantasms of the Living*. London: Trubner and Co.

Hadfield, P. (1991). 'Japanese Find Death a Depressing Experience'. *New Scientist*, vol. 132, no. 1797, p. 11.

Hallowell, A. I. (1967). 'Spirits of the Dead in Salteaux Life and Thought'. In *Culture and Experience*, A. I. Hallowell, New York: Shocken. Originally published in 1940 in *Journal of the Royal Anthropological Institute*, vol. 70, pp. 29–51.

Hamilton, D. (2008). *How Your Mind Can Heal Your Body*. Australia, Canada, Hong Kong, India, South Africa, United Kingdom, United States: Hay House.

Hamilton, D. (2010). *Why Kindness is Good for You*. Australia, Canada, Hong Kong, India, South Africa, United Kingdom, United States: Hay House.

Hampe, J. C. (1979). *To Die is Gain: The Experience of One's Own Death.* London: Darton, Longman and Todd.

Hardy, Sir A. (1979). *The Spiritual Nature of Man.* Oxford: Clarendon Press.

Hay, D. (1982). *Exploring Inner Space: Is God Still Possible in the Twentieth Century?* Middlesex: Penguin Books.

Hayes, E. R. and Orne, R. M. (1990). 'A Study of the Relationship Between Knowledge and Attitudes of Nurses in Practice Related to Near-Death Experience'. *Loss, Grief and Care,* vol. 4, nos 1–2, pp. 71–80.

Healy, F. and Persinger, M. A. (1996). 'Enhanced Hypnotic Induction Profile and the Sense of a Presence Following Application of Burst Firing Magnetic Fields Over Right Temporoparietal Lobes: A Replication'. *International Journal of Neuroscience,* vol. 87, pp. 201–7.

Heim, A. (1892). 'Notizen uber den Tod durch Absturz'. *Jarbuch des Sweizer Alpenclub,* vol. 27, pp. 327–37. Translated as 'The Experience of Dying from Falls' by Noyes, R. and Kletti, R. (1972). *Omega,* vol. 3, pp. 45–52.

Hemingway, A. (2008). *Practicing Conscious Living and Dying.* Winchester, UK and Washington, DC: O Books.

Henderson, Y. and Haggard, H. W. (1927). *Noxious Gases and the Principles of Respiration Influencing their Action.* New York: American Chemical Society.

Herzog, D. and Herrin, J. (1985). 'Near-Death Experiences in the Very Young'. *Critical Care Medicine,* vol. 13, no. 12, pp. 1074–5.

Hoffman, E. (1992). *Visions of Innocence: Spiritual and Inspirational Experiences of Childhood.* London: Shambhala Publications Inc.

Holden, J. M. (1988). 'Visual Perception During Naturalistic Near-Death Out-of-Body Experiences'. *Journal of Near-Death Studies,* vol. 7, no. 2, winter, pp. 107–20.

Holden, J. M. (1989). 'Unexpected Findings in a Study of Visual Perception During the Naturalistic Near-Death Out-of-Body Experience'. *Journal of Near-Death Studies,* vol. 7, no. 3, spring, pp. 55–163.

Holden, J. M. and Joesten, L. (1990). 'Near-Death Veridicality Research in the Hospital Setting: Problems and Promise'. *Journal of Near-Death Studies,* vol. 9, no. 1, fall, pp. 45–54.

Holden, J. M., Long, J. and McClurg, J. (2006). 'Out-of-Body Experiences: All in the Brain?' *Journal of Near-Death Studies,* vol. 25, no. 2, winter, pp. 99–107.

Hood, R. (1976). 'Conceptual Criticisms of Regressive Explanations of Mysticism'. *Review of Religious Research,* vol. 17, pp. 179–88.

Hood, R. W. (1979). 'Personality Correlates of the Report of Mystical Experience'. *Psychological Reports*, vol. 44, no. 3, pp. 804–6.

Houck, J. A. (2005). 'The Universal, Multiple, and Exclusive Experiences of After-Death Communication'. *Journal of Near-Death Studies*, vol. 24, no. 2, winter, pp. 117–27.

Howarth, G. and Kellehear, A. (2001). 'Shared-Death and Related Illness Experiences: Steps on an Unscheduled Journey'. *Journal of Near-Death Studies*, vol. 20, no. 2, winter, pp. 71–86.

Hyslop, J. H. (1908). *Psychical Research and the Resurrection*. Chareleston, SC: Bibliobazaar. Reprinted 2008.

Irwin, H. J. (1993). 'The Near-Death Experience as a Dissociative Phenomenon: An Empirical Assessment'. *Journal of Near-Death Studies*, vol. 12, no. 2, pp. 95–103.

Iwasaka, M. and Toelken, B. (1994). *Ghosts and the Japanese*. Logan, UT: Utah State University Press.

Jakobsen, M. D. (1999). *Negative Spiritual Experiences: Encounters with Evil*. Lampeter, Wales: Religious Experience Research Centre. Occasional paper.

Jansen, K. L. R. (1997a). 'The Ketamine Model of the Near-Death Experience: A Central Role for the NMDA Receptor'. *Journal of Near-Death Studies*, vol. 16, no. 1, fall, pp. 3–26.

Jansen, K. (2001). *Ketamine: Dreams and Realities*. Florida: Multidisciplinary Association for Psychedelic Studies (MAPS).

Jung, C. G. (1996). *The Archetypes and the Collective Unconscious*. London: Routledge. Second edition. First published in England in 1959.

Kalweit, H. (1988). *Dreamtime and Inner Space: The World of the Shaman*, trans. W. Wunsche. Boston, MA: Shambhala.

Kason, Y. (2000). *Farther Shores: Exploring How Near-Death, Kundalini and Mystical Experiences Can Transform our Ordinary Lives*. Ontario: Harper Collins Publishers Ltd.

Keable, R. (1921). 'A People of Dreams'. *Hibbert Journal*, vol. 19, pp. 522–31.

Kellehear, A. (1990). 'The Near-Death Experience as a Status Passage'. *Social Science and Medicine*, vol. 31, pp. 933–99.

Kellehear, A. (1993). 'Culture, Biology and the Near Death Experience'. *Journal of Nervous and Mental Disease*, vol. 181, no. 3, pp. 148–56.

Kellehear, A. (1996). *Experiences Near Death*. New York: Oxford University Press.

Kellehear, A. (2001). 'An Hawaiian Near-Death Experience'. *Journal of Near-Death Studies*, vol. 20, no. 1, fall, pp. 31–5.

Kellehear, A. (2008). 'Census of Non-Western Near-Death Experiences to 2005: Overview of the Current Data'. *Journal of Near-Death Studies*, vol. 26, no. 4, summer, pp. 249–65.

Kellman, R. (2004). *Matrix Healing*. London, Toronto, Sydney, Auckland and Johannesburg: Bantam Books.

Kelly, E. F., Williams Kelly, E., Crabtree, A., Gauld, A., Grosso, M. and Greyson, B. (2007). *Irreducible Mind: Toward a Psychology for the 21st Century*. Lanham, MD, and Plymouth, UK: Rowman & Littlefield Publishers Inc.

Kessler, D. (1997). *The Rights of the Dying*. London: Vermillion.

King, M. (1985). *Being Pakeha: An Encounter with New Zealand and the Maori Renaissance*. Auckland: Hodder and Stoughton.

Kircher, P. M., (1995). *Love is the Link: A Hospice Doctor Shares her Experience of Near-Death and Dying*. New York: Larson Publications.

Knoblauch, H., Schmied, I. and Schnettler, B. (2001). 'Different Kinds of Near-Death Experience: A Report on a Survey of Near-Death Experiences in Germany'. *Journal of Near-Death Studies*, vol. 20, no. 1, fall, pp. 15–29.

Kreps, J. I. (2009). 'The Search for Muslim Near-Death Experiences'. *Journal of Near-Death Studies*, vol. 28, no. 4, summer, pp. 67–86.

Kuhn, T. (1996). *The Structure of Scientific Revolutions*. Chicago, IL: University of Chicago Press. Third edition.

LaGrand, L. E. (1997). *After-Death Communication: Final Farewells*. St Paul, MN: Llewellyn.

LaGrand, L. E. (2005). 'The Nature and Therapeutic Implications of the Extraordinary Experiences of the Bereaved'. *Journal of Near-Death Studies*, vol. 24, no. 1, fall, pp. 3–20.

Lawrence, M. (1995). 'The Unconscious Experience'. *American Journal of Critical Care*, vol. 4, no. 3, pp. 227–32.

Lawrence, M. (1998). *In a World of their Own: Experiencing Unconsciousness*. Westport, CO and London: Bergin and Garvey.

Lerma, J. (2009). *Learning from the Light*. Pompton Plains, NJ: Career Press.

Lhermitte, J. (1939). 'Les Phenomenes Heautoscopiques, les Hallucinations Speculaire et Autoscopies'. In *L'Image de Notre Corps*, Lhermitte, J., Paris: L'Harmattan.

Lhermitte, J. (1951). 'Les Phenomenes Heautoscopiques, les Hallucinations Speculaire'. In *Les Hallucinations. Clinique et Physiopathologie*, Lhermitte, J., Paris: G. Doin.

# References

Lindley, J., Bryan, S. and Conley, B. (1981). 'Near-Death Experiences in a Pacific Northwest American Population: The Evergreen Study'. *Anabiosis – The Journal for Near-Death Studies,* vol. 1, no. 2, winter, pp. 104–24.

Lipton, B. (2005). *The Biology of Belief.* Llandeilo: Cygnus Books.

Long, J. and Holden, J. (2007). 'Does the Arousal System Contribute to Near-Death Experiences? A Summary and Response'. *Journal of Near-Death Studies,* vol. 25, no. 3, spring, pp. 135–69.

Long, J. P. and Long, J. A. (2003). 'A Comparison of Near-Death Experiences Occurring Before and After 1975: Results from an Internet Survey'. *Journal of Near-Death Studies,* vol. 22, no. 1, fall, pp. 21–32.

Longaker, C. (1997). *Facing Death and Finding Hope.* London: Arrow Books.

Lukianowicz, N. (1958). 'Autoscopic Phenomena'. *A.M.A. Archives of Neurology and Psychiatry,* vol. 80, pp. 199–220.

Luks, A. (1991). *The Healing Power of Doing Good: The Health and Spiritual Benefits of Helping Others.* New York: Ballantine.

Lundahl, C. R. (1993). 'A Nonscience Forerunner to Modern Near-Death Studies in America'. *Omega,* vol. 28, pp. 63–76.

Marsh, M. (2010). *Out-of-Body and Near-Death Experiences: Brain State Phenomena or Glimpses of Immortality.* Oxford and New York: Oxford University Press.

Marshall, R. S., Lazar, R. M., Spellman, J. P. et al (2001). 'Recovery of Brain Function During Induced Cerebral Hypoperfusion'. *Brain,* vol. 124, pp. 1208–17.

Maslow, A. (1954). *Motivation and Personality.* New York: Harper & Row.

Maslow, A. (1964). *Religions, Values and Peak Experiences.* Columbus, OH: Ohio State University Press.

Masters, R. and Houston, J. (2000). *The Varieties of Psychedelic Experience: The Classic Guide to the Effects of LSD on the Human Psyche.* Rochester, VT: Park Street Press. First published in 1966.

Matthews, C. (2009). 'Addressing the Need of Near-Death Experience Survivors to Find The Soul's Mission in Life'. Masters of Transpersonal Arts. Virginia Beach, VA: Atlantic University.

Mavromatis, A. (1987). *Hypnagogia.* New York: Routledge & Kegan Paul.

McClelland, D. C. and Kirshnit, C. (1988). 'The Effect of Motivational Arousal through Films on Salivary Immunoglobulin A'. *Psychology and Health,* vol. 2, no. 1, pp. 31–52.

McClenon, J. (2006). 'Kongo Near-Death Experiences: Cross-Cultural Patterns'. *Journal of Near-Death Studies,* vol. 25, no. 1, fall, pp. 21–34.

# References

McDonagh, J. M. (1979) 'Bibliotherapy with Suicidal Patients.' Paper presented at the 87th Annual Convention of the American Psychological Association, New York.

McDonagh, J. M. (2004) 'Introducing Near-Death Research Findings into Psychotherapy'. *Journal of Near-Death Studies*, vol. 22, no. 4, summer, pp. 269–73.

McInroy, A. and Edwards, S. (2002). 'Preventing Sensory Alteration: A Practical Approach'. *Nursing in Critical Care*, vol. 7, no. 5, pp. 247–54.

McFarland, R. A. (1932). 'The Psychological Effects of Oxygen Deprivation (Anoxaemia) on Human Behaviour'. *Archives of Psychology*, Columbia University, vol. 145, pp. 1–135.

Meduna, L. J. (1950). 'The Effect of Carbon Dioxide upon the Functions of the Brain'. In *Carbon Dioxide Therapy*, Meduna, L. J. , Springfield, IL: Charles C. Thomas.

Milner, Q. J. and Gunning, K. E. (2000). 'Sedation in the Intensive Care Unit'. *British Journal of Intensive Care*, vol. 10, pp. 12–17.

Mitchell, E. D. (1974). *Psychic Exploration.* New York: Putnam.

Monroe, R. (1974). *Journeys Out of the Body.* London: Corgi Books.

Moody, R. A., Jnr. (1975). *Life After Life.* New York: Mockingbird/Bantam Books.

Moody, R. A. (1992). 'Family Reunions: Visionary Encounters with the Departed in a Modern-day Psychomanteum'. *Journal of Near-Death Studies*, vol. 11, no. 2, winter, pp. 83–121.

Moody, R. A. (1999). *The Last Laugh: A New Philosophy of Near-Death Experiences, Apparitions, and the Paranormal.* Charlottesville, VA: Hampton Roads Publishing Company Inc.

Moody, R. and Perry, P. (1995). *Reunions: Visionary Encounters with Departed Loved Ones.* London: Warner Books. First published in the United States by Villard Books in 1993.

Moody, R. A. with Perry, P. (2010). *Glimpses of Eternity: Investigation into Shared Death Experiences.* London, Sydney, Auckland and Johannesburg: Rider Books.

Moore, L. H. (1994). 'An Assessment of Physicians' Knowledge of and Attitudes Toward the Near-Death Experience'. *Journal of Near-Death Studies*, vol. 13, no. 2, winter, pp. 91–102.

Moorjani, A. (2012). *Dying to be Me: My Journey from Cancer, to Near-Death to True Healing.* London: Hay House.

Morris, L. L. and Knafl, K. (2003). 'The Nature and Meaning of the Near-Death Experience for Patients and Critical Care Nurses'. *Journal of Near-Death Studies*, vol. 21, no. 3, spring, pp. 139–67.

Morris, R. L., Harary, S. B., Janis, J., Hartwell, J. and Roll, W. G. (1978). 'Studies in Communication During Out-of-Body Experiences'. *Journal of the American Society for Psychical Research*, vol. 72, pp. 1–22.

Morse, M. with Perry, P. (1990). *Closer to the Light: Learning from Children's Near-Death Experiences.* New York: Villard Books.

Morse, M. with Perry, P. (1993). *Transformed by the Light.* London: Piatkus.

Morse, M. with Perry, P. (1994). *Parting Visions: Uses and Meanings of Pre-Death, Psychic and Spiritual Experiences.* New York: Villard Books.

Morse, M. with Perry, P. (2000). *Where God Lives: The Science of the Paranormal and How our Brains are Linked to the Universe.* New York: Cliff Street Books.

Morse, M., Conner, D. and Tyler, D. (1985). 'Near-Death Experiences in a Pediatric Population'. *American Journal of Diseases of Children*, vol. 139, pp. 595–600.

Morse, M., Castillo, P., Venecia, D., Milstein, J. and Tyler, D. C. (1986). 'Childhood Near-Death Experiences'. *American Journal of Diseases of Children*, vol. 140, pp. 1110–14.

Morse, M., Venecia, D. and Milstein, J. (1989). 'Near-Death Experiences: A Neurophysiological Explanatory Model'. *Journal of Near-Death Studies*, vol. 8, no. 1, fall, pp. 45–53.

Muldoon, S. (1965). *The Projection of the Astral Body.* London: Rider.

Muldoon, S. and Carrington, H. (1974). *The Projection of the Astral Body.* New York: Samuel Weiser.

Mundigler, G., Delle-Karth, G., Koreny, M. et al (2002). 'Impaired Circadian Rhythm of Melatonin in Sedated Critically Ill Patients with Severe Sepsis'. *Critical Care Medicine*, vol. 30, pp. 536–40.

Murphy, T. (2001). 'Near-Death Experiences in Thailand'. *Journal of Near-Death Studies*, vol. 19, no. 3, spring, pp. 161–78.

Musgrave, C. (1997). 'The Near-Death Experience: A Study of Spiritual Transformation'. *Journal of Near-Death Studies*, vol. 15, no. 3, spring, pp. 187–201.

Nahm, M. (2009a). 'Four Ostensible Near-Death Experiences of Roman Times with Peculiar Features: Mistake Cases, Correction Cases, Xenoglossy and a Prediction'. *Journal of Near-Death Studies*, vol. 27, no. 4, summer, pp. 211–22.

Nahm, M. (2009b). 'Terminal Lucidity in People with Mental Illness and Other Mental Disability: An Overview and Implications for Possible Explanatory Models'. *Journal of Near-Death Studies*, vol. 28, no. 2, winter, pp. 87–106.

Nahm, M. and Greyson, B. (2009). 'Terminal Lucidity in Patients with Chronic Schizophrenia and Dementia: A Survey of the Literature'. *Journal of Nervous and Mental Disease*, vol. 197, no. 12, December, pp. 942–4.

Nahm, M. and Nicolay, J. (2010). 'Essential Features of Eight Published Muslim Near-Death Experiences: An Addendum to Joel Ibrahim Kreps's "The Search for Muslim Near-Death Experiences"'. *Journal of Near-Death Studies*, vol. 29, no. 1, fall, pp. 255–63.

Nataraja, S. (2008). *The Blissful Brain: Neuroscience and the Proof of the Power of Meditation*. London: Gaia Books Ltd.

Neihardt, J. G. (1995). *Black Elk Speaks*. Lincoln, NB, and London: University of Nebraska Press. Eighth cloth printing. Originally published in New York by William Morrow & Company in 1932.

Nelson, K., Mattingly, M., Lee, S. A. and Schmitt, F. A. (2006). 'Does the Arousal System Contribute to Near-Death Experience?' *Neurology*, vol. 66, pp. 1003–9.

Nelson, K., Mattingly, M. and Schmitt, F. A. (2007). 'Out-of-Body Experiences and Arousal'. *Neurology*, vol. 68, pp. 794–5.

Nouri, F. M. and Holden, J. M. (2008). 'Electromagnetic After Effects of Near-Death Experiences'. *Journal of Near-Death Studies*, vol. 27, no. 2, winter, pp. 83–110.

Noyes, R. and Kletti, R. (1976). 'Depersonalisation in the Threat of Life Threatening Danger: A Description'. *Psychiatry*, vol. 39, pp. 19–27.

Noyes, R. and Kletti, R. (1977). 'Panoramic Memory: A Response to the Threat of Death'. *Omega*, vol. 8, pp. 181–94.

Noyes, R., Jnr, Hoenk, P. R., Kuperman, S. and Slymen, D. J. (1977). 'Depersonalization in Accident Victims and Psychiatric Patients'. *Journal of Nervous and Mental Disease*, vol. 164, pp. 401–7.

Noyes, R. and Slymen, D. (1979). 'The Subjective Response to Life Threatening Danger'. *Omega*, vol. 9, pp. 313–21.

Olson, M. and Dulaney, P. (1993). 'Life Satisfaction, Life Review, and Near-Death Experiences in the Elderly'. *Journal of Holistic Nursing*, vol. 11, no. 4, December, pp. 368–82.

Orne, R. M. (1986). 'Nurses' views of NDEs.' *American Journal of Nursing*, vol. 86, pp. 419–20

# References

Ornstein, R. and Sobel, D. (1987). *The Healing Brain*. Cambridge, MA: Makor Books.

Osis, K. (1972). 'New ASPR Research on Out-of-the-Body Experiences'. *Newsletter of the American Society for Psychical Research*, no. 14, pp. 2–4.

Osis, K. and Haraldsson, E. (1977). *At the Hour of Death*. New York: Avon Books.

Owens, J. E., Cook, E. W. and Stevenson, I. (1990). 'Features of Near-Death Experience in Relation to Whether or Not Patients Were Near Death'. *Lancet*, vol. 336, pp. 1175–7.

Oyama, T.Y., Jin, T., Yamaga, R., Ling, N. and Guillemin, R. (1980). 'Profound Analgesic Effects of Beta-Endorphin in Man'. *Lancet*, vol. 1, pp. 122–4.

Parnia, S., Waller, D. G., Yeates, R. and Fenwick, P. (2001). 'A Qualitative and Quantitative Study of the Incidence, Features and Aetiology of Near Death Experiences in Cardiac Arrest Survivors'. *Resuscitation*, vol. 48, pp. 149–56.

Pasricha, S. K. (2008). 'Near-Death Experiences in India: Prevalence and New Features'. *Journal of Near-Death Studies*, vol. 26, no. 4, summer, pp. 267–82.

Pasricha, S. and Stevenson, I. (1986). 'Near Death Experiences in India: A Preliminary Report'. *Journal of Nervous and Mental Disease*, vol. 174, no. 3, pp. 165–70.

Pelletier, K. R. (1994). *Sound Mind, Sound Body: A New Model for Lifelong Health*. New York, London and Toronto: Simon and Schuster.

Penfield, W. (1955). 'The Role of the Temporal Cortex in Certain Psychic Phenomena'. *Journal of Mental Science*, vol. 101, pp. 451–65.

Penfield, W. (1975). *The Mystery of the Mind: A Critical Study of Consciousness*. Princeton, NJ: Princeton University Press.

Penfield, W. and Kristiansen, K. (1951). *Epileptic Seizure Patterns*. Springfield, IL: Charles C. Thomas.

Penfield, W. and Perot, P. (1963). 'The Brain's Record of Auditory and Visual Experience'. *Brain*, vol. 86, pp. 595–695.

Perera, M., Padmasekara, G. and Belanti, J. (2005). 'Prevalence of Near-Death Experiences in Australia'. *Journal of Near-Death Studies*, vol. 24, no. 2, winter, pp. 109–16.

Persinger, M. A. (2003). 'Experimental Simulation of the God Experience: Implications for Religious Beliefs and the Future of the Human Species'. In *Neurotheology: Brain, Science, Spirituality, Religious Experience*, Joseph, R. A. (ed.), San Jose, CA: University of California Press.

# References

Persinger, M. A. and Healey, F. (2002). 'Experimental Facilitation of the Sensed Presence: Possible Intercalation Between the Hemispheres Induced by Complex Magnetic Fields'. *Journal of Nervous and Mental Diseases*, vol. 190, pp. 533–41.

Planck, M. (1948). *Wissenschaftliche Selbstbiographie. Mit einem Bildnis und der von Max von Laue gehaltenen Traueransprache*. Leipzig: Johann Ambrosius Barth Verlag, p. 22, as translated in *Scientific Autobiography and Other Papers*, trans. F. Gaynor (New York, 1949), pp. 33–4.

Pommaret, F. (1989). *Les Revenants de l'Au-dela dans le Monde Tibetain: Sources Litteraires et Tradition Vivante*. Paris: Editions du Centre National de le Recherché Scientifique.

Putnam, F. W. (1991). 'Dissociative Disorders in Children and Adolescents: A Developmental Perspective'. *Psychiatric Clinics of North America*, vol. 14, pp. 519–31.

Rawlings, M. (1979). *Beyond Death's Door* . . . London: Sheldon Press. Third impression. First published in the United States in 1978 by Thomas Nelson Inc.

Rawlings, M. (1993). *To Hell and Back*. Nashville, TN: Nelson.

Rees, W. D. (1971). 'The Hallucinations of Widowhood'. *British Medical Journal*, vol. 4, no. 778, pp. 37–41.

Rein, G., McCraty, R. M. and Atkinson, M. (1995). 'Effects of Positive and Negative Emotions on Salivary IgA'. *Journal for the Advancement of Medicine*, vol. 8, no. 2, pp. 87–105.

Ring, K. (1980). *Life at Death: A Scientific Investigation of the Near-Death Experience*. New York: Coward, McCann and Geoghegan.

Ring, K. (1984). *Heading Toward Omega: In Search of the Meaning of the Near-Death Experience*. New York: William Morrow.

Ring, K. (1992). *The Omega Project: Near-Death Experiences, UFO Encounters and Mind at Large*. New York: William Morrow.

Ring, K. (1994). 'Solving the Riddle of Frightening Near-Death Experiences: Some Testable Hypotheses and a Perspective Based on *A Course in Miracles*'. *Journal of Near-Death Studies*, vol. 13, no. 1, fall, pp. 5–23.

Ring, K. (1995). 'The Impact of Near-Death Experiences on Persons who Have Not Had Them: A Report of a Preliminary Study and Two Replications'. *Journal of Near-Death Studies*, vol. 13, no. 4, summer, pp. 223–35.

Ring, K. and Cooper, S. (1999). *Mindsight: Near-Death and Out-of-Body Experiences in the Blind*. Palo Alto, CA: William James Center for Consciousness Studies, Institute of Transpersonal Psychology.

Ring, K. and Rosing, C.J. (1990). 'The Omega Project: An Empirical Study of the NDE Prone Personality'. *Journal of Near-Death Studies*, vol. 8, no. 4, summer, pp. 211–39.

Ring, K. and Valarino, E. (1998). *Lessons from the Light*. New York and London: Insight Books, Plenum Press.

Roberts, B. and Chaboyer, W. (2004). 'Patients' Dreams and Unreal Experiences Following Intensive Care Admission'. *Nursing in Critical Care*, vol. 9, no. 4, pp. 173–80.

Rodin, E. (1989). 'Comments on "A Neurobiological Model for Near-Death Experiences"'. *Journal of Near-Death Studies*, vol. 7, no. 4, summer, pp. 255–9.

Rogo, D. S. (1978). *Mind Beyond the Body*. New York: Penguin.

Rominger, R. A. (2009). 'Exploring the Integration of Near-Death Experience Aftereffects: Summary of Findings'. *Journal of Near-Death Studies*, vol. 28, no. 1, fall, pp. 3–34.

Rommer, B. (2000). *Blessing in Disguise: Another Side of the Near-Death Experience*. St. Paul, MN: Llewellyn Publications.

Rosen, D. H. (1975). 'Suicide Survivors'. *Western Journal of Medicine*, vol. 122, pp. 289–94.

Ruttan, L. and Persinger, M. A. (1990). 'Enhancement of Temporal Lobe-related Experiences During Brief Exposures to Milligauss Intensity Extremely Low Frequency Magnetic Fields'. *Journal of Bioelectricity*, vol. 9, no. 1, pp. 33–54.

Sabom, M. (1982). *Recollections of Death: An Investigation Revealing Striking New Medical Evidence of Life After Death*. London: Corgi.

Sabom, M. (1998). *Light and Death: One Doctor's Fascinating Account of Near-Death Experiences*. Grand Rapids, MI: Zondervan Publishing House.

Sanders, M. A. (2007). *Nearing Death Awareness*. London: Jessica Kingsley Publishers.

Sartori, P. (2008). *The Near-Death Experiences of Hospitalized Intensive Care Patients: A Five-Year Clinical Study*. New York and Lampeter: Edwin Mellen Press.

Sartori, P. (2010a). 'Spirituality 1: Should Spiritual and Religious Beliefs be Part of Patient Care?' *Nursing Times*, vol. 106, no. 28, pp. 14–17.

Sartori, P. (2010b). 'Spirituality 2: Exploring How to Address Patients' Spiritual Needs in Practice'. *Nursing Times*, vol. 106, no. 29, pp. 23–5.

Sartori, P. (2010c). 'Understanding the Subjective Experiences and Needs of Patients as they Approach Death'. *Nursing Times*, vol. 106, no. 37, pp. 14–16.

# References

Sartori, P., Badham, P. and Fenwick, P. (2006). 'A Prospectively Studied Near-Death Experience with Corroborated Out-of-Body Perceptions and Unexplained Healing'. *Journal of Near-Death Studies*, vol. 25, no. 2, winter, pp. 69–84.

Saunders, N., Saunders, A. and Pauli, M. (2000). *In Search of the Ultimate High: Spiritual Experience through Psychoactives.* London, Sydney, Auckland and Johannesburg: Rider Books.

Saver, J. L. and Rabin, J. (1997). 'The Neural Substrates of Religious Experience'. *Journal of Neuropsychiatry and Clinical Neurosciences*, vol. 9, pp. 498–510.

Schenk, P. (2006). *The Hypnotic Use of Waking Dreams: Exploring Near-Death Experiences without the Flatlines.* London: Crown House Publishing.

Schoolcraft, H. R. (1975). *Travels in the Central Portions of the Mississippi Valley: Comprising Observations on its Mineral Geography, Internal Resources, and Aboriginal Populations.* Millwood, NY: Kraus Reprint. First published 1825.

Schwaninger, J., Eisenberg, P. R., Schechtman, K. B. and Weiss, A. N. (2002). 'A Prospective Analysis of Near-Death Experiences in Cardiac Arrest Patients'. *Journal of Near-Death Studies*, vol. 20, no. 4, summer, pp. 215–32.

Serdahely, W. (1990). 'Pediatric Near-Death Experiences'. *Journal of Near-Death Studies*, vol. 9, no. 1, fall, pp. 33–9.

Serdahely, W. (1991). 'A Comparison of Retrospective Accounts of Childhood Near-Death Experiences with Contemporary Pediatric Near-Death Experience Accounts'. *Journal of Near-Death Studies*, vol. 9, no. 4, summer, pp. 219–24.

Sheeler, R. D. (2005). 'Teaching Near-Death Experiences to Medical Students'. *Journal of Near-Death Studies*, vol. 23, no. 4, summer, pp. 239–47.

Shelly, M. P. (1993). 'Sedation for the Critically Ill Patient: Current Thoughts and Future Developments'. In *Intensive Care Britain*, Rennie, M. (ed.), London: Greycoat.

Sogyal, R. (1995). *The Tibetan Book of Living and Dying.* London: Rider Books. First published 1992.

Sotelo, J., Perez, R., Guevara, P. and Fernandez, A. (1995). 'Changes in Brain, Plasma and Cerebrospinal Fluid Contents of B-Endorphins in Dogs at the Moment of Death'. *Neurological Research*, vol. 17, pp. 223–5.

Spencer, M. (1996). 'Dissociation: Normal or Abnormal?' *Journal of Near-Death Studies*, vol. 14, no. 3, spring, pp. 145–57.

Spiegel, D. and Cardena, E. (1991). 'Disintegrated Experience: The Dissociative Disorders Revisited'. *Journal of Abnormal Psychology*, vol. 100, pp. 366–78.

Stevenson, I. and Cook, E. W. (1995). 'Involuntary Memories During Severe Physical Illness or Injury'. *Journal of Nervous and Mental Disease*, vol. 183, pp. 452–8.

Storm, H. (2000). *My Descent into Death*. London: Clairview Books.

Stout, Y. M., Jacquin, L. A. and Atwater, P. M. H. (2006). 'Six Major Challenges Faced by Near-Death Experiencers'. *Journal of Near-Death Studies*, vol. 25, no. 1, fall, pp. 49–62.

Strassman, R. (2001). *DMT: The Spirit Molecule*. Rochester, VT: Park Street Press.

Sutherland, C. (1992). *Transformed by the Light: Life After Near-Death Experiences*. Sydney: Bantam Books.

Sutherland, C. (1995a). *Children of the Light*. London: Souvenir Press.

Sutherland, C. (1995b) *Reborn in the Light: Life After Near-Death Experiences*. New York, Toronto, London, Sydney and Auckland: Bantam Books.

Swaddling, M. (2006). *Telling Tales: 'Life as it Was – Told by those who Lived it'*. Aldershot: Pavilion Housing Association.

Tachibana, T. (1994). *Near-Death Experience*. Tokyo: Bungei Shunju (Japanese only).

Talayesva, D. (1942). *Sun Chief: The Autobiography of a Hopi Indian*. New Haven, CT: Yale University Press.

Tart, C. (1968). 'A Psychophysiological Study of the Out-of-Body Experiences in a Selected Subject'. *Journal of the American Society for Psychical Research*, vol. 62, no. 7, pp. 3–27.

Tart, C. (1998). 'Six Studies of Out-of-Body Experiences'. *Journal of Near-Death Studies*, vol. 17, no. 2, winter, pp. 73–99.

Taylor, E. (2011). ABC News interview broadcast 23 March 2011. http://abcnews. go.com/WNT/Video/elizabeth-taylor-death-experience-13201786.

Thrum, T. (1907). *Hawaiian Folk Tales: A Collection of Native Legends*. Chicago, IL: A. C. McClurg.

Twemlow, S. W. (1977). 'Epilogue: Personality File'. In *Journeys Out of the Body*, Monroe, R. A. (ed.), New York: Anchor Press/Doubleday.

van Lommel, P. (2004a). Personal communication.

van Lommel, P. (2004b). 'About the Continuity of our Consciousness'. In *Brain Death and Disorders of Consciousness*, Machado, C. and Shewmon,

D. A. (eds), New York, Boston, Dordrecht, London and Moscow: Kluwer Academic/ Plenum Publishers.

van Lommel, P. (2010). *Consciousness Beyond Life: The Science of the Near-Death Experience*. New York: Harper One.

van Lommel, P., van Wees, R., Meyers, V. and Eifferich, I. (2001). 'Near-Death Experience in Survivors of Cardiac Arrest: A Prospective Study in the Netherlands'. *Lancet*, vol. 358, pp. 2039–45.

Varela, F. J. (ed.) (1997). *Sleeping, Dreaming, and Dying: An Exploration of Consciousness with the Dalai Lama*. Boston, MA: Wisdom Publications.

Vaughan, L. (1920). *Answered or Unanswered? Faith in China*. Philadelphia: Christian Life Literature Fund.

Wade, J. (2003). 'In a Sacred Manner we Died: Native American Near-Death Experiences'. *Journal of Near-Death Studies*, vol. 22, no. 2, winter, pp. 83–115.

Wallis Budge, E. A. (2008). *The Egyptian Book of the Dead (Penguin Classics)*. London and New York: Penguin Books.

Warner, L. (1937). *A Black Civilization: A Social Study of an Australian Tribe*. New York: Harper and Brothers.

Whinnery, J. E. (1990). 'Acceleration-Induced Loss of Consciousness: A Review of 500 Episodes'. *Archives of Neurology*, vol. 47, pp. 764–76.

Whinnery, J. (1997). 'Psychophysiologic Correlates of Unconsciousness and Near-Death Experiences'. *Journal of Near-Death Studies*, vol. 15, no. 4, summer, pp. 231–58.

White, P. R. (1997). 'The Anatomy of a Transformation: An Analysis of the Psychological Structure of Four Near-Death Experiences'. *Journal of Near-Death Studies*, vol. 15, no. 3, spring, pp. 163–85.

Wilber, K. (1991). *Grace and Grit*. Boston, MA, and London: Shambhala.

Winkler, E. (1996). *Das Abendlandische Totenbuch* (The Occidental Book of Death and Dying). Hamburg: Corona.

Winkler, E. (2003). 'The Elias Project: Using the Near-Death Experience Potential in Therapy'. *Journal of Near-Death Studies*, vol. 22, no, 2, winter, pp. 79–82.

Woerlee, G. M. (2003). *Mortal Minds: A Biology of the Soul and Dying Experience*. Utrecht: de Tijdstroom.

Woerlee, G. M. (2004). 'Cardiac Arrest and Near-Death Experiences'. *Journal of Near-Death Studies*, vol. 22, no. 4, summer, pp. 235–49.

Woodrow, P. (2000). *Intensive Care Nursing: A Framework for Practice*. London: Routledge.

Wren-Lewis, J. (2004). 'The Implications of Near-Death Experiences and Understanding Posttraumatic Growth'. *Psychological Inquiry*, vol. 15, pp. 90–2.

Yanagita, K. (1975). *The Legends of Tono*. Tokyo: Japan Foundation Translation Series. Originally published 1910.

Zaleski, C. (1987). *Otherworld Journeys: Accounts of Near-Death Experiences in Medieval and Modern Times*. New York and Oxford: Oxford University Press.

Zhi-ying, F. and Jian-xun, L. (1992). 'Near-Death Experiences Among Survivors of the 1976 Tang Shan Earthquake'. *Journal of Near-Death Studies*, vol. 11, no. 1, fall, pp. 39–49.

# Index

# Index

Brayne, S. 86
British Psychological Society
  Transpersonal Section Annual
  Conference 96
Buddha Amitabha 75
Bush, Nancy 3, 17–18, 22–3

cancer/lymphoma 13, 21, 34, 42, 88,
  99, 106, 108
  disappearance after NDEs 3, 46
  premonition of 91
car and bicycle accidents 15, 20, 21,
  25, 49, 63, 65, 76, 154, 155–6
carbon dioxide *see* hypercarbia
cardiac arrests xix, xv, 2, 19, 27, 29,
  53, 57, 58, 63, 112, 129, 130, 133,
  134, 140, 141, 154, 168, 177, 187
  proportion of NDEs reported 113,
  129
cardiopulmonary resuscitation (CPR)
  xv, 187–8
Carter, Chris 179
Catholicism 20, 36, 76, 156
childbirth 18, 30, 76, 125, 164
childhood and teenage NDEs 10,
  16–17, 21, 40–1, 43–4, 46, 53–69,
  82, 83
  after effects 40–1, 46, 64–5, 66–9,
  168
children's deathbed vision 86
Chinese NDEs 75–6
Chitragupta 72
Christianity 15, 51, 75–6, 79
collective unconscious 23, 83
comas 3, 4, 20, 38, 54, 61, 62, 96, 110,
  174
coming back to life
  being called back by living relatives
  30, 54, 60
  being drawn back by thoughts of
  relatives 68, 80
  being given the choice 30, 32, 50,
  54, 55
  being sent back 6, 8, 9, 13, 37, 46,
  56, 58, 59, 60, 62, 66, 74, 75, 77,
  78, 79, 82, 83, 89, 131
  needing to come back to care for
  children 6, 20, 30, 33, 76

re-entering the body 6, 9, 13–4, 32,
  35–6, 46, 131
compassion 30, 153
  and IgA 170
  increased after NDEs 30–1, 167,
  169, 171, 179, 183
  increased with awareness of NDEs
  2, 153, 167, 168
complementary therapies 67
consciousness
  continuation after death 123–4
  expansion due to drugs 114
  heightened during NDEs 8, 114
  relationship with the brain 1, 4,
  116, 133, 139, 143, 173, 178–9,
  180–1
  transformation for the planet 171
  understanding of 143, 171
Corazza, Ornella 74, 114
Cornwell, Hazel 88–9, 104–5
Counts, Dorothy 78
critical-care units xvii, 123, 144, 152,
  164, 174, 175
cultural conditioning 23, 53, 71, 83
cultural variations in NDEs 70–84

Darwin, Charles 169
death xvii, xx
  approach, and lights around the
  body 88–9
  cultural variations in concept and
  definitions 70, 73
  how and when to broach the
  subject 158–63
  medicalization 110, 144–8
  need for education of healthcare
  workers 152, 175
  *see also* fear of death
death denial 147, 148, 174, 176
deathbed visions 72, 85–8, 109, 110,
  132–3
  cross-cultural study 72, 75, 86
  people with Alzheimer's 100–1
deceased loved ones
  after-death communications 14, 90,
  98, 104–9
  deathbed visions of 85, 86, 87, 88,
  100–1, 133

230

# Index

Gaia Hypothesis 171
Galileo 180
Gallup, George 70
Germany, prevalence of NDEs 70
God (Heavenly Father) 19, 56, 131
   appearance in NDEs 54, 57, 75, 146
   appearance in precognitive dreams 92
'God helmet' 118
gravitational-induced loss of consciousness (G-LOC) 112
Grey, Margot 3, 17, 23
Greyson, Bruce 3, 17–18, 125, 139, 165, 168
Greyson NDE scale 71, 114, 129
grief therapy 104, 166–7, 176–7, 179
Grossman, Neal 168–9
Guam NDEs 78

hallucinations
   deathbed visions compared 86
   deathbed visions ascribed to 87
   distinguishing from spiritual expressions 164
   drug-induced 86, 115, 131, 134, 136–9, 140
   NDEs regarded as xvii, 2, 153, 178
   NDEs distinct from xix, 124–5, 131, 136, 138–9, 140
Hamilton, David 170
Hampe, Johan 2, 174
Hata, Yoshia 74
Hawaiian NDEs 82
healing ability/being healed
   after empathic death experience 99
   after NDEs 46–9, 132, 178, 179–80
healthcare
   acknowledging and responding to NDEs 152–8
   spiritual aspects of patient care 149–50, 175
   unbelievable 'scientific' statements 181
healthcare workers
   need for knowledge about death and dying 109–10, 152
   need for knowledge of NDEs xviii, 150–2, 153, 154, 158, 172, 177, 189

hearing news of being close to death 5, 10–11, 41, 154
heart attacks 7, 23, 29 *see also* cardiac arrests
heautoscopy 117
heaven/paradise 146
   in NDEs 2, 22, 72, 73, 74, 78, 88
   in precognitive dreams 93–4
   as state of mind 191
   *see also* other realms
hell 16, 17, 18, 21, 22, 23, 72, 73, 79, 130, 136, 138
Holden, Janice 3, 121, 128
Horizon Research Foundation, UK 3, 154
hospices 30, 86, 87, 110, 164, 175, 188
hypercarbia (high carbon dioxide levels) 18, 113, 139–40, 178
hypnagogia 122
hypnopompia 122
hypoxia 111–13
Hyslop, James 86

India
   deathbed visions 86
   NDEs 72
Induced After Death Communication (IADC) 167
ineffability 9–10, 49, 71
Intensive Therapy Units (ITUs)/intensive care units xx, 3, 29, 34, 38, 102–3, 110, 165, 166
   allaying the fear of death 159–63
   denial of death and dying 147–8, 173–5
   encounter with dying patient xvi–xvii, xviii, 189, 190
   expansion 110, 147
   hallucination/ITU psychosis 124–5
   poor knowledge of NDEs 151
   research on children 53
   resuscitation scenarios xv–xvi, 123, 187–9
   *see also* five-year prospective study of NDEs
interconnectivity/unity 9, 158, 167, 169–70, 171, 185, 186
   with the universe 114

International Association of Near-
Death Studies (IANDS), USA 3,
25, 153–4, 168

Japanese NDEs 74–5
Jesus 54, 75, 76, 77, 79, 114, 130, 131,
146
*Journal of Near Death Studies* 123,
125
joyful/blissful feelings
and after-death communications
104–5
during NDEs 8, 11, 13, 15, 29, 30,
130
and empathic death experiences 94,
95
judgement of souls 18, 74, 78, 82, 146
Jung, Carl 83

karma 73, 74
Kason, Yvonne 46, 151, 164
Kellman, Raphael 149
Keltner, Dacher 169
ketamine experiences 114–15
Kikuchi, Matsunojo 74
Kongo NDEs 79
Kübler-Ross, Elisabeth 2, 97

Lawrence, Madeleine 3, 128
Leese, Heather 38–9
Lerman, John 54, 103
life expectancy, cultural variations
70–1, 78
life reviews 5, 7–8, 16, 42, 76, 83, 146
childhood NDEs 55, 56
distressing 18
and interconnectivity 169, 186
ketamine experiences 114
as a psychological process of
reminiscence 123–4
Lifebridge Foundation, New York 127
light or lights
around the body at time of death
88–9
ketamine experiences/NDEs
compared 114
in NDEs 42, 74, 75, 83, 88, 95,
129–30

*see also* beings of light; stairway and
light; tunnel/shadow and light
light sensitivity 4, 28, 45, 67
Long, Jeffrey 83, 121
Long, Jodie 83
love
and enhancement of recovery 150
enveloping, in NDEs 10, 13, 30, 32,
65, 66, 156, 157
and evolution 169
immeasurability 180, 183
lovingness increased after NDEs
30–1, 167
surrounded by, at moment of death
of a loved one 97–8
'Love Project' 168
Lovelock, James 171
Lyons, Jules 10–14, 23, 176–7, 182,
185

Maori NDEs 77–8
Mapuche NDEs 82–3
Masau'u 82
Maslow, Abraham 171
materialism 22, 144, 171
criticised in *Ars Moriendi* 145
lessened after NDEs 31, 167
materialist explanations of NDEs
111–26, 143, 168–9, 178, 183
Matthews, Carolyn 34
Mayan civilization 145
McClurg, J. 121
McDonagh, J. M. 166
meditation 66, 97, 171
mediums 96
Meduna, Charles 113
Melanesia/Western New Britain 70
NDEs 78
meningitis 4, 32, 46, 54
midazolam 165
Middle Ages
attitudes and concepts of death
145–6
NDEs/otherworld journeys 2, 16,
71
mind models 134
mind-body dualism 180
mind-body-spirit connection 150

# Index